# Prison Officers and Their World

# Prison Officers
## and
# Their World

**Kelsey Kauffman**

Harvard University Press
Cambridge, Massachusetts
London, England
1988

*Library of Congress Cataloging in Publication Data*
Kauffman, Kelsey.
  Prison officers and their world/ Kelsey Kauffman.
    p.   cm.
  Bibliography: p.
  Includes index.
    1. Prisons—Massachusetts—Officials and employees—Case studies.
I. Title.
HV9475.M4K38 1988                              88-468
331.7′613659744—dc19                            CIP
ISBN 0-674-70716-8 (alk. paper)

In loving memory of
my father and mother
Draper Lawrence Kauffman
and Margaret Tuckerman Kauffman
and of my friend and mentor
Lawrence Kohlberg

# Acknowledgments

First and foremost, I should like to acknowledge my great debt to the prison officers who participated in this study. Over a four-year period, they responded to my questions with patience, candor, and a genuine effort to communicate to someone outside the prison system what was happening inside. I gained from them a deeply enriched appreciation of human capacity for insight, courage, and growth. They have my respect and my thanks.

Three individuals had substantial influence on the writing of this book: Bruce Stinebrickner, Lawrence Kohlberg, and Gordon Hawkins. For eighteen years, Bruce Stinebrickner has taken an active interest in my prison work and research, first as a good friend and then as my husband. In all phases of the study reported here, I turned primarily to him for advice and criticism. His influence can be found on every page; as befits his training as a political scientist, it is probably greatest in Chapter 4, "Power in a Prison." In addition to his rich insights and analytical skills, he is also as fine and careful an editor as any author might hope to find. Much of the credit for whatever good qualities this book possesses belongs to him.

I first met Lawrence Kohlberg in 1972 when he was a professor at Harvard University and I was a prison officer at the Connecticut state prison for women in Niantic, Connecticut. I was assigned to work in an experimental unit at the prison that was structured according to principles of democracy and justice developed by Kohlberg. He worked patiently to defuse my hostility to the academic world, and encouraged me to go to graduate school and write about officers. As a generation of students at the Harvard Graduate School of Education was fortunate enough to learn, having Larry Kohlberg as a dissertation supervisor meant acquiring an intellectual mentor of considerable renown, and a friend and father-figure as well. Our friendship deeply enriched my life.

My debt to Gordon Hawkins is unusual. I was briefly a student of his in 1977 at the Institute of Criminology, University of Sydney, Australia, and have not seen him since then. Yet, over the years, he has always responded with helpful criticisms to drafts of papers and chapters that I have sent him. Ill health in my family seemed for a time to postpone completion of this study interminably. I am not certain whether I would have persisted had it not been for his encouragement.

Although this book focuses on the Massachusetts prison system, my ideas about prisons and prison officers were initially shaped when I was an officer in the Connecticut prison system. The officers and inmates of the women's prison in Niantic, Connecticut, taught me a great deal about prisons, and even more about myself. Joseph Hickey and Robert J. Brooks were administrators with the Connecticut Department of Correction during the 1970s, and had considerable influence on my ideas about prisons and prison officers. William Gimignani was the tough-talking captain who trained me as a recruit, and the warm human being who first exposed me to the moral dilemmas that officers face.

The research reported here could not have been undertaken without the support and cooperation of administrators in the Massachusetts Department of Correction. Commissioner Frank Hall inherited a troubled department in 1973, and throughout his five years in office faced criticism from many parties. Nevertheless, he readily approved investigation by outsiders. The superintendents of Bridgewater, Concord, Norfolk, and Walpole prisons kindly consented to the research. Members of their staffs were unfailingly courteous and helpful in arranging for interviews with officers during their duty hours, no mean task given the severe shortage of officers throughout the system.

The director of the Massachusetts Department of Correction training academy, George Fosque, and his entire staff went to great lengths to facilitate the research and provide background information on the prison system. The staff of the Department of Correction research office also provided invaluable assistance and information. My thanks to Francis Carney, the director, and to his assistant, Dallas Miller, who ably handled a seemingly endless series of questions from me.

Stanton Wheeler, James F. Gilligan, and Keith Nightenhelser generously read and criticized earlier versions of the book. Substantial improvements resulted from their comments. Robert Palmer, George Fosque, and Rachel Kurshan also read drafts of chapters and made helpful suggestions. Maria Ascher, Michael Aronson, and Joan Mark of Harvard University Press capably guided the transformation of a doctoral dissertation into a book. I was fortunate to find a sympathetic copy editor in Kate Schmit at the Press.

Transcription of interviews was made possible by a grant from the National Institute of Mental Health. Arthur Lcabman and Ecford Voit of NIMH provided assistance in completing my grant application and offered thoughtful criticisms of the project, especially in regard to its ethical implications. Susan Kauffman and Susan O'Loughlin painstakingly transcribed most of the tapes, a laborious task. Susan Bush located hundreds of newspaper articles on the Massachusetts prison system. Useful background information on Massachusetts prisons was provided by Jerry Taylor of the *Boston Globe* and by the staff of former state senator Jack Backman. Many friends, especially Caroline Frazer, Barbara Gillies, and Dianne Hardin, provided assistance along the way. Taren Stinebrickner-Kauffman helped proofread and ably distracted her little brother, Aden, at crucial times.

Finally, I should like to thank my parents, Draper L. Kauffman and Margaret T. Kauffman, and my aunt, Elizabeth Bush. They were more than a little bit surprised when I became a prison officer, and were never convinced that researching and writing this book deserved a large portion of my life. But they steadfastly believed that whatever I chose to undertake must be worthwhile, and gave me the unquestioning love and encouragement that most writers so desperately need. I regret that neither of my parents lived to see *Prison Officers and Their World* completed. I hope they would have liked it.

# Contents

# Prison Officers and Their World

# 1

# The Other Prisoners

The years 1971 to 1980 were violent and tumultuous in American prisons. It was a decade marked at beginning and end by two of the bloodiest prison upheavals in American history. In 1971, New York authorities crushed a four-day rebellion at Attica prison, killing twenty-nine inmates and ten hostages in the process. Nine years later, inmates at New Mexico State Prison took over the institution, brutally murdering thirty-three of their fellow prisoners and torturing scores of other inmates and officers before surrendering.

Events at Attica and New Mexico prisons were the most dramatic and best publicized of the decade, but few state prison systems escaped without confrontation and bloodshed. The Massachusetts prison system was one of the most seriously and persistently afflicted. Murders, suicides, riots, strikes, and mass escapes were only the most obvious manifestations of a system in turmoil. Attempts to implement radical changes within Massachusetts prisons met with fierce resistance by important sectors of the community, most notably prison officers. Throughout much of the decade, administrators, officers, and inmates were locked in conflict within the state's prisons while public debate over the proper governance and future of the prison system raged outside.

This book focuses on one of the major groups of protagonists within the Massachusetts prison system during this period, the officers. It is based on interviews with sixty prison officers conducted between 1976 and 1980 at the four major state prisons for men: the maximum-security prison, Walpole; the medium-security prison, Norfolk; the reformatory for young adult males, Concord; and the state hospital for the criminally insane, Bridgewater. It is the *officers'* story I seek to tell, and not that of inmates, administrators, or institutions as a whole. Wherever possible, I attempt to let officers describe for themselves the prison world and their own lives within it. Although I examine the lives and subculture of officers at all four prisons, my primary focus is the maximum-security prison, Walpole. That was the institution in which problems in the Massachusetts prison system surfaced most dramatically, in which officers were tested most sorely, and in which the contours of the officer subculture were in sharpest relief.

This study is intended not to be an exposé of the Massachusetts prison system, but rather an analysis of life inside one prison system, during one decade, from the perspective of one key group inside that prison system. Although specific events discussed are unique in time and place, the underlying problems are not. In varying intensity, they afflict most prisons most of the time. The histories of prisons and prison systems tend to be cyclical in nature, periods of turmoil alternating with periods of relative calm. Like prisons in many other states, those in Massachusetts experienced disturbances in the 1950s and 1970s, yet were largely quiescent during the 1960s and 1980s. Throughout their cycles, most prisons remain citadels of brutality and despair.

Over the past fifty years, a large body of scholarly literature has accumulated concerning penal institutions. Almost invariably, the focus has been on inmates. Researchers have examined their subculture, delved into their sex lives, traced their origins, recorded their idiom, and reported their attitudes. Systematic attention has been paid to variations among inmates within single institutions, as well as to the effect on inmates of differences among institutions. Meanwhile, most researchers have proved indifferent to prison officers and have shed little light on the problems and perspectives of either the individual officer or officers as a group. As Gordon Hawkins has pointed out in *The Prison: Policy and Practice* (1976, p. 85):

> It is in fact remarkable how little serious attention has been paid to prison officers in the quite extensive literature on prisons and imprisonment. It is almost as though they were, like the postman in G. K. Chesterton's celebrated detective story, so commonplace and routine a feature of the scene as to be invisible. Yet their role is clearly of critical importance . . . Within penal institutions their influence is inevitably predominant.

I became interested in studying prison officers because I was one. Early in the 1970s I worked for a year as a correctional officer at the state prison for women in Niantic, Connecticut. The institution housed approximately 150 inmates, including all women sentenced to prison terms in Connecticut as well as those awaiting trial without bail. The most unusual feature of Niantic prison at that time was a "democratic unit" of thirty inmates and six staff that operated on the principle of "one person (inmate *or* officer), one vote" in regard to all matters arising within the unit. I worked in the democratic unit for part of my tenure as an officer. With its small inmate population, picturesque setting, and relatively benevolent administration, Niantic prison was atypical. Nevertheless, officers there, myself included, shared many of the problems of officers in mainstream penal institutions.

I did not become an officer with the intention of studying prisons or my co-workers, but during my year at Niantic I came to believe that those who work in prisons—"officers," "guards," "turnkeys," "screws"—are badly misunderstood and often maligned by the general public, by social scientists, and by those who govern prisons. Failure to understand officers—their characters and motivations, problems and perspectives—has inevitably undermined efforts to reform prisons and has contributed to the everyday misery of those who live and work behind the walls. My purpose in undertaking the research was to investigate the officer subculture in a range of penal institutions, to document the often devastating effect that prison work has on officers, and to communicate to those concerned with prisons the importance of understanding the officers' predicament and the necessity of considering officers and their needs in any effort to restructure prisons.

I brought to the research a basic sympathy toward prison officers, although not toward prisons. I liked the officers who had been my co-workers and those who were part of this study very much indeed. I do not share the perspective that officers are, by their natures, different from the rest of society. Yet their lives are deeply affected by their experiences within prisons, especially if they work in prisons as violent and chaotic as the ones described in this book. Officers are both agents and victims of a dehumanizing system, but they are *not* its architects. I agree with one of the prison officers I interviewed:

> We get this impression . . . from Hollywood. We see pictures of prisons and state hospitals and we say, "Oh, look at them screws and look how they treated [the inmates]!" But you've got to remember, the officer . . . [was] the simple person who had a job

to do and he was told to do it and he did it. Guards may have started trouble; inmates have started trouble. But neither one of them would have been there unless the society decided to make this prison this way. They built up the wall . . . It wasn't the guard who decided it, he just went along with it.

I interviewed two samples of Massachusetts officers. One sample consisted of twenty officers at Walpole prison who were interviewed in 1976–77. Fifteen of the twenty were randomly selected from among the 226 officers and senior officers employed at Walpole. Five were chosen because they played important roles within the prison by virtue either of their formal or informal leadership among officers or their unusual styles as officers.

The second sample was longitudinal. It comprised forty officers who were interviewed before they had begun work in prisons and then reinterviewed two years and, in some cases, also four years later. I interviewed them for the first time in 1976 when they were recruits at the Massachusetts Department of Correction Training Academy. On completing their training course the forty recruits (all of whom were men) were assigned to the four major state prisons for male offenders. Thirteen were sent to Walpole, eleven to Norfolk, five to Concord, and eleven to one of the four correctional facilities at Bridgewater (Hospital for the Criminally Insane, Treatment Center for Sexually Dangerous Persons, Addiction Center, and Southeast Correctional Center).

In 1978, I reinterviewed all twenty-eight of the original sample who were still employed by the Department of Correction (twenty-two were still officers, six had become prison social workers, teachers, or the like). Of the twelve men who had already left the department, I located and reinterviewed ten. By 1980, only seventeen members of the original sample of forty were still employed by the Department of Correction, all of them as officers. I conducted a third round of interviews with six of them as well as with six who had left the department subsequent to the 1978 interviews.

The 110 interviews that I conducted with the two samples of Massachusetts officers lasted approximately 250 hours. With the permission of those interviewed, most of the interviews were tape recorded and fully transcribed. I have taken few liberties in quoting officers. I have, of course, consistently altered identifying information such as age, marital status, and location of an incident within a particular institution in order to protect the identity of interviewees. But I have not attempted to "polish" interviews. With few exceptions—the use of empty phrases such as "you know," for example, or needless repetitions—all words, phrases, or sentences missing from passages quoted in the book are indicated by ellipses. On two occasions I have rearranged the order of sentences that were not consecutive in their respective interviews in order to make the meaning of a story or passage clearer. (The sentences in question are, of course, separated by ellipses.) When quoting officers I have used square brackets—[ ]—to indicate words inserted by me to clarify meaning, and braces—{ }—to indicate words or passages that could not be understood with certainty from the tapes. With the exception of Chapters 1, 9, 10, and 11, all unattributed quotes in the book are from Walpole officers unless the context of a passage makes clear that I am quoting an officer from another Massachusetts prison. In the Appendix to this book I discuss some procedural and ethical problems encountered in the course of my research. Further details on research design and execution, as well as references to scholarly literature and a more comprehensive history of the Massachusetts prison system than that provided in Chapter 2 below, may be found in Kauffman (1985).

Finally, a note on terminology. I depart from the standard practice of referring to individuals employed to maintain security within prisons as "guards" or "correction[al] officers." My use of the term "prison officer" reflects my orientation toward those I studied and their role within prisons. "Guard" is too suggestive of a static relationship, something one does with inanimate objects. In any case, its connotations are derogatory and belittling. "Correction officer" conveys a fanciful (and, to my mind, unseemly) notion of the relationship between keeper and kept. "Prison officer" simply denotes an individual granted official authority within the specific domain of a penal institution.

# 2

# Decade of Turmoil

The 1970s began in Massachusetts in a spirit of reform. Before then, the Department of Correction had been tradition-bound and lethargic. Individual prisons were run according to the philosophies of their own superintendents and officer union leaders. In the wake of the Attica rebellion and less serious disturbances in the Massachusetts prison system, Governor Francis Sargent proclaimed a new era in Massachusetts corrections. He proposed sweeping changes in prison legislation and appointed a new commissioner of correction who was committed to radical reform of the state's prison system, including deinstitutionalization of most offenders, sharing of authority with inmates who remained in institutional settings, and participation of the "free" community in the internal affairs of the state's prisons.

## The Boone Era

The new commissioner, John Boone, was a black Southerner who had begun his career as an officer in the federal prison system and had most recently been superintendent of a prison in Virginia. On assuming the position of commissioner in January 1972, he appointed progressive superintendents for the state's maximum-security prison, Walpole, and medium-security prison, Norfolk, and moved swiftly to implement change within the Department of Correction.

Despite promises of reform, tensions remained high within the prisons. Violence escalated. On 17 March 1972, less than three months after the new commissioner had been appointed, Walpole exploded in a riot that resulted in extensive damage to the institution though no loss of life. Commissioner Boone scored "lack of training of guards" as the main cause of the riot (quoted in the *Boston Globe*, 23 March 1972), and both he and the prison's new superintendent publicly expressed sympathy for inmate grievances. In the wake of a second, smaller disturbance a few days later, the superintendent apologized to the inmates over the prison's public-address system for having failed to seek their advice and assistance. In a startling departure from traditional prison management, the commissioner invited citizen observers into Walpole to participate in negotiations with inmates and to monitor interactions between inmates and officers. It was a form of community participation within the prison that was to become the hallmark of his administration. For more than a week, some 150 citizens drawn from the Junior Chamber of Commerce, churches, businesses, colleges, and activist groups provided around-the-clock surveillance within the prison.

Many officers were unhappy about these developments. They felt their traditional authority was being undermined by administrators from outside the system, by the legitimacy newly accorded to inmate activists, and now by the presence of civilian observers. Officers at Walpole in particular perceived that their institution had become a more dangerous place in which to work since Boone had arrived. Most galling of all, they found themselves being blamed for the problems of the prison system itself.

On 1 May 1972, 250 officers and civilian employees at Walpole and two other state prisons participated in a one-day "sick-out" to highlight their disaffection. Boone responded by suspending 34 Walpole employees for a week without pay. Officers were bitter about the fact that, as one put it, "Inmates do one million dollars damage and [Boone] gives them amnesty, but officers stay out one day and he takes disciplinary action" (*Boston Globe*, 5 May 1972). Officers saw their authority further eroded when, over the objections of the superintendent, the commissioner permitted Walpole inmates to form a union with prison-wide elections.

Amidst continuing violence, officers charged that large volumes of weapons and drugs were circulating within Walpole. These charges were given dramatic support when an inmate with radical political leanings blew up himself and another inmate in the process of making a bomb in the prison foundry. On searching the two inmates' cells, officials discovered a handmade shotgun, two zip guns, a two-way radio, a pocket telescope, ammunition, and other weapons and explosives.

Officer leaders responded to these developments with what was to become an all-out campaign for Boone's removal—a campaign in which they were joined by conservative state legislators and one of Boston's two major newspapers, the *Herald*. Two events during the summer of 1972 fueled opposition to Boone and the reforms he was introducing. The first was the resignation of Walpole's new superintendent after only four-and-a-half months in office, partly due to differences with Boone regarding governance of the institution. The second event was violent. A Norfolk inmate acquired two guns and ammunition, probably smuggled in to him by his wife on a visit. In an apparent escape attempt, the inmate shot and killed an officer and a civilian employee and critically injured another officer before taking refuge with his wife in one of the prison's dormitories. (The lives of several other staff members were saved by inmates who hid them.) After a siege that lasted several hours, the inmate killed his wife and himself.

Officers and the commissioner immediately blamed each other for the shooting. Boone accused the officers on duty at the time of a "breach of security" and called for "the indictment of the guard responsible for allowing [the inmate's wife] into the prison without searching her" (*New York Times*, 1 August 1972). Officers retorted that regulations restricting searches of visitors had allowed the guns to be smuggled into the prison. (No metal detector was in use at Norfolk and female visitors were not usually searched because of an absence of female staff.) The superintendent of Norfolk acknowledged that several days before the shooting he had been forewarned by state police of an escape attempt to be led by the inmate in question. Boone publicly reprimanded the superintendent for "poor judgment" in not preventing the tragedy (*Boston Globe*, 3 August 1972). But, in fact, the superintendent's request that the inmate be transferred to a more secure prison on the basis of the rumored escape plan had not been approved by department officials. (Boone was apparently out of town at the time and the two ranking deputy commissioners were serving as acting superintendents at Walpole and Concord prisons. The request for a transfer had been handled by Boone's executive assistant, himself a former inmate in the federal prison system, and the deputy commissioner for personnel and training.) In any case, officers at the prison had apparently not been advised to place the inmate or his visitors under special surveillance. When Governor Sargent attended the funeral of the slain officer, he was greeted with boos and shouts of "murderer" from some of the 300 officers in attendance.

For most of 1972, the state's reformatory for young men, Concord, had been relatively quiet, but during the fall it, too, began to unravel. In October several officers were hurt in a minor riot. A month later, fourteen Concord inmates escaped during a disturbance—the largest mass escape from a Massachusetts prison. In their increasingly vitriolic exchanges, Boone and officer union leaders once again publicly accused each other of responsibility for events.

Meanwhile, problems were again mounting at Walpole, which had gained an unenviable reputation as one of the nation's most violent prisons. A series of interim superintendents attempted to govern the prison from Boston while a search was made for a permanent superintendent. With the prison's national reputation for trouble, there were few who were willing to take on the job. Finally in November a new superintendent was appointed. The day after he arrived at Walpole, an inmate was murdered. Three weeks later another inmate was killed—stabbed more than fifty times. Shortly before Christmas, seven inmates reportedly held an officer hostage for several hours before releasing him unharmed.

The new superintendent responded to these events by imposing the longest institution-wide lockup in Massachusetts prison history. A cell-by-cell shakedown produced a large assortment of weapons and narcotics, as well as charges by inmates of officer brutality. By the time the inmates were finally released from their cells in mid-February 1973, they had been in almost continuous lockup for seven weeks. As one department official was to recall, "when they started unlocking the institutions people weren't walking out of those cells, they were flying out of those cells and they were ready to kill anybody that happened to be standing in their way" (quoted in Konefsky, Peers, and Simon, 1977, pt. 2, p. 30).

To help defuse the situation, Boone once again invited civilian observers into Walpole. Over the next three-and-a-half months, hundreds of citizens were to take part in twenty-four-hour-a-day surveillance within the prison, including some men who had themselves served time at Walpole and at least one who was on parole.

Inmates were adamant that the superintendent who had imposed the lockup be dismissed. In support of that and other demands, they declared a work strike and refused to clean up food and debris that had been thrown on the cell block floors. Amidst the continuing turmoil, the superintendent quit, citing difficulties with the commissioner, officers, and inmates. On announcing his resignation he declared, "it is physically, mentally and administratively impossible to run this institution" (*Herald*, 3 March 1973). Having achieved their principal demand, inmates ended their work strike and entered into negotiations with a new acting superintendent, a psychologist who had been serving as an executive assistant to the commissioner. Over the coming days, many of the inmates' demands were granted. Next on their list was for the department to comply with one of its own regulations and release men from the segregation unit who had been held for more than fifteen days without a hearing—a move officers adamantly opposed.

Walpole was now being governed by inmate union leaders, outside observers, and an acting superintendent. The officers, it seemed, were the odd men out. Far from quiescent, they threatened a work stoppage of their own if the administration released from segregation inmates whom the officers considered dangerous. On 13 March, officers were ordered to release the inmates in question. It was, as one officer was to recall, "the straw that broke the camel's back." The long-standing feud between the officers and the commissioner was about to come to a head.

In the upheavals that had occurred since Boone's arrival, officers had lost much of the power that they had formerly exercised within the institution. The commissioner had at times dealt directly with the inmates to secure their support. Now his representatives were meeting daily with inmate leaders to negotiate matters central to governance of the institution. Nor were inmate leaders the only ones in the cell blocks who were competing with officers for authority. Outside observers were there as well, and few if any of them were seen as sympathetic to officers. The officers saw themselves gradually losing all control. The midday count was no longer taken with inmates in their cells as officers insisted was necessary. Many of the inmates whom officers considered most dangerous were being released from segregation and strict limits were to be placed on the use of segregation in the future. Further erosions in the officers' powers seemed inevitable. On 15 March 1973 all members of the day and evening shifts walked out on strike, the first prison officer strike in Massachusetts history.

For more than a year, Commissioner Boone had been attempting to bring about what he and many of his supporters saw as one of the great revolutions in American penology. He had had the support of the governor and large segments of the state's population, yet he had been thwarted by the officers. The illegal strike presented Boone with the opportunity to break officer resistance and in the process to demonstrate the viability of some of his most radical reforms—the sharing of power with inmates and participation of the "free" community in the affairs of the prison.

In a televised address to the state, Governor Sargent described Walpole as the "last stronghold of the old way" and declared, "The guards are on strike because I refused to turn over control of Walpole prison to the guards' union and because I insisted the Corrections Department and not the *employees* of the Corrections Department run that prison." State police were called in to man gun towers and patrol the outside perimeter of the prison. Administrative and treatment staff from Boston along with several "cadet officers" were sent to work inside Walpole. There they were joined by a large contingent of outside observers who were continuing their around-the-clock surveillance of the prison. The striking officers, meanwhile, were immediately suspended for five days without pay while a court order against the strike was sought.

Any officers who had hoped that in their absence Walpole would soon be in tumult were sorely disappointed. By all accounts, the prison was the calmest it had been in a long time. Inmates passed the time playing ball in the yard, relaxing in the blocks, and enjoying the company of visitors who were entering the prison unimpeded by searches. Some inmates were cleaning the blocks while others were working in the kitchen. Leaders of the inmate union declared that "the prison has been running perfectly" (*Boston Globe*, 17 March 1973).

Four days after the strike had begun, the Supreme Judicial Court issued a preliminary injunction ordering the officers back to work. But "back to work" was to have a new meaning. If the officers were to return at all, it was going to be on the administration's terms. When the day and evening shifts reported for duty, only a quarter were permitted to work, and then only at positions in which they would have no contact with inmates. The remainder of the officers were informed they must undergo "reeducation" (Boone, 1973). Although Boone cancelled the five-day suspensions he had imposed on the striking officers, he announced that the 180 officers and 25 civilian employees at Walpole who had refused to work would face disciplinary hearings as a result of which they could be fired, suspended, transferred to another institution or job, demoted, or subject to cuts in pay. Reported one newsman, the Department of Correction now had the "guards in a hammerlock" (*Boston Globe*, 21 March 1973).

A few days after the officers ended their strike, Walpole received a new acting superintendent, the third acting superintendent the institution had had since the officer strike began, its fourth superintendent since the beginning of the month. The new acting superintendent's job was made more difficult in the weeks ahead by the absence of a deputy superintendent, the transfer of the assistant deputy superintendent, the retirement of the business manager, the illness of the treatment director, and continued resignations of officers and other staff.

For the next two months officer shifts worked at half strength while men were undergoing compulsory "retraining." Meanwhile, civilian observers and officer cadets were overseeing activities in the cell blocks. When small numbers of officers were ordered to work inside, they initially refused. They were afraid of inmates who had formerly been in segregation and were now free in the institution, and they anticipated lack of support from civilian employees, temporary appointees, and outside observers if they did run into trouble. In the face of contempt charges, however, even this resistance crumbled.

As late as the middle of May (two months after the officer strike was over), direct supervision of inmates was, according to the acting superintendent, still largely in the hands of civilian observers and cadet officers. When the observers had first arrived in early March many inmates and their supporters hailed them as a force for rationality within the institution. They hoped the observers would temper the actions of both prisoners and guards. But as an officer insightfully inquired at the time, "They're here now, but when they're gone, what happens then? If they did stay more than two weeks, wouldn't they become just as familiar as guards to inmates? Where would you be then?" (Officer John Moore, *Boston Globe*, 18 March 1973). During the first few weeks when the officers were withdrawn from the prison and civilian observers were the principal representatives of the outside world in the cell blocks, Walpole was remarkably quiet—but it was a situation that could not last. Gradually, the presence of the observers lost its effect. Levels of violence within the prison rose steadily until stabbings and beatings were once again routine. Large quantities of contraband had reportedly entered the

institution through unchecked visitors. Thousands of pills had disappeared from the prison infirmary. Idleness pervaded the institution. Inmate leaders were unable to maintain control without
themselves resorting to strong-arm tactics, which they did with
increasing regularity.

On Friday, 18 May, the acting superintendent of Walpole announced that beginning the following Monday a forty-eight-hour
lockup and shakedown of the institution would take place. Inmate
leaders were outraged that there had not been "any inmates on the
task force that planned the shakedown" (*Boston Globe*, 20 May
1973). They were not appcased by the superintendent's plea that he
had announced the shakedown in advance because inmates had
objected in the past when they had not been given prior notice. A
major riot resulted, lasting most of the night and causing a million
dollars' worth of damage, although again no loss of life. In the early
hours of the following morning, state police regained control of the
institution. The inmates were locked for nearly a week while a
shakedown was conducted. Violence then resumed unabated; inmates were stabbed; officers and civilian employees were beaten.

On 12 June an event occurred that was gruesome even by Walpole's standards. While the inmates were locked in their cells for the
night, one inmate began throwing flammable liquid on another
inmate who had been asleep in the adjacent cell. For nearly fifteen
minutes screams filled the block while the man methodically
reached through the bars and doused his terrified quarry. On the
undermanned night shift, no officers were in the area, only civilian
observers. A frantic effort was made to find someone with keys to
open the cells, or at least some fire extinguishers (there were none in
the institution). Just as help finally arrived, the inmate tossed lighted
matches through the cell door, instantly incinerating his victim and
filling the block with smoke.

Four days later an inmate was stabbed twenty times and his body
flung from the second tier onto the concrete flats below. More
assaults and attempted murders followed. On 19 June, two inmates
reportedly attempted to hang themselves, four others slashed themselves in an apparent bid to be transferred out of the prison, and one
inmate and two officers were assaulted. That night a sizable number
of inmates refused to be locked in their cells in another dispute over
shakedowns. State police were once again asked to stand by. Walpole prison was in a state of virtual anarchy.

For almost two years, the prison system had dominated headlines in Massachusetts. Throughout his tenure as commissioner, Boone had enjoyed the backing of the governor, the *Boston Globe*, and important segments of the community, but his support was rapidly eroding. Just when the officers had ended their strike in March and were being forced to accede to the administration's will, an inmate who had been convicted of first-degree murder escaped while on furlough from Walpole and remained at large for a month. As a member of the commissioner's task force on furloughs later recalled, "I think what we did was we scared the hell out of the people of the Commonwealth of Massachusetts" (quoted in Konefsky, Peers, and Simon, 1977, pt. 2, p. 26). Walpole seemed to be in a state of perpetual chaos. Attempts to govern the prison without the officers had apparently failed, and relations between the commissioner and the officers were so poisoned that a rapprochement seemed impossible. Conservative legislative leaders were threatening to repeal reform legislation that provided not only for furloughs, but also for halfway houses and work release programs. Amidst the continuing violence, even liberals were abandoning Boone. As he was to recall their betrayal later,

> You see, liberals can't stand when there's so much blood, so much violence. I'll never forget, when we were discussing the Walpole situation, someone telling me, "Oh, but the blood and the killing!" But you should understand, I know that once you get a decent superintendent at Walpole, everything was going to work out. But those liberals just had taken as much as they could take. (Quoted in Konefsky, Peers, and Simon, pt. 3, pp. 20–21)

By mid-June, Boone was all but alone in believing that "everything was going to work out."

On 21 June 1973, eighteen months after Sargent had invited Boone to Massachusetts to revolutionize the prison system, the governor fired him. In a televised address to the people of the state, Sargent praised Boone as "a brave man" who had taken important strides in moving Massachusetts toward a system of community corrections but whose effectiveness had been lost.

Boone and his supporters laid blame for his downfall squarely on the officers. Certainly the animosities that existed between the officers and Boone were far greater than those ordinarily found between line staff and their superiors in a prison system. From the beginning, the officer corps at Walpole had been unenthusiastic about Boone and his reforms. And, from the beginning, Boone had been determined to push through his reforms with or without the officers' acquiescence. Boone's grievances against the officers had considerable merit. Not only had they actively campaigned for their commissioner's dismissal, but they also, according to Boone, had done "everything that they possibly could to undermine progressive tools—to destroy our concepts and implementation of re-integration" (*Boston Globe*, 26 January 1975). Time and again, Boone had publicly accused officers of incompetence and malfeasance. He blamed recurrent crises on a "guard culture" whose members were untrained, resistant to change, and determined to restore their century-old domination of the prison system (*Boston Globe*, 10 March 1973).

But the officers were only part of the problem. Removed from the passions of the times, many of the charges against them seem unfair. For example, the commissioner repeatedly criticized officers for being poorly trained, yet officer training was a departmental responsibility. Officers were accused of moonlighting and of holding second jobs during a year when they were frequently required to work twelve-hour shifts six and seven days a week and then were not being paid for their efforts for months, even years. (By the fall of 1973, officers were owed a million dollars for overtime dating back to 1971.) Officers calling in sick or seeking out posts as far removed from the conflict as possible were accused of malingering at a time when superintendents and acting superintendents were regularly taking leaves of absence on "doctors' orders." At the end of a year during which more than half the officer corps had resigned, Boone charged that the officers had "organized to take care of themselves" and that their demands for rules and regulations within the institution were a mere "smokescreen" for "fear of change" (*Boston Globe*, 10 March 1973). Amidst the unending violence and chaos within the prison, and in the context of officer deaths not only in other states but recently in the prison next door, officers' fears for their own physical safety were dismissed as just one more manipulation by men seeking dictatorial rule. Officers were even criticized for the injuries they, themselves, sustained. After an officer was stabbed with a sharpened television antenna thrust through the bars of an inmate's cell, Boone publicly asserted that the man had been the victim of his own incompetence. The commissioner helpfully advised, "You don't get close enough for [an inmate] to stick you," and suggested that in the federal prison system an officer foolish enough to get himself stabbed in such a fashion would justifiably face suspension (*Boston Globe*, 10 March 1973). For months the commissioner and his officers had communicated with each other largely through critical statements in news media. The absence of direct dialogue inevitably led to misunderstandings and furthered bad feelings on both sides.

In correctly discerning some of the worst attributes of the "guard culture," Boone apparently failed to see beyond it to the very real problems that individual members of that culture were facing as a consequence of changes he was introducing into the system. Boone had tremendous compassion for inmates and seemed to feel personally the misery and injustice that they suffered. But at least in his public pronouncements, he failed to evidence the same compassion and understanding for the plight of the officers. If the primary goal of officer union leaders was to oust Boone and return to the old ways, the primary goal of most of the rank and file was a good deal more mundane. It was, as one officer put it, "to see if you could make it through the day." Those who could quit, did. Those who stayed "had nowhere else to go." A man who was deputy commissioner at the time, himself a former Walpole officer, explained,

> Many of the most experienced men—the men we had counted on to train newcomers—simply couldn't stand it any more. Those who could took retirement. Others were out with real or imagined sicknesses. We [had] averaged five retirements a year, but by that time about 160 out of the 240 man staff [at Walpole] were new . . . The job of [correction officer] was impossible. (Quoted in Campbell, 1976, pt. A, p. 31)

It was little wonder that many of the officers who did stay sought refuge from the conflict by sitting in towers and other spots removed from inmate contact, thus exacerbating the problem of lack of men and lack of experience within the institution. As the president of the officers' union was to recall,

> The officers had no power. It was mass confusion. So the easiest thing to do was to go in there, stay away from the inmates, and take your pay. It wasn't what you wanted, but it was safest. The officers who tried to do their jobs ended up with high blood pressure, heart attacks, and nervous breakdowns. The tension was incredible. (Quoted in Campbell, 1976, pt. A, p. 31)

Few beyond the officers and their families seemed to appreciate just how depleted the officers had become in strength and in spirit.

Boone and many of his supporters believed that racism played a major role in his downfall. One of Governor Sargent's top aides ascribed Boone's difficulties to "an enormous cultural gap between a Southern black and Irish rednecks" (quoted in Konefsky, Peers, and Simon, 1977, pt. 3, p. 16). Although racism on the part of officers undoubtedly exacerbated hostility toward Boone, the substantial differences over policy and style that divided the commissioner and his officers appear to have overwhelmed whatever role race played in their relationship. Little evidence exists that officers would have taken any more kindly to Boone's radical changes and the way in which he attempted to introduce them if he had been white.

One of the ironies of the Boone administration was that, years later, officers who had worked at Walpole before Boone became commissioner and stayed on at the prison after he left often voiced support for changes that Boone tried to introduce while still expressing bitterness about the way he tried to do it. As one recalled, "There's a lot of things probably that changed in [19]72 that should have changed. But they changed too quick . . . It only took three days to change it from Walpole State Prison to Walpole Correction Institution with all the trimmings." Worse yet, Boone tried to introduce change while overlooking the officers. Nobody consulted them; nobody even told them why things were happening as they did. "Something was done and all you could think about was, 'It's going to be no good, I know it's going to be a failure,' because you didn't understand where he was going, why he was doing this, why he was either lightening up or tightening up." Four years after Boone's departure this officer was able to recognize the substantial contribution the former commissioner had made to the prison system, even to express sympathy for him as a person. At the same time, however, he criticized Boone's methods:

A lot of Boone's ideas I agree with. A lot of them we are carrying out today and [the officers] are accepting them. But . . . [Boone] didn't want to wait. We'd been stagnant for fifty years, so tomorrow we are changing it and we are changing it completely. And I think that was just as bad as no change, to change it so quickly and so fast that people didn't have a chance to slowly accustom themselves to the change. That's like being in a tee-shirt in Bermuda and flying a quick sonic jet to Alaska and walking out still in the tee-shirt. You shiver and you can't get used to the cold no matter how much clothes you put on. Like how you are when you get a cold wet, it goes right through your body. It was the same thing. You were blind to where we were going and you just wouldn't accept it.

And I was the same way. I had the same faults. Later on as you read more about Boone or you heard more about the policies and you see them today—if you are not blind . . . you [can] see these things that are happening today are basically the same things then—you understand him more as a person. But I still totally disagree with his implementation of his program, his plan, and how he did it.

In his speech removing Boone from office, Governor Sargent described the commissioner as a victim of Walpole. But so, too, were most of the men who lived and worked there. During Boone's eighteen-month tenure, eight inmates had been murdered at Walpole and several score stabbed. Countless others had been raped and beaten. Hopes for substantial improvement in their lives had been dashed. Conditions under which they lived were worse than before their struggles had begun. Unlike neighboring Norfolk prison, no Walpole officers had been killed or suffered serious permanent injury, but most had been psychologically scarred by events. More than half had quit. The only time officers seemed in control of the institution was when they were backed by state police. They were distrustful of all administrators and advocates of reform. For the rest of the decade, Walpole would remain violent and chaotic; relations among officers, inmates, and administrators would be strained and would often flare into open conflict.

## The Hall Era

During Boone's tenure as commissioner, the prison system had become "an extraordinarily visible and explosive issue in Massachusetts" (Campbell, 1976, pt. A, p. 35). Governor Sargent's first order of business on firing Boone was to find a successor who could take prisons—especially Walpole—off the front pages without betraying the promise of reform. After a search that lasted several months, the governor appointed Frank Hall, a thirty-three-year-old, white, deputy commissioner of the North Carolina prison system. A surprising choice given his youth, Hall proved to be an able administrator.

When Sargent (a Republican) was defeated for reelection a year later, his successor, Michael Dukakis (a Democrat), kept the young commissioner on. Hall stayed in office until Dukakis was himself defeated four years later in the 1978 Democratic primary election by Edward King, a "law and order" candidate who went on to win the general election.

Governor Dukakis inherited a prison system still in crisis—and an appreciation of the volatility of the prison issue in Massachusetts politics. According to a 1978 *Boston Globe* editorial, "Governor Dukakis, influenced perhaps by the heavy political costs his predecessor paid for becoming too closely identified with prison reform, has kept the issue at arm's length" (12 August 1978). Although Dukakis espoused reform of the prison system, he did not provide strong leadership toward that goal. On leaving office in 1979, Dukakis cited Walpole as one of two problems to which he would have accorded top priority had he been elected to a second term. "Had I been re-elected we would have produced a plan and recommended very strongly to the legislature that we proceed with the construction of one or possibly two maximum security institutions to replace Walpole, as rapidly as possible" (*Herald*, 3 January 1979). When Dukakis regained the governorship four years later, however, his interest in replacing Walpole and reforming prisons had apparently waned.

Compared to any previous Massachusetts commissioner of correction except Boone, Hall was, as a staff member put it, a "screaming liberal." But next to Boone, Hall was cautious and methodical. In his first year in office he was able gradually to defuse public and legislative hostility to the furlough program and quietly pressed ahead with development of community corrections. By the time Hall left in 1979, twenty-seven pre-release and drug treatment centers housed 15 percent of the department's inmate population. Forty percent of all inmates spent time in one of these centers prior to their release. In addition, several new medium- and minimum-security institutions had been opened, no small feat given strident opposition by residents in each local community when their area came under consideration as the site for a new facility.

Hall brought with him a number of administrators from the South to fill key posts. Over the next few years, he was able to attract and keep reasonably competent staff members at upper and middle management levels, although turnover among superintendents remained high. Because the new commissioner was able to fill a large number of vacancies immediately both in the central office and at each of the major prisons except Bridgewater, centralization of control within the department was greatly accelerated.

Although Hall brought important management skills to the department and proved adept at relations with the legislature and news media, the department under his leadership failed to gain mastery over Walpole or to put an end to chaotic conditions at Concord. High levels of violence continued within the state's prisons. The only major riot during Hall's tenure occurred at Concord in 1976, causing extensive damage to the institution but, again, no serious injury or loss of life. Individual acts of violence, however, more than made up for the lack of collective violence. In the five-and-a-half years during which Hall was commissioner, at least fifteen inmates were murdered (thirteen of them at Walpole); at least eighteen others committed suicide (five of them at Walpole). Attempted murders, serious assaults, rapes, and beatings by inmates of inmates were legion, especially at Walpole and Concord. Periodic shakedowns routinely yielded a wide assortment of weapons and narcotics. An exceptionally large number of inmates from throughout the prison system were in "protective custody" (tantamount to solitary confinement) *at their own insistence* because they feared living in the inmate population.

The situation was almost as precarious for officers. A total of eight guns with ammunition were discovered in various parts of Walpole and Norfolk while Hall was commissioner. On all but one of these occasions the weapons were found before they were used. The exception occurred in March 1975, when a Norfolk inmate shot two officers with a gun that had allegedly been inside the institution for two years. One of the officers was shot in the head, leaving him permanently and severely disabled. Although no other officer during the remainder of Hall's tenure was as seriously injured, assaults on officers were frequently reported, especially at Walpole and Bridgewater. In addition, officers were twice taken hostage at Walpole and once at the women's prison, Framingham. In each case they were released unharmed.

Officers, meanwhile, gave almost as much as they got. Accusations of officer brutality precipitated numerous official investigations, including ones by the United States attorney, the Massachusetts attorney general, the local district attorney, and the Massachusetts Department of Correction itself. (Chapter 6 deals at length with officer violence during this period.)

Not all battles for control of the prisons involved bloodshed. Both officers and inmates had learned a great deal during the early seventies about the use of collective action in influencing prison policies and procedures. At Norfolk, an institution that still boasted a profitable industrial sector, inmates used work strikes with some success. But officers, especially those at Walpole, were the ones who resorted most often and with greatest effect to the use of collective action in achieving their aims.*

Massachusetts, generally speaking, had a contentious public-employee sector during the 1970s, but no state employees rivaled prison officers for militancy. When other branches of the state employees' union were merely threatening to strike about pay and contract issues, prison officers were already out on the picket lines. More important, during the mid- and late 1970s, Walpole officers repeatedly threatened to strike, and frequently went out on strike, over issues regarding governance of the prison itself. "You've got a three-way battle there," explained a Walpole officer toward the end of the decade. "If we didn't get along with what the administration said and they were giving it to the cons, we walked. And when the cons weren't getting their way, they'd have to do something or they'd strike. It was a never ending battle."

In January 1979, Hall offered his resignation to the newly elected governor, Edward King, and left Massachusetts to become the head of New York State's Division of Youth. During his five years as commissioner, Hall had accelerated the movement toward community corrections, saved the furlough program, and strengthened centralized control over the prison system. But, as the editors of the *Boston Globe* (23 January 1979) pointed out,

> if Hall stood in the way of retrogression, he never emerged as a
> champion of change. Conditions at the state's most volatile

---

* Prison officer associations had long been a key element in the operation of the state's penal institutions. Prior to 1973, officers at each prison had had their own unions which, though affiliated with one another, negotiated separate contracts regarding working conditions. (Until 1973, Massachusetts public employees were denied the right to bargain over wages.) When Massachusetts passed a comprehensive collective-bargaining law for state employees in 1973, the state's prison officers voted to join the statewide employees' association (the American Federation of State, County and Municipal Employees). Some differences that had existed in regard to working conditions at the different prisons were incorporated in the new statewide contract. The most important of these was that officers at Walpole and Concord, and to a limited extent Norfolk, retained the right to select on the basis of seniority bid their own post, shift, days off, and vacation time.

prison, Walpole, continued to deteriorate during Hall's tenure as the prisons' chief . . . Murder and assault remain as commonplace there today as they were when Hall became commissioner in 1973.

## The End of the Decade

Governor King failed to appoint a permanent commissioner of correction for the first nine months of his administration. During that time the department exerted even less influence than usual over the internal dynamics of its maximum-security prison. Inmates were murdered, stabbed, and beaten; hostages were taken; officers went out on strike; grand juries investigated. "Who's in charge at Walpole?" cried newspaper headlines. It was not an unreasonable question. In explaining what he would do—nothing—about officers who had refused direct orders to unlock inmates' cells, the secretary of human services declared, "The prisons of this commonwealth are run by the administrators of the prisons. They are not run by prisoners and they are not run by the guards" (*Worcester Telegram*, 16 August 1979). His was a protestation echoing back through the decade. If neither the officers nor the inmates were running the prison, it was not because the administration was in control.

Finally, in September 1979, a new commissioner was named. Although he stayed in office for only twelve months, his appointment ushered in a new era within the department, one in which the emphasis officially shifted from reform to control. The spirit of rebellion among inmates and officers had by then been largely spent. After eight wearying years, officers and administrators moved into greater alignment and accord. The turmoil of the 1970s gave way to an exhausted calm.

# 3

# Prison Life

During the 1970s, the Massachusetts Department of Correction operated four maximum- and medium-security prisons for men and one for women, several minimum-security prisons, three forestry camps, and a number of pre-release and drug rehabilitation centers. (A separate system of county jails and houses of correction under local government jurisdictions housed minor offenders.) The major state prisons had always enjoyed considerable autonomy from the central administration. Inmates were frequently transferred from one prison to another, but administrators and officers usually spent their entire careers at only one institution. Consequently, rules and customs developed idiosyncratically. At each prison, "long-time staffers were mental repositories of the complex administrative processes, both official and unofficial" (Konefsky, Peers, and Simon, 1977, pt. 1, p. 8). Despite efforts to centralize the prison system during the 1970s, the four major prisons for men continued to differ substantially from one another both formally and informally.

## Walpole

The flagship institution for the entire state prison system was the maximum-security prison for men located in South Walpole, a rural community twenty-three miles southwest of Boston. Walpole was built in the mid-1950s to replace what was at the time the oldest state prison still in use in America. With its larger cells, dining room, and, best of all, running water and toilets, it was considered a major advance over its antiquated predecessor. Yet within twenty years the Governor's Advisory Committee on Corrections (1974,

p. 3) described the institution as "a badly conceived, poorly designed multi-million dollar mistake." In 1978 the local district attorney pronounced the prison already "outdated" and declared, "As a physical facility to house a significant criminal population, Walpole is a failure" (Delahunt, 1978, pp. 38, 39). The same year, an investigation by the Department of Public Health "revealed a facility that is suffering from poor design, chronic neglect, disrepair, inmate damage, unsanitary conditions, and an overwhelming infestation of rodents and cockroaches" (Wensley, 1978, p. 1). Parts of the institution were declared "unfit for human habitation."

Fit for habitation or not, Walpole was home for approximately six hundred inmates throughout the 1970s and the work place for half that number of staff. The traditional prison world of towering walls, dreary concrete expanses, and clanging metal doors was made all the more oppressive by Walpole's reputation for sudden violence and chronic despair. "I can imagine how the inmate walking into Walpole for the first time, how he must feel," remarked an officer with empathy. "He must feel like he's going to be eaten alive."

*Inmates and their environment.* A new inmate arrived at Walpole shackled hand and foot. Odds were that he was no older than twenty-five and had never completed high school. Although only 3 percent of Massachusetts residents were black, there was a 35 percent chance that he was black (and an additional 7 percent chance that he was Spanish speaking). Despite his youth, his commitment to Walpole probably did not mark his first stay in a penal institution. His current conviction was likely to have been for a crime of actual or threatened violence such as armed robbery, murder, assault, or rape, for which he would spend at least three years at Walpole before being released or moved to a less secure prison. One in five of his fellow inmates was serving a life sentence.

Like anyone entering the main part of the prison, be he inmate or officer, visitor or superintendent, the new inmate did so via the "trap," a narrow enclosure with heavy metal sliding doors at each end, only one of which could be opened at a time. Through the trap and across a small yard lay the heart of the prison: thirteen cellblocks jutting out from a long central corridor. Toward one end of the corridor were eight maximum-security ("max") blocks and the old death row. Toward the other end were three minimum-security cell blocks and the segregation block (see Figure 1).

The new inmate began his stay at Walpole in neither a maximum-nor minimum-security block, but rather in a subterranean "new

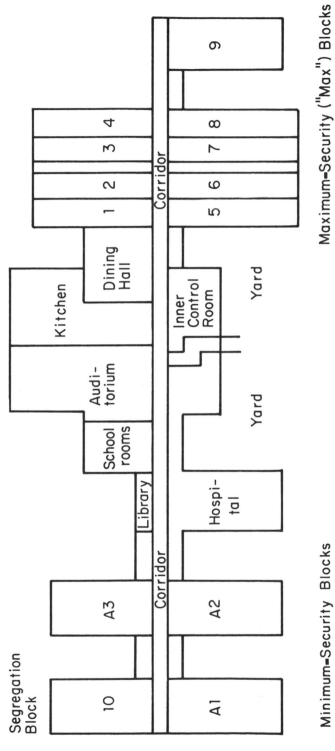

Segregation Block

Minimum-Security Blocks

Maximum-Security ("Max") Blocks

*Figure 1.* Floor plan of Walpole prison (adapted from Campbell, 1976, p. 40).

man's section" that had "a total lack of either natural or mechanical ventilation as well as a total lack of natural and only minimal artificial lighting"; lack of ventilation greatly exacerbated the problem of "multiple water leaks . . . and raw sewage periodically backing up through the floor drains" (Wensley, 1978, p. 2). Here the new inmate languished in his cell twenty-three-and-a-half hours a day, often waiting for months for assignment to a regular block. An officer lamented this neglect:

> If a guy committed a crime . . . [and was] sentenced to Walpole, it would be great if he came in, went through some kind of . . . indoctrination, he's given some kind of medical check-up, given an opportunity to see his family and friends . . . if he was given clean clothes, a bar of soap and a toothbrush and toothpaste the first day. But he's not. Guys have been here for *weeks* and don't get an initial issue of clothing!

In theory each new inmate was evaluated and assigned to a cell block according to his behavior and future prospects; in practice he was sent to wherever there was an empty cell. Officers were as critical of the situation as the inmates.

> A lot of inmates that get into Walpole, they go up the wall just staying in that new men's block . . . If they're lucky enough, they get out of the new men's block after . . . 3, 4, 5 months, whatever and they go down to the minimum end . . . [But] they haven't even done anything wrong and they end up in the maximum blocks because there's no room down at the minimum end . . . If the guy seems to be pretty straight, doesn't get into any trouble, stays clean, why throw him in the max block? . . . He'll meet all the real {beauties} in there and maybe end up just as bad.

If the new inmate did indeed end up in the more populous maximum end of the prison, he found somewhat better lighting and fresher air than in the new man's section, but also a far more precarious existence. The maximum-security blocks were cavernous places with "intractable" ventilation problems that resulted in extreme heat or cold depending on the season (Wensley, 1978, p. 2). Each block contained three tiers of fifteen windowless cells with barred doors facing out onto a solid concrete wall across a concrete floor or "flats" below. The four-by-six-foot cells each housed a single inmate and contained a bed, sink, and toilet in addition to whatever personal belongings its occupant could fit inside. (The 1978 Health Department inspection revealed that many of the toilets and sinks were broken and no cleaning supplies were available for those that were operational. Despite the filth, many inmates resorted to placing milk bottles in their toilet bowls as a crude form of refrigeration.) While inmates were permitted electrical appliances such as televisions, radios, and hot plates in their cells, they had no electrical outlets into which they could plug them. They were thus forced to improvise wiring from the single light fixture in their cell, creating a fire hazard. The blocks were strung like spiders' webs with makeshift television antennas—long wires extending from inmates' television sets, through the barred cell doors, over the flats to the opposing wall, stuck there by wads of wet toilet paper thrown from the tiers.

Unsoiled toilet paper was among the less offensive items thrown off the tiers. Food, feces, and other garbage littered the walls and flats below and served as a ready source of food for the "overpowering population of insects and rodents" (Wensley, 1978, p. 2). An inmate, Jerry Pierce, wrote to his wife,

> They put my styrofoam food container on the floor and right away a big rat started chewing on it. By the time I picked it up and threw it out of the cell, the rat had almost chewed through it and when it landed three other rats were on it. The cockroaches are all over. I sleep with the light on to keep them away but they are making us shut the lights now to save on electricity. (*Boston Globe*, 16 April 1980)

An inmate housed in the max end spent virtually all his time in his own block. Several times a week he was permitted out of the block for closely supervised visits with family or friends. Participation in most prison programs was denied; opportunity for outdoor recreation was "extremely limited" (Wensley, 1978, p. 2). All meals were served on the flats. Periodic counts were taken with inmates in their cells. For most of the rest of the day, inmates were free to wander on the flats or tiers in their own block, but did so without formal activity or opportunity for lawful recreation. Drug use was rampant; rape, assault, and extortion commonplace; murder a real and ever-present threat. Inmate Pierce described his block,

> This place is like a madhouse. There are guys who haven't been out with the rest of the [inmate] population in years. They're all

packing [carrying weapons]. The guards are scared of them. No one will even walk at the edge of the tier because they might get pushed over because the people on this block are just insane. There are kids in here who never did drugs before in their life and now they are junkies. There are rapes all over the place. Guys get whacked out on pain-killers. I have to be real careful that I don't get caught up in the craziness. I want to be out of here before the summer when things start boiling. (*Boston Globe*, 16 April 1980)

One week later, Pierce, who was serving time for forgery, was found strangled in his cell.

Prison administrators justified conditions in the "max" blocks by reference to a crude form of behavior modification theory: if an inmate found life sufficiently unbearable in the "max" blocks, he would be spurred to improve his own behavior in order to gain transfer to one of the three "minimum-security" cell blocks (assuming, of course, that there was an empty bed in a minimum block).

Conditions in the minimum blocks were indeed better. Each block contained seventy-two single occupancy cells arrayed three tiers high against the three external walls of the block. In an important departure from the max blocks, every cell had its own window facing out onto the prison yard which provided natural light and air as well as some contact with the world outside the cell blocks. In addition, cell doors were solid, not barred, and thus provided a degree of privacy and security in a world where men had little of either.

An inmate in the minimum-security blocks enjoyed access to activities outside his block including regular outdoor recreation, school, and work in various parts of the prison or in one of the outmoded industrial shops, as well as meals in the prison dining hall. In the evenings, he was not only permitted to visit within his own block, but often also in the other two minimum-security blocks as well (a privilege periodically granted and withdrawn during the 1970s).

Yet for all their advantages, the minimum blocks were plagued by most of the same problems as the rest of the institution. There were the ubiquitous rats and roaches, broken sinks and toilets, and lack of cleaning equipment. Opportunities for work or involvement in educational, therapeutic, or recreational activities were very limited.

And there were as many murders, rapes, assaults, and acts of extortion in the minimum blocks as elsewhere in the institution. For the two hundred inmates who lived there, the minimum-security blocks were, as often as not, just that—minimally secure.

If an inmate feared for his life whether he lived in the maximum or minimum end, he had an option, albeit an extreme one. He could request "protective custody," thereby effecting his removal from the regular blocks to an area specifically set aside for inmates in protective custody. There he would spend his time in solitary confinement with very limited time out of his cell each week for individual exercise, visits, or showers. It was not a move an inmate undertook lightly. Protective custody bears such stigma within the prison world that, once requested, an inmate usually feels compelled to serve the rest of his time in that status.

Despite these drawbacks, an exceptionally large number of Walpole inmates requested protective custody or "PC" status during the 1970s. "PC's" occupied the old death row, the hospital, at least one of the maximum-security blocks, and often parts of the disciplinary unit. In 1978 the president of the officers' union estimated that one-quarter of all Walpole inmates were PC's, an extraordinary statistic. But even PC's died violent deaths at Walpole. After one such murder, a *Boston Globe* editorial commented, "Maximum security, it is obvious, is a term used for the comfort of those outside the walls. Within Walpole, security doesn't exist" (20 November 1978).

If an inmate chose to respond to the horrors of his prison world not by withdrawal but by violence or active defiance, he, too, would find himself in solitary confinement, this time in the infamous Departmental Segregation Unit. Block 10, as the segregation unit was better known, was home to the "screw-ups of the screw-ups," the sixty inmates deemed most intractable by prison authorities. Despite its physical separation from the rest of the institution, Block 10 was considered a barometer for the prison. From here inmate leaders led strikes, issued manifestos, and fought daily fights with their captors. The president of the officers' union observed, "As Block 10 goes, so goes the institution" (*Boston Globe*, 19 August 1978).

Block 10 consisted of four self-contained units of fifteen cells. Each inmate's physical environment comprised a bed, sink, and seatless toilet inside three solid concrete walls and a barred cell door through which he could gaze out across a narrow corridor at another concrete wall. Depending on recent events in the block and the philosophy of the supervisor in charge, inmates were permitted a range of personal items as well, including at times radios and televisions. Some light and fresh air were provided in the block by a row of windows placed above eye level on the outside wall.

An officer recruit recalled his first visit to Block 10. "I walked in. I said to myself, I haven't even seen zoos where animals live like this. There was shit, garbage, everything, thrown all over the place. Human shit. And it stunk." Conditions in the rest of the prison paled in comparison. Exclaimed a Block 10 officer, "It's incredible how filthy it is. You think the max blocks are dirty—they're clean!" The walls and floors were caked with excrement and garbage, pungent mementos of past altercations. "I've walked in that place where there was garbage [knee] high on the floors—feces, urine, everything, *everything*. There was an inch of slime on the floor so when it was wet outside and the walls used to bleed, you couldn't walk. You'd slide down the corridors." Rats and roaches were everywhere, swarming over the block and its inhabitants. "You've got platoons of cockroaches up there. First platoon, second platoon, third platoon . . . Thousands of them!" An inmate likened living there to being "three inches big . . . standing facing the gutter. There are walls beside you and a wall behind you and bars in front of you and you are looking into the gutter . . . all you can see is a wall with shit on it" (*Boston Globe*, 6 May 1979). (Reasons why sanitary conditions in Block 10 and the rest of the prison remained so bad for so many years despite the revulsion of most inmates and officers will be explored in Chapter 4.)

As constrained as an inmate's world might have been in Block 10, it could be made even more so. In addition to the standard barred cell door, half the cells had solid metal doors with one tiny window in them. The cells themselves had no windows, and once the metal door was closed the cell's occupant was effectively sealed off from the rest of the world. Some inmates spent months at a time in "punitive isolation" under conditions they likened to being in "a box or tomb" (*Boston Globe*, 11 December 1979). In a revealing commentary on "contemporary standards," the Massachusetts Supreme Judicial Court held in 1982 that confinement in "box car" cells was not "repugnant to contemporary standards of decency," nor did it constitute cruel and unusual punishment (*Libby v. Commissioner of Correction*, 1982, p. 421).

Alternatively, an inmate could be placed in one of Block 10's punishment cells known as the "blue rooms." They were bare rooms with solid doors and no windows, toilets, sinks, or furniture other than a urine-stained mattress on the floor. An officer likened the blue rooms to a

> ceramic tile shower stall. That's what the floor and the walls and the ceilings are. The drain is like a shower drain and that's where they go to the bathroom. And it's filled with water, and everything's floating around in there. The mattress {is covered with} maggots and cockroaches. Guy'll be sleeping and you walk down there and they'll be crawling all over him.

Block 10 was, as a *Boston Globe* editorial phrased it, "Massachusetts' own version of the black hole of Calcutta" (7 May 1979).

*Officers.* Charged with controlling and maintaining the inmate population at Walpole was a staff of approximately 350, a ratio of fewer than two inmates for every staff member. Included among the staff were the superintendent, his deputies, and their assistants; social workers, teachers, and chaplains; and secretarial and maintenance workers. But the vast majority were "protective service" staff—correction officers, senior officers, and their supervisors.

In contrast to the inmates, most of whom came from the Boston metropolitan area, Walpole officers traditionally hailed from the small towns and communities of southeast Massachusetts down to the old whaling ports of New Bedford and Fall River. Many were immigrants or sons of immigrants, but few were members of racial minority groups. Like the inmates, most officers were in their twenties. Turnover rates among officers were very high throughout the 1970s. In 1976, when research for this book began, two-thirds of all Walpole officers had worked there less than five years; one in four had been there less than a year. (A profile of men who became officers—their backgrounds, attitudes, and motivations—is provided in Chapter 7.)

Officers were organized into three permanent shifts: the "7-3" (7 A.M. to 3 P.M.), the "3-11" (3 P.M. to 11 P.M.), and the "11-7" (11 P.M. to 7 A.M.). Each shift had its own chain of command with officers, senior officers, shift supervisors, and shift commanders, the last reporting directly to the deputy superintendent for security.

As in most prisons, the three shifts served as an organizational device not only for the officers but also for the institution as a whole. The day shift was "complete chaos." Administrators, social workers, lawyers, teachers, visitors, and other "outsiders" were all in the institution. Inmates from the minimum end were out of their cell blocks working and attending classes. Visits and programs were in progress. The corridors were filled with activity.

And then, "the 3-to-11 comes on and boom!" "It's like someone rings a bell and everything is different." The inmates were locked for a headcount, most organized activities ceased, and the institution was left to the officers and inmates. It was a time of stricter security and greater control despite a smaller complement of officers. It was also the time of greatest conflict and violence between officers and inmates.

By the time the skeletal 11–7 shift arrived, the inmates were already locked in their cells for the night. The "graveyard shift" counted sleeping bodies and patrolled the shadows of the institution until the 7–3 shift arrived to begin another day's activity.

On the 7–3 and 3–11 shifts at Walpole, a single officer was assigned to each max block, one or two officers to each minimum block, and up to a dozen officers to the segregation unit, Block 10. These men were known as "block officers." Just as the cell blocks constituted the heart of the prison, the block officers held the most critical posts within it. They were the principal representatives of the prison establishment (and thus of the world outside) in those parts of the prison that mattered most to inmates. They had the greatest contact with inmates, the primary responsibility for supervising and controlling them, and the first (and often only) opportunity to identify and resolve problems affecting inmates in their charge. By their actions and interactions, they set the tone for relations between officers and inmates throughout the prison. Block officers' intimate contact with inmates and their relative isolation from other officers made their posts by far the most dangerous ones in the prison.

At Walpole, block officers were severely hampered in carrying out their principal tasks of security and control by defects in design of the prison itself. In the maximum end, the officer's desk was located just inside the door to the block. But the "cell blocks in the maximum section have been designed to place the doors to the block in the one location that makes it impossible for an officer at the door to observe activity in that section of the block housing the inmates" (Jenkins, 1978, p. 85). If an officer dared venture far from his desk onto the flats to observe what was happening in the cells, he risked being struck by heavy objects (such as mop wringers or full cans of soup) hurled from the tiers above. If he dared to go up onto the tiers alone, he risked assault, capture, or being tossed over the railing onto the flats below.

Although each block officer bore primary responsibility for control of his own block, he was not the only one charged with surveillance. High above the blocks ran a network of galleries with windows overlooking the tiers. It was from there that the cell doors below were electronically opened and shut. In theory, the gallery officer, shrouded in semi-darkness, should have been able to monitor the cell blocks below him. Whoever designed the galleries, however, was unacquainted with the defiance of human captives and their resentment against prying eyes. The gallery windows could not be cleaned from inside the gallery, and over the years inmates had thrown enough food and excrement to make the windows nearly opaque.

In the minimum blocks, the cells formed a horseshoe around three walls with the officer's desk next to the door at the open end of the block. Opportunities for surveillance were thus better (unless there was insufficient lighting to see to the end of the block, a situation officers complained often prevailed).

The most serious problems existed in Block 10. Cells in the segregation unit faced out across a corridor that was only a few feet wide onto a solid wall. The only means of observing inmates or having contact with them (to serve meals, distribute medicine, remove men for visits, and so on) was for an officer to go down the tier. But as soon as he had gone past the first cell door, he became a ready target for objects thrown through the bars. Officers routinely wore raincoats or garbage bags to ward off excrement as they ventured down the tier, but such garments provided little defense against more dangerous weapons—boiling water or, worse, sharpened broom handles, television antennas, or whatever weapons inmates could forge from their meager belongings. Officers frequently found themselves trapped on the tier, a situation made more precarious by the absence of adequate lighting. "At night you couldn't even see who [the inmates] were or *where* they were." At one point, only seventeen of 160 light fixtures were reportedly working in the block. In what was no doubt an understatement, the president of the officers' union observed, "Working in this condition presents a degree of horror for the officers. If an officer walks as much as fifteen feet down the upper tier at night, his fellow officer standing watch loses sight of him in the darkness" (*Herald*, 27 March 1979).

A block officer typically spent his entire shift in his own block. Security and control within his block were his foremost responsibilities. (In the event of trouble elsewhere in the prison, he was expected to lock his own block door and go to the aid of his fellow officers.) But more mundane tasks demanded most of his attention, especially on the 7–3 shift: answering the telephone, checking inmates in and out of the block, distributing meals, mail, and medicine, processing new arrivals, tracking down television sets lost in the prison delivery system. For hours at a time, however, he might sit inside the cell block door doing nothing, waiting for something to happen.

Although life within the prison centered on the cell blocks, only about one-quarter of all Walpole officers were assigned to blocks. The remainder of the officer corps worked in inner and outer control centers, monitored inmate work and recreation areas, manned gun towers, and provided the myriad backup services necessary for running a large institution—handling mail, ordering supplies, running the inmate canteen. Many of these positions were far removed from life in the blocks. Some, like gun tower duty, involved no direct contact with inmates at all.

Individual officers were not assigned to various posts according to their capacities or skills. Rather, prior to the 1970s, *officers at Walpole had acquired the right to select their posts for themselves on the basis of seniority alone.* Whenever a particular post on a particular shift became available, any officer could bid for that position. Whichever officer expressing interest had worked the longest time at Walpole automatically got the job. Once an officer successfully bid for a post, he could remain in that position, on the same shift, with the same days off, until he retired or was able to bid onto a more desirable post and shift. "More desirable post" at Walpole during the 1970s almost always meant one further removed from the inmates. In fact, a general maxim about Walpole would have been that the greater an officer's experience, the less he had to do with inmates. As a consequence, the most important and hazardous posts within the prison—those of cell block officer—were invariably filled by the least experienced officers. The New York State Special Commission on Attica concluded that a seniority bid system in effect at the time of the Attica uprising had "left the daily supervision of the inmate population to inexperienced young officers, often no older than the young inmates they confronted. With no supervisory training or experience, they were totally unprepared for the jobs left to them by older officers" (*Attica*, 1972, p. 126). The seniority bid system had an equally disastrous effect at Walpole.

Seniority bid contributed to another important problem at Walpole, differences between work shifts. Such differences can be found at almost any prison, but they were particularly marked at Walpole. The 7–3 and 3–11 shifts were as "different as black and white," and considerable hostility existed between them. Officers with seniority were able to bid onto the day shift with its better work hours, leaving the 3–11 shift to younger, less experienced officers who were generally "more gung-ho . . . Whereas an older officer, he's mellowed." As will be discussed in Chapter 8, differences between the two shifts of officers reflected not only their ages and experiences, but also the styles and philosophies of the men who were in charge of the shifts.

A study of Walpole commissioned by the Department of Correction in 1979 scored lack of cooperation and communication between shifts.

> There is a dichotomy between correctional staff. Each staff member views his shift as a separate and independent function. There is no formal log passed from one Shift Commander to the next. The only form of communication is from word of mouth. (National Institute of Corrections, 1979, pp. 72–73)

Lack of briefings for officers on incoming shifts led to some extraordinary situations. One officer reported that he did not find out that an inmate had been murdered during the preceding shift *in that officer's own cell block* until he walked into the block and found state police investigating the death. Worse yet, officers on one shift were allegedly not told when officers on a preceding shift had been stabbed. Oblivious to the danger, two more officers were injured on the incoming shift under similar circumstances. A fight brewing, a door jammed, a sudden influx of drugs—such information is the lifeblood of a prison. That it was not always or even commonly passed on from shift to shift at Walpole bespoke remarkable incompetence (or indifference) at the supervisory level, and mutual hostility at the officer level.

*Officers and administrators.* Antagonism between shifts was a minor problem at Walpole compared to hostility that existed between officers and administrators throughout the decade. Overriding all else, officers saw administrators "from the top echelons on down" as uncaring about officers and willing to betray them if necessary to purchase a transient peace. As an officer described their feelings, "We're alone. We have only each other. The administration does not give a shit for us."

Officers viewed the prison's administrators as weak, incompetent, vacillating, petty, and uncaring, afraid even to venture inside the prison.

> They had all kinds of nicknames, "Rainbow so-and-so," because he was only out in good weather and he was gone in the storms, and "Shaky." There were different nicknames for different people in authority that were making decisions. People would say, "I wonder where they hid the ouiji board to make this decision." . . . There was not much common sense behind [them].

To the officers, especially those on the 3–11 and 11–7 shifts, administrators were phantom men who rarely made their presence felt within the institution. What did officers think was the worst thing they could do in the eyes of the administration? Not fail to prevent an escape or bring drugs into the prison or somehow disgrace their uniform. Rather, it was to take too many sick days. "As long as you were in there working, that's all they cared about."

What an officer did once inside the prison seemed of little concern to the administration. He was not, as was the case in other prison systems, "evaluated in terms of the conduct of the men he controls" (Sykes, 1958, p. 56). Nor did "a troublesome, noisy, dirty cell block" (p. 56) affect his future in terms of pay, promotion, or job assignment, these being almost exclusively determined by state contract, written examination, and seniority bid. Even if the administration did not like the way an officer handled his position, what were they going to do—relieve him? fire him? replace him with whom? "At Walpole they're not going to send you home . . . Because they need the help . . . They need a body. Even if the guy's no good they need that man in there."

In any case, the administration could not evaluate what it knew nothing about and, according to the officers, their superiors rarely availed themselves of the opportunity to see firsthand what was happening. "I don't know if the administration really knows what is going on," observed one officer in 1978. "You never see them in there," commented another. Added a third, "As far as the administration, I've never dealt with any of them. To be honest, I don't even know any of them [by] name . . . I had no dealing with them." If the administration ignored the officers, the officers largely ignored the administration. "A lot of times the officers up there, if they got an order that they didn't like, they just wouldn't do it."

During the middle and late 1970s, the administration effectively conceded control over the day-to-day life of the institution to the officers and inmates. The power struggles that ensued between officers and inmates, largely in the absence of the administration, are discussed in the next chapter.

## Concord

Concord prison, built in 1878, served briefly as the state's maximum-security prison before being turned into a reformatory for young men. By the 1970s Concord was in a state of disrepair, its external wall crumbling, its cell blocks cramped, its industries antiquated. The century-old prison was, by then, incongruously situated near the heart of one of Boston's most exclusive suburbs. Multimillion-dollar efforts to rejuvenate the institution were severely hampered in the 1970s by political corruption (part of a broader construction scandal in Massachusetts) and conflicting demands of a rapid succession of prison superintendents.

*Inmates and their environment.* Inmates at Concord were "young kids" doing "short time." They ranged in age from seventeen to twenty-five and usually spent six months or less at the prison. Few, however, were novices in the criminal justice system. Most had been arrested for the first time by the age of fifteen, had previously been incarcerated in an adult or juvenile institution, and were presently serving time for a crime of violence.

The Governor's Advisory Committee on Corrections noted in 1978 (p. 28):

> Concord, which houses the youngest and most vulnerable male inmates in the system, operates at 160% of capacity. The facility is designed to hold 220 inmates, however, 347 are placed there currently. Concord inmates are routinely double bunked or placed in overcrowded, insufficiently supervised, dormitory facilities. Assaults, rapes and beatings are commonplace. Conditions for inmates and staff are intolerable.

For want of space anywhere else, new arrivals were placed in an "overcrowded, unsanitary" hospital ward. It had been designed for eight sick inmates but often housed more than thirty inmates, well and sick, in triple bunk beds and mattresses on the floor. Whenever space permitted, inmates were moved from the hospital to the "New Line"—a cell block with 106 inmates double bunked in cells so small that only one man could stand comfortably at a time. Inmates were supposed to be held in the New Line for a month while they were diagnosed and classified. Instead, most remained there four to six months, locked in their cells twenty-three hours a day with an unwelcome companion, awaiting a bed somewhere else.

If an inmate was not released before he had finally been "classified," he was moved to a recently constructed, poorly designed building "in which the officers' station is located in the only position on the floor that guarantees minimal visual observation of the areas of activity" (Jenkins, 1978, p. 85). As inmates and officers know only too well, "Violence within an institution setting is facilitated by problems in the construction of the physical plant" (p. 86). Poorly designed buildings housing young, idle inmates in cramped, ill-supervised quarters were major factors in the high levels of individual and collective violence that characterized Concord throughout the decade.

*Officers and administrators.* Inmates were not the only ones engaged in conflict. Nowhere in the state prison system were relations between officers and administrators worse than at Concord. The officer corps there had long been the most insular in Massachusetts. Most officers came from Lowell, at one time a major textile manufacturing center although most of the mills had since closed. For some families, employment at Concord went back generations.

> They called it "the place of the forty cousins." It was all relatives. And that wasn't just officers; it was the administration, it was the secretaries, it was the social workers, the counselors, the whole bit . . . They were very cohesive . . . And they were very union-oriented.

Concord officers were particularly resistant to efforts by the Department of Correction to assert central authority over the state prisons during the 1970s. "They don't like Central Office, they didn't like the philosophies of Central Office. And it seemed like Central Office had very little power over them." The department was considered remote, its administrators indifferent to the officers' fate.

> The administration has no control over the officers. And if there's a riot or something . . . [and] the administration decided to do something, and if the officers didn't think it was wise, I think they might not do it . . . I'd follow [an officer] first before anyone from the Central Office because, number one, I know they have no regard for me whatsoever as an officer.

Concord officers had been the most militant supporters of an illegal statewide employees' strike in 1976. In the aftermath of the strike, Concord officers saw themselves as singled out for harsh treatment by the department. During the latter part of the decade, officers there reported "a tremendous breakdown in morale throughout the entire institution." Feeling "more frustration from the problems they have with the administration than they do from the problems they have with the inmates," officers quit in record numbers. They were replaced for the most part by new officers who came from outside the Lowell area. Concord officers did not support a 1978 wildcat strike led by Walpole officers over the failure of the legislature to pass the state budget on time. They continued to manifest their defiance of the administration in individualistic ways, but they rarely seemed able to organize themselves in effective opposition to the administration. The hold of the old corps of officers was for the most part broken, yet a succession of superintendents failed to gain mastery over the institution. For much of the 1970s Concord drifted—grossly overcrowded, violent, largely out of control.

## Norfolk

A few miles from Walpole stood the state's medium-security prison for adult males, Norfolk. It was built in the early 1930s as a radically new type of prison for men, one based on a "community" model. Inmates were housed not in a fortress-style prison but in a series of residential buildings around an open yard, albeit surrounded by a traditional prison wall and gun towers. Inmates enjoyed limited self-governance and were expected to be employed within the institution. Officers were divided between those who acted as the "cop on the beat" (the "uniformed officers") and those who wore civilian clothes and interacted with inmates in the residential buildings as counsellors and caseworkers (the "house officers"). The experiment was short-lived. Upheavals within the institution led to increased restrictions on the inmate population and adverse publicity about events inside. Only three years after the prison opened, its reformist superintendent was dismissed. Although the prison henceforth assumed more traditional custodial goals and procedures, Norfolk retained some characteristics of its early, innovative years.

*Inmates and their environment.* During the 1970s (and before), inmates were not sentenced directly to Norfolk. Instead they were transferred there from other state prisons, principally Walpole and Concord. As an officer explained, "We get them from Walpole if they've been good and from Concord if they've been bad." Norfolk inmates tended to be older than inmates at the other two prisons and serving longer sentences. The 700 to 750 inmates lived in groups of fifty in three-story "houses" situated around a large "yard" with walkways, grass, and occasional flowers. Most inmates spent their days working in various parts of the institution, participating in training programs, or attending school. After returning to their own houses for dinner, they were free to roam the yard until nightfall.

Despite a relatively relaxed environment, Norfolk was not insulated from the turmoil of the decade. On a number of occasions inmates engaged in strikes or other protest actions, at times with considerable tenacity and effect. During the summer of 1978, all 750 inmates went on strike to protest restrictions on visitors to the institution. In a time-honored response to protests at Norfolk, inmate leaders were quickly transferred out of the institution. But the rest of the inmate population maintained solidarity, effectively shutting down all of the prison's industries for three months and forcing employees to perform kitchen, janitorial, and clerical chores normally done by inmates (unlike Walpole and Concord, Norfolk continued to operate profitable industrial shops during the 1970s). Only when the administration rescinded new regulations regarding searches of visitors and participation of outsiders in prison programs did inmates return to work.

Violence was not common at Norfolk. Although Norfolk was the scene of the only staff fatalities in Massachusetts prisons during the 1970s, only four inmates were murdered there during the same period, and serious assaults on inmates and officers were rare. Day-to-day relations between officers and inmates were not marred by the raw antagonisms evident at Walpole and Concord. As one Norfolk officer observed, "For this type of environment with so many supposedly dangerous, no-good people, it runs pretty smooth."

*Officers and administrators.* The original division of Norfolk officers into "uniformed officers" and "house officers" persisted over the years. The majority were uniformed officers. As their title suggests, they bore traditional responsibilities for security and control within the prison: supervising inmates outside the houses, manning gun towers, handling emergencies. House officers were in a sense analogous to cell block officers at other prisons, but with important differences. In role and appearance, they often resembled social workers as much as prison officers. They wore civilian clothes (and in the 1970s often modishly long hair and beards), served on classification committees and disciplinary boards dealing with inmates in their house, and spent much of their day interacting with inmates in a relatively informal residential setting.

Norfolk officers had the right to determine on the basis of seniority bid whether they would work as uniformed officers or house officers. Uniformed officers could also decide by seniority which shift (8–4, 4–12, 12–8) they would work (all house officers worked swing shifts). But unlike officers at Walpole and Concord, uniformed officers at Norfolk did not have the right to choose their own post within the prison—that important power remained with their superiors. House officers, on the other hand, could bid for positions within specific houses.

Prior to the 1970s, house officer positions were popular. Five or six years of seniority were usually necessary to bid onto one; once in a house, officers often stayed there for years. But as the prison system overheated, house officer positions became less and less attractive. By the mid-1970s, officers with just a few months experience were able to obtain house officer posts. Soon thereafter, rookie officers were being drafted directly into houses, and they were bailing out of them as soon as they had sufficient seniority. As at Walpole, the most sensitive and important jobs within the prison were being relegated to the least experienced officers.

Officers at Norfolk felt considerable hostility to certain administrators and administrative policies and were not hesitant about expressing grievances to their superiors. In 1975, for example, union officials called a press conference to express displeasure over delays in purchasing an X-ray machine with which to examine incoming packages (this in the wake of the shooting of two officers). Other protests were less public. An officer recalled the attempts of a supervisor on the midnight shift to impose a new method of counting inmates that involved locking an officer inside the inmates' sleeping area while he counted. "Of course, nobody did it. We paid no attention to it . . . [The officers] went to the superintendent next day; everybody [on the midnight shift] just stayed over [until the superintendent arrived] . . . They wouldn't put up with that." The new policy was quickly abandoned. For the most part, though, relations between officers and the administration were stable at Norfolk. Officers, meanwhile, complained of lack of unity within their own ranks; hence, many were reluctant to become actively involved in union activities, especially strikes. During a strike over "payless paydays" led by Walpole officers in 1978, Norfolk officers voted unanimously to continue working.

## Bridgewater

The state's largest prison complex was situated on fourteen hundred acres near the town of Bridgewater in southeastern Massachusetts. The site was first used as an almshouse in 1855, then as a workhouse for "vicious paupers" and short-term offenders who were compelled to work surrounding state farmland. When leveled by fire in the 1880s, the "State Farm" was rebuilt to house a remarkable assortment of human beings: the "criminally insane," "defective delinquents," "inebriates," and, eventually, "sexually dangerous persons."

In the 1970s Bridgewater contained four separate facilities to which inmates and officers were permanently assigned. The two facilities that were part of this study were the State Hospital for the Criminally Insane and the Treatment Center for Sexually Dangerous Persons. (The other two were an addiction center for alcoholics and a minimum-security prison for inmates who had been transferred from Walpole, Concord, and Norfolk because they were nearing release or were in special need of protective custody.)

*State Hospital for the Criminally Insane.* Until 1974, inmates at the State Hospital were housed under conditions "that would have shamed the Middle Ages . . . [L]arge groups of men, naked or half-clothed, milled about through the litter in large, dimly lit, barn-like rooms, hallucinating, talking to themselves and gesticulating, living in conditions worse than we permit for animals in zoos" (James F. Gilligan, personal communication, February 1987). The shocking conditions of confinement and harsh treatment of "patients" revealed in Fred Wiseman's brilliant documentary film, *Titicut Follies,* contributed to public pressure for a new facility which was built immediately adjacent to the old one. The new hospital was a dramatic improvement. In place of the labyrinth of old dungeons, which the Governor's Advisory Committee on Corrections had aptly likened to a "stage set for a Dickensian movie," was a series of modern, airy, well-equipped buildings around a grassy compound surrounded by a high chain-link fence. The man who was to become the medical director of the institution wryly observed that, with the move to the new facility, "Bridgewater went from somewhere in the

Dark Ages (say around the tenth century) to something at least approximating the twentieth century" (Gilligan, pers. com., 1987).

The new hospital held approximately 350 adult males who had been committed by courts for pre-trial observation and evaluation; found not competent to stand trial; found not guilty by reason of insanity; transferred from another state or county prison because of mental illness; or transferred from a nonpenal mental institution because of violent or aggressive behavior. Although approximately half of the "patients" were civil, not criminal, commitments, the hospital was under the direct authority of the Department of Correction. Beginning in the mid-1970s, however, psychiatric services were contracted to a private psychiatric institution with a director who was independent of the Department of Correction. Under this "split administration," the superintendent retained sole authority over correctional staff and responsibility for safety and security within the institution, while the medical director assumed responsibility for care and treatment of patients. In practice, their spheres of influence often conflicted.

*Treatment Center for Sexually Dangerous Persons.* Massachusetts was unusual in the 1970s in having 150 of its hard-core sex offenders segregated in a single institution—the "Treatment Center" located in some of the oldest buildings at Bridgewater. A 1958 law defined a sexually dangerous person (SDP) as:

> Any person whose misconduct in sexual matters indicates a general lack of power to control his sexual impulses, as evidenced by repetitive or compulsive behavior and either violence, or aggression by an adult against a victim under the age of 16 years, and who, as a result is likely to attack or otherwise inflict injury on the objects of his uncontrolled or uncontrollable desires.   (Powers, 1973, p. 131)

In order to incapacitate such men (there were no women) until they were no longer deemed sexually dangerous, all SDPs were committed to the Treatment Center, the date of release depending on the local district courts' agreement (or disagreement) with the most recent annual psychiatric evaluation. The institution was placed under the joint administrative control of the Department of Mental Health and the Department of Correction, a cumbersome arrangement which resulted in hostility among staff members and neglect by both departments.

*Inmates, officers, and administrators.* Bridgewater had a history of independence from the rest of the Department of Correction. The special inmate population—insane, retarded, alcoholic, sexually deviant—rendered many department policies inapplicable there, and commissioners and superintendents of other institutions tended to treat Bridgewater as outside their sphere of influence as long as the institution was operating quietly, which it usually was. For nearly half a century, a succession of two powerful superintendents controlled Bridgewater. Strong political ties of their own insulated them and the prison from political and administrative changes affecting the rest of the department.

Life for officers and inmates at Bridgewater was quite different from life in the state's other prisons. Because inmates at the State Hospital and Treatment Center were formally considered "patients," they could not be forced to work. Most spent their days in idleness; many were heavily medicated. Although inmates at the State Hospital were prone to sudden, spontaneous acts of violence, they were almost never armed with weapons and were largely incapable of engaging in collective violence. By 1980, six years after the facility had opened, no homicides and only one suicide had occurred among the thousands of inmates admitted.

Although relations between officers and administrators were often antagonistic at Bridgewater, especially on an individual basis, officers did not attempt to affect prison governance through collective action and only weakly supported strike actions taken by officers at other institutions. Compared to the rest of the prison system, officer turnover was very low.

# 4

# Power in a Prison

Prison officials face a daunting task in fulfilling the mission of the modern penitentiary. As Gresham Sykes (1958, p. 18) pointed out in his classic study of a New Jersey prison,

> Somehow [the administrator of the maximum-security prison] must resolve the claims that the prison should exact vengeance, erect a specter to terrify the actual or potential deviant, isolate the known offender from the free community, and effect a change in the personality of his captives so that they gladly follow the dictates of the law—and in addition maintain order within his society of prisoners and see that they are employed at useful labor.

In short, prison officials are expected to punish, deter, isolate, and rehabilitate offenders while at the same time maintaining order and inmate productivity.

But external pressures to pursue multiple goals are not necessarily felt within a prison at the level where officers and inmates interact. Walpole is a case in point. Few people, least of all the officers, suggested that Walpole rehabilitated anyone. As one officer exclaimed, "Massachusetts Correctional Institution, shit! It's the state prison." Walpole certainly did punish, but aside from some officers who sought to make the going particularly rough on certain types of offenders (such as child molesters), few saw themselves exacting punishment beyond confinement for offenses committed *outside* of Walpole. (Some saw no need to improve conditions because of the types of crimes the inmates had committed, but that is a somewhat different matter.) Soaring crime rates and their own experiences with the prison's "revolving door" had relieved them of any delusions that they were deterring crime. In years past, Walpole allegedly had a thriving industrial section, but by the late 1970s it was obsolete and employed but a few dozen inmates. In any case, inmate productivity was not a matter that appeared to concern any of the officers interviewed.

Walpole officers were thus left with two aims: prevention of escape (isolation) and maintenance of internal order. The officers took isolation of the inmates from the community outside very seriously, and they performed the task exceptionally well. By 1980 only two prisoners had ever escaped from inside Walpole. As for internal order, it is a task they had pared to the bone: the prevention of large-scale riots and of injury to officers. The blood- and excrement-stained walls of Walpole attested to their inability to prevent much else. Thus, of the diverse and often conflicting expectations of prisons, Walpole officers concerned themselves with only two reasonably compatible ones: prevention of escape and maintenance of a minimum of internal control.

Not only were Walpole officers able to concentrate their energies on the accomplishment of two complementary tasks, but by the mid-1970s they were also free of many of the external constraints that encumber officers in many other prisons in carrying out those tasks, especially in regard to use of physical force and coercion. Yet one needed only to walk into Walpole with its stench, its sullen inmates, its officers afraid to venture onto the flats or the tiers to know how tenuous was the officers' control, particularly in comparison with maximum-security prisons in other states where more formal constraints on officers existed. Why, despite the lack of external constraints, did officers at Walpole fail so conspicuously to control the inmates?

Power is the ability to get an individual to do as one wants when the individual otherwise would not do so. Commonly recognized forms of power include authority, persuasion, inducement, manipulation, force, and coercion. In trying to understand why officers at Walpole, and to a lesser extent the other Massachusetts prisons, proved unable to control their respective inmate populations, I shall consider how officers (and inmates) attempted to use each of these six forms of power.

## Authority

Authority is commonly viewed as a power relationship in which the commands and desires of one individual or group are accepted as legitimate and thus are automatically complied with by another individual or group. Because compliance is automatic, in most circumstances authority is the most desirable and economical means of effecting control.

Richard Cloward (1960, pp. 20–21) observed regarding the use of authority in prisons,

> In a stable society most institutions succeed in converting force into authority. People conform not so much because they must as because they feel they should; that is, most institutions successfully motivate individuals to want to do what they have to do. *But this conversion does not take place in the penal environment.* (Emphasis added.)

Sykes (1958, p. 48) singled out officers' lack of authority as a, perhaps *the*, prime defect in their power over inmates. At Trenton prison he observed the "apparent contradiction" wherein inmates recognized the legitimacy of the officers' control over them but felt no corresponding obligation to obey. At Walpole in the 1970s he would perhaps have observed a grimmer situation for the officers. There—partly as a result of the politicization of inmates, which affected officer-inmate relations throughout the nation, and partly as a result of sustained conflict at Walpole itself—Walpole officers appeared to have been denied both elements of authority: they were daily surrounded by inmates who not only flaunted an attitude that they had no obligation to obey their captors, but also openly challenged the right of the officers to rule at all.

On the other hand, to say that officers at Walpole or elsewhere exercise *no* authority overstates the case. At each of the institutions studied here, *most* officers exercised authority over *some* aspects of inmates' lives—that is, inmates recognized the legitimacy of the officers' control in certain spheres and obeyed. The problem besetting officers was not that they had no authority within the prison, but rather that the scope of their authority was insufficient for the accomplishment of necessary tasks, limited though those tasks may have been. Moreover, the strength of their authority was insufficient to overcome opposing forms and sources of power within the institution, principally use of force and coercion by inmates. Let us look for a moment at the authority officers did have.

"The first month-and-a-half I really didn't know how to cope with the job," recalled one Walpole officer. "I was at the point where I was so scared working in there or so nervous or whatever—the frustration—that I wasn't sure I wanted to do that kind of work." One day he told the inmates in his block they would be unable to go out to the yard. They responded by "picking up everything they could get their hands on and throwing it" at the officer. "I was actually at the point where I was losing my temper. I almost wanted to . . . go out there to fight with them." With the inmates heaping refuse and abuse on the officer, his claim to authority seemed tenuous indeed. The officer reflected on the seeming impossibility of the job. "Everybody tells you you've got to make the inmates do this, you've got to make the inmates do that, and you're trying to control the situation. There they are—all of them. They're throwing things at you and they're yelling at you, swearing at you." Standing alone, what could he do?

Yet, like many other officers before him, he was able to come to grips with his authority.

> I was thinking at the time I'm going to control this situation if I have to go out there and beat some heads. And that's when I started thinking, well, gee, that's no good. I can't go in there and fight with forty guys. I mean, I've got to be able to *tell* them that I don't want them to do that and they've got to listen to me . . . There's a way to handle this job that's better than being all worked up and yelling and screaming and fighting with everybody.

At that point, two inmates

> started fighting. And so all I told them was to break the fight up. I said, "I don't care how you do it, I want that fight broken up right now." And sure enough . . . just like that, they broke the fight up . . . There was ten guys standing around watching the fight . . . and they just jumped {right in} and grabbed them and pulled them out. And that was the end of it.

The officer described this situation as the "turning point" in his career. From that day onward he found he was able to accomplish his essential duties by *telling* the inmates what he wanted without recourse to threats of force or physical coercion.

I recall a similar incident at Niantic prison when as a new officer

I first became aware of how much authority I had. I was taking a group of twenty or more inmates on a walk accompanied by another officer even newer than myself. After about ten minutes—when we were well out of sight or hearing of any other officer and next to an open field that led to a forest and freedom—two inmates got into an ugly quarrel. Other inmates appeared to be choosing sides. With the situation getting out of hand I announced in a quavering voice that the fighting inmates should stop it that instant and that everyone was to return to the housing unit immediately. Turning around, I headed toward the unit. To my very considerable relief, everyone reversed direction and trooped back behind me. They did not do this out of any personal loyalty or respect, for I had not been there long enough to establish such feelings; nor did they stop fighting and follow me out of anticipation of reward for doing so or much in the way of punishment for failure to comply (had things gotten really out of hand it would have reflected more on me than on them); nor just because my directions may have been appropriate under the circumstances, for I do not think that any of the inmates could have gotten similar compliance, and certainly none as new or young as myself. Rather it was the position I held, coupled with some claim to reasonableness of my directions (Friedrich, 1958), that resulted in my being obeyed. In short, it was my authority over the group.

Most experienced officers at Walpole and the other Massachusetts prisons felt they had established authority over inmates regarding their basic responsibilities—doing counts, locking and unlocking cells, distributing food, breaking up fights, rescuing suicides—and had done so by virtue of the reasonableness of their own behavior and recognition on the part of most inmates that they were only doing their job. "If you just did your job, you'd get no hassle with them, they'd get no hassle with you. They know you're just doing your job. They're not stupid."

Among the institutions studied, officers at Norfolk appeared to exercise the most authority. Nowhere was their authority more evident than out in the prison yard during the evenings when nearly seven hundred inmates were supervised by only four officers working in pairs. A Norfolk officer marveled, "They're all walking around doing what they want to do. There's two of you walking around telling them what to do. You says, 'Why are they listening to me?' Why would they? But they do." Another Norfolk officer who had worried about his ability to exercise authority over inmates discovered, "Most people don't really have to be dominated to be told to do something because you can just say you need something done and they recognize your authority." When conflict arose with an inmate, "99 percent of them would back down, not for me, but from the authority that was behind me."

An exception to the officers' authority at Norfolk was the housing unit "called the Mafioso House. Out of forty-two [inmates] . . . there were twenty-six known Mafia people and at least another six were trying to get in on the periphery." One officer described Norfolk in the mid-1970s as an institution with two administrations—the official administration and "an administration also on the inside that has its own chain of command" whose members inhabited that house. Good communication between the administration and the inmate hierarchy, and the privileged position of inmates in the "Mafia House," reportedly were factors in Norfolk's smooth operation. "It's a very handy device to control" the inmates, one officer observed, but it also "made it hard for the officers to work [that unit]." The administration's failure to back up officers' efforts to enforce institution-wide rules in that unit (and its apparent failure to take action once in the late 1970s when an officer was injured there by assailants unknown) led "the house officers that normally work there . . . [to] walk around on tiptoes."

Some officers, of course, try to take the authority conferred on them as officers further than "just doing their job." A Walpole interviewee particularly sensitive to the subtleties of the officers' authority observed:

> [Some officers] don't understand what authority is and what bounds you have within that authority . . . I think everyone interprets it to meet their own image of themself. "I'm a corrections officer [slams table]! You sit here! [Slam!] You sit there!" Rather than "I'm a *person* who has limited authority. So, you know, I'm sorry gentlemen, but you can't sit there. You are going to have to sit over there. That's just the rules," and explaining or something like that the reason why.

While some officers attempted to stretch their claims to authority too far, a more common complaint among interviewees was that officers too often failed to use what authority (as opposed to other forms of power) they did have. The Walpole officer whose discovery of his own authority was described at the beginning of this section recalled a situation where a group of officers were about to go down the tiers to disarm a violent inmate. "I didn't think there was any need to put up a big hassle. They wanted to go right down and go in his room, take everything apart, find the [weapon]. And I said, 'Well there's no need for that. Why don't you just go down and *tell* the guy to give it to you?' " When he did just that the inmate quietly surrendered the weapon. "They couldn't understand why I would do something like that. And I said, 'Well, it's a lot easier just to go down and tell the man to give you what you want, and if he gives it to you, then you don't have to go through all that trouble. If he doesn't give it to you, well, okay, then you go in and get it.' " The interviews produced numerous stories of officers (not always the interviewee himself) who accomplished by command or request—that is, by authority—what others felt could be accomplished only by coercion or force or could not be accomplished at all.

Moreover, some interviewees believed that most inmates (especially those at violence-plagued Walpole and Concord) yearned for officers to exercise *more*, not less, authority over the prisons. "I think a lot of them look for restrictions . . . I think there are only a few who want everything loose." The instability of a prison like Walpole and the precariousness of the inmates' situation there must have made life nearly intolerable. Why else would up to one-quarter of the inmate population at Walpole have been in protective custody at their own request? This is not to say that most inmates there would have welcomed wholesale intrusions into their lives. But were the officers, for example, to have failed to regulate the distribution of food, it seems very likely that some Walpole inmates would have ended up overfed while a good many others went hungry. And the inmates must have been aware that the mayhem that occurs at some institutions (for example, at New Mexico state prison in 1980) takes place after the complete removal of even a weak and corrupt officer corps.

Walpole officers clearly exercised some authority within the prison and probably had the potential for exercising more, but their actual and potential authority fell far short of allowing them to accomplish basic tasks of prison governance. They were unable, for example, to prevent by command inmate butchery of other inmates or widespread drug dealings or even the smearing of excrement on walls. Authority failed the officers in their quest to control the prison in part because the behavior officers sought to compel of inmates so often violated what inmates considered to be in their own self-interests: to enter cramped cells where they would be locked for hours if not days or weeks, to refrain from sexual contact or the use of depression-relieving drugs, to restrict themselves to miserly consignments of material goods. This conflict between desire and obedience may seem obvious to those outside prisons contemplating what life must be like for those inside. But authority also failed officers at a prison like Walpole because it was too weak a competitor with *inmate* power, especially coercion and force used by inmates against fellow inmates. The question is not whether most inmates felt they *ought* to obey, but rather whether they perceived they *could* obey without serious risk to limb or life. This was not a simple case of peer pressure to defy authority. "If an inmate bucks the system that they have then they're going to find him dead somewhere. It's just as simple as that. He *will* end up dead."

## Persuasion

What an inmate cannot be commanded to do he may, of course, still be persuaded to do by means of rational argument alone. In prisons, where so much that is required of an inmate is obviously counter to his self-interest, recourse to persuasion as a means of control may seem ludicrous. Yet, even at Walpole, officers found they could "rationalize" with most inmates, to try to persuade them of—or perhaps more often, to dissuade them from—a course of action. "I'd say, 'Hey, look, I know what's going on. It'd be to your advantage if it stopped before anything came down.' And they would." As one Walpole officer observed, a prison is a place where "you talk yourself out of 99.9 percent of crises." "The only weapon you have is your head. It's not an offensive weapon. It's a defensive weapon."

Different officers, and in particular different work shifts, at Walpole varied in the frequency of their recourse to persuasion as a means of influence. Observed an officer on the 7–3 shift:

> Three-to-eleven [shift] has the reputation of handling situations in a way that they won't bargain with you as much as some other shifts will. We [the day shift] will try to explain things, try and present it to you, to tell you. The day shift might say, "Well, look, this is for your own good. Why don't you smarten up and do the right thing. If you don't you're going to get in trouble, you're going to lose your visits, you're going to get set back [by the parole board] . . . Why blow all this? Why don't you just put the chair down or put the fire out or give us the home brew or give us the knife that we know you have?"

In these instances, officers sought to persuade by making reference to sanctions *over which the officers had no control* (such as parole or loss of visits). But "persuasion" at Walpole too often became a mere preamble to coercion where the threatened sanctions *were* under the officers' control. "I'd say, 'Look, I'm putting the handcuffs on you. You may be bigger than me, but I'm putting the handcuffs on you because I can get ten guys to help me but you can't get anybody to help you. So just let's put the handcuffs on and go.' And so we'd go. Nothing to it." Another officer who described himself as a "good talker" recalled his efforts to persuade a "tall, skinny" inmate to permit a search of his cell. "For five minutes we went back and forth. I says, 'We got to come in. It's got to be done. Now let's do it as easy and non-violently. I don't want to burn up all my calories and I know you don't either, you can't afford to.' " When talk failed he pushed the inmate down and handcuffed him. "Then I very quietly, so I wouldn't embarrass him or anything, I got right up to his ear and I says, 'If you don't stop I'm going to break your fucking wrist.'. . . So he said, 'Okay, man, okay.' "

While many Walpole officers could and did attempt to persuade inmates to do some things by force of argument alone, the opportunities for reasoned communication that would have been essential for persuasion to become a major source of influence within that prison were lacking.* On the institutional level, prison officials in the mid- and late 1970s did not engage in propaganda to win the hearts or minds of their captives. On the individual level, officers and inmates avoided sustained communication as too likely to arouse suspicion on all sides that the inmate was ratting, the officer "lugging" (carrying in contraband), or both (see Chapter 5). In any

---

* In the Democratic Unit at Niantic prison in Connecticut, persuasion, next to authority, was the principal source of influence. Whenever problems arose, a meeting was called of all inmates and officers on duty in the unit and the issue was debated until a resolution had been achieved acceptable to a majority of those present. Officers were, of course, considerably outnumbered by inmates. These meetings were known to last ten or twelve hours at a stretch, continuing late into the night if necessary. Through open and ready dialogue, the officers (and many inmates) achieved substantial if erratic influence. But such an attempt to govern by persuasion, especially in a prison context, requires a small community where virtually unlimited time and energy can be devoted to resolution of problems. As such it is not a model appropriate to institutions with large inmate populations. Easton (1958, p. 185) has pointed out that in the absence of authority, "the outlay of energy involved in having to force, manipulate, or persuade members into conformity with a decision would exceed the resources of any but the smallest face-to-face political system."

case, those who could be persuaded by words alone had to pay greater heed to those who sought to "persuade" them by other means, namely force and coercion.

## Inducement

What inmates will not do out of moral or rational conviction, they may still willingly do out of self-interest. "You'd be surprised what an extra piece of cake will get you," observed one Walpole officer. A piece of cake, a carton of milk, a book of matches, a roll of toilet paper, the Friday sports section: these were the small change with which officers could purchase occasional compliance or could, as one officer put it, at least "pacify them to make me get through another day."

More systematic rewards were required for sustained cooperation. Those few inmates who actually worked in any of the prisons received miserly wages—poor inducements in themselves. Officers in charge of work areas commonly fell back on informal systems of rewards to motivate their men. A Bridgewater officer in charge of the kitchen stated, "I do certain things for my workers that I wouldn't do for anybody else just to keep them satisfied because sixty cents a day isn't too much pay. Let them score a little bit more . . . I mean, that's the system. You got to pay them off to work." At Walpole inmate workers from throughout the institution were permitted to "score" food from the kitchen. (Inmates apparently were not the only ones "scoring." The Walpole staff dining room was losing an estimated $55,000 a year in unpaid officers' meals.) Even the performance of small tasks by an inmate commonly called for a payoff. As a Concord officer observed, "Guy does something for you, you buy him a pack of butts. Big shit. He sweeps the floor, you get him a coke. No shit. Like, you don't have to do that, but just to show him that you appreciate it. And that'll give him more to do it for you." Officers, of course, were not limited to a "pack of butts" to pay off cooperative inmates. They could offer substantial rewards by importing contraband (especially drugs), exchanging important information, and ignoring inmate offenses.

Amidst great deprivation, one might expect that the power to reward would be potent within a prison. But officers' attempts to purchase compliance encounter serious difficulties.

First, inducement is nearly always a double-edged sword: I get what I want in exchange for your getting what you want. If officers may be said to reward good inmate behavior with extra food, inmates may be said to reward with their good behavior those officers who pass out extra food. (Inmates, of course, have more than cooperation to offer. They may seek to corrupt their captors with money, sex, or a variety of services. Allegations of officer corruption are often made—at Walpole as elsewhere—but are difficult to prove.)

Second, the risk is ever present that what inmates gratefully received yesterday they may expect today—and demand tomorrow. Furthermore, the possibility always exists that rewards illicitly granted once may be used as blackmail by inmates wishing to ensure that those rewards are granted repeatedly, in which case inmates end up controlling officers at least as much as officers are controlling inmates.

Third, a prison is a society of relative scarcity where the division of any new spoils is likely to lead to contention, if not violence, among inmates. Unless rewards are uniformly distributed (in which case they come to be viewed as rights, not rewards), they may result in less, not more, stability and control. The more valuable the reward (especially drugs), the more inevitable the conflict that is engendered.

Fourth, an officer who attempts to purchase peace (or anything else) from inmates runs the very real danger of crossing his fellow officers. This risk is especially great in regard to lugging drugs, which if discovered may incur severe sanctions, including physical reprisal or expulsion by fellow officers for compromising their own safety and control. (See Chapter 5 for a discussion of officer lugging and sanctions for engaging in it.) Even extra pieces of cake or cartons of milk can lead to complications because then the inmates "are going to get on somebody else's case, they're going to say, 'Hey, look, [this officer] is giving me this, why can't you give me this?' " Resentment can build quickly at a prison against an officer seen as coddling inmates and may lead to sustained harassment by fellow officers.

Finally, the rewards available to officers are too often inadequate to the task of inducing compliance. Sykes (1958, pp. 51–52, 61) pointed to the "pathetic collection" of rewards with which officers might win compliance as an important defect in their power. As a Concord officer observed of the entire Massachusetts Department of Correction, "It's a system of punishment and reward. However, there's no reward anywhere you go. It's all punishment." Nowhere was the lack of meaningful rewards more painfully obvious than in the rather crude attempt of the Department of Correction to use behavior modification theory at Walpole. Wretched conditions in the segregation block (Block 10) and the maximum-security blocks were justified on the grounds that they made transfer to a minimum block seem a major reward for good behavior. But beyond the reward of moving from one punitive environment to another, slightly less punitive environment, this "behavior modification system" was almost wholly devoid of positive reinforcement as a means of shaping specific behaviors. As such, it violated one of the basic tenets of behavior learning theory. In practice, even this one "reward" often failed. Overcrowding was so severe that availability of beds was as likely to determine block assignment as was an individual inmate's behavior.

But even a more substantial collection or sophisticated system of rewards would probably have proved unequal to the task. It takes a lot of cartons of milk or pieces of cake to induce an inmate to risk assault or death. And once again, on matters big and seemingly small, those were indeed the stakes at Walpole.


## Manipulation

Where a sense of obligation is lacking and neither persuasion nor inducement can secure compliance, willing if uncomprehending cooperation can still be obtained through manipulation. "Conning"—prison slang for manipulation—involves getting someone to do as the manipulator wants by means of misleading or deceitful communication. Conning is an important facet of prison life and is symptomatic of a situation in which many individuals are denied more legitimate means of obtaining what they want.

That inmates tend to use manipulation vis-à-vis officers more than the other way around reflects their lesser access to other means of influence, as well as their greater strategic advantage. The term *con* accurately reflects how most officers regard most inmates, especially at prisons like Walpole. "You always find that they are trying to get something from you. You don't get nothing for nothing in here . . . They want to see how much they can get away with." They often got away with a lot.

The "good con," which in a prison refers less to the well-behaved inmate than to the successful duping of officials, requires careful thought and knowledge of one's quarry. Any halfway intelligent inmate has the time and perspective to gain both. "They're in there for twenty-four hours a day, every day of the week, and all they have to do is sit in there and scheme on some way to get over on you." While an inmate has all day to observe a handful of officers, each officer has but a single shift to observe and assess dozens of inmates. The advantage goes to the captives. "Someone who has twenty-four hours a day to just think about ways to get something and be cozy about it and get that system perfected. Phew! You can do it." Bridgewater State Hospital, where most inmates did not have the mental wherewithal to con officers, was the only institution where officers did not report conning to be a significant frustration of their job.

New officers, in particular, are easy targets for the con and are often distressed by it. A Walpole officer recalled,

> At first I didn't know they were conning me. I was real vulnerable to it. Boy, they got away with a lot of stuff . . . I took it personally. "What do you think I am, a dummy?" or something like that. And after they conned me and got themselves out of the block for one reason or another I would say, "Ah!" It hit me, they're not supposed to be doing that. Or I'd get a phone call from someone saying, "What's he doing out here?" And then I'd get chewed out and then I'd get all upset because of this guy. That would make me angry.*

This officer learned to handle conning the way many officers do: by "conning the cons," "playing a little game back with them." Manipulation became a few officers' own principal style of interaction with inmates. Asserted one, "They knew I could play their con game better than they could sometimes. And I was able to con them. I had to con them just as much as they had to con me." His advice: "You just got to be cool at everything you do and you got to be able to con with the cons." (Some officers eventually found themselves using

---

* I empathized with this officer's anger and frustration. I found conning to be one of the most dispiriting aspects of prison work. I recall one incident in particular as a new officer. A recently admitted inmate was in tears on being placed in a room formerly inhabited by an inmate who had died and allegedly still haunted the place. Taking pity on the woman, I took her to the kitchen for a glass of milk and a calming chat and then moved her to the one other vacant room. As it turned out, this other room happened to be right next to the woman's long-standing girl friend. When I learned of this the next day (from my unimpressed supervisor), I was outraged at the deception and bore it with none of the good humor it no doubt deserved. As deceptions go, it was, after all, well acted and imaginative, to say nothing of perceptive of my own gullibility.

manipulation as a primary form of influence beyond the officer-inmate arena. Said one of relations with the administration and the world at large, "You get to be like the inmates after a while. You have to start conning to [get] things that you want.")*

Manipulation, though ubiquitous in prison, has serious flaws as a form of power, there as elsewhere. Although potent in the single instance, the pattern of deceit required for sustained usage can rarely be maintained. This may be particularly true in prisons where so much of what occurs is on public display. More important, manipulation, once unveiled, characteristically leads to a diminution in power. Those officers who sought to "con the cons" often succeeded, but once their deceptions inevitably became known, their every word and action were scrutinized for deceit. Even their ability to use other forms of power suffered: their authority was eroded, their ability to persuade undermined, their offers of inducement suspected. Moreover, each recourse to manipulation served to erode the credibility of officers as a group. Although there were officers who had abjured deceit over the years and thus were known for their integrity, the presumption of veracity in a prison is one hard earned, never easily granted.

## Force

When cooperation cannot be secured through duty, logic, reward, or deceit, compliance can be compelled by force or coercion. These two forms of power are often considered jointly by penologists who, in recent decades, have downplayed their importance in the modern American prison. Richard McCleery (1961b, p. 153) warned that "the illusion, fostered by certain physical appearances in the prison, that control rests on the instruments of force rather than the procedures for creating consensus is a rich source of error for inexperienced scholars or officials." Yet the interviews with officers in this study lead to the inescapable conclusion that at least at Walpole and the Bridgewater State Hospital, instruments of force and coercion as

---

* Toward the end of his twenty-year imprisonment for Nazi war crimes, Albert Speer (1977, p. 487) wrote of the deceit regularly practiced by prisoners and their guards: "All these years I have had the feeling of walking on unstable ground. I have never been able to do more than guess what was intended honestly and what hypocritically. In this prison world, dissimulation became second nature on both sides . . . Somewhere I once read that prison is the university of crime; it is, at least, the university of moral corruption."

a means of compelling compliance had not been relinquished. On the contrary, throughout the 1970s they remained central to efforts by officers to maintain control. I shall discuss first the use of pure force and then will turn in the following section to coercion.

Force, which I take to mean "stripping" an individual of the "choice between compliance and noncompliance" (Bachrach and Baratz, 1970, p. 28), plays a part in virtually every prison principally by limiting inmate mobility and capacity to resist. The very act of physically confining someone to a prison against his or her will is one of force if we assume that it is at least in part the physical constraints of the prison that keep that person there. ("Secure" prisons are built at great public expense on just that premise.) Shooting someone who attempts to overcome those physical constraints is also, of course, an act of force. Within a prison, inmates usually spend at least part of their time locked in their cells. A prisoner who rebels may be forcibly restrained, bodily removed, and placed in an isolation cell where he is further constrained by mortar and steel. If he riots, he may be incapacitated by chemical means. If he goes berserk, he may be subdued by forcible injection of drugs.

The use of force, like other forms of power, varies markedly from prison to prison. At "campus-style" prisons like Norfolk, its overt use may be rare, although even there some inmates are housed in secure units and all are locked in their buildings at night. The "Pennsylvania" or "separate" system devised in the early 1800s perhaps went further than any other in physically constraining inmates, short of shackling them to the walls. Under this system, each inmate was confined to a solitary cell with thick walls and a solid door, deprived of contact even with the guards who, silent and faceless, served meals through a slat in the door. Remnants of the separate system existed in the United States until recently (and had more lasting impact abroad). Some of the old-time Walpole officers recalled that at the maximum-security prison that predated Walpole particularly difficult inmates might spend years all but forgotten in solitary confinement.

The contemporary version of long-term solitary confinement in a cell is long-term sedation. Modern psychopharmacology has the potential for treating many otherwise intractable mental illnesses. If properly prescribed and supervised, drugs can play an important role in alleviating some of the individual and collective miseries of prison life. But drugs are widely misused as a means of control in American prisons. Too many prison physicians (and the administrators who employ them) are content to allow as many inmates as possible to serve their sentences in a drug-induced haze. A Walpole officer wagered that "we give out more drugs here than at Mass[achusetts] General [Hospital]."*

Most inmates, of course, are willing recipients of the drugs that they receive. Many come into prison already drug addicted and happily assent to sleeping away their time in prison. But officers at all the prisons studied assailed the practice of heavily medicating inmates. During the 1970s, officers were usually not informed about the nature, purpose, or likely consequences of specific drugs, and they often felt considerable hostility toward medical staff because of what they viewed as indiscriminate prescription of powerful drugs. An officer working with criminally insane inmates at Bridgewater State Hospital asserted that inmates there "don't know anything. From day to day, they're all messed up on drugs. I mean, like, tranquilizers, highs, ups, lows. And they give them this to bring them up and this to bring him down, this to keep him in between. And the guy is walking around in a circle." A fellow officer concurred, "You watch them come in in good shape, and then after a year they're all fat, sloppy looking and some of them are so burnt out on medication . . . Like you're talking twenty-five pills three times a day, handfuls, like candy. It's too much medication, too, too much." Yet as this Bridgewater officer admitted, drugs were invaluable in the control of the most violent and unpredictable inmates. He recalled an inmate who had long ago succumbed to the "thorazine shuffle. He'd be standing there all day long once he got the medication. It would just totally mess the guy up. You felt bad. But when he wasn't on the medication, he'd be totally different. He'd be so violent it would be incredible."

Regardless of the means by which officials seek to incapacitate inmates, force has important flaws as a form of power within a prison. Legal limits exist on the length of time an inmate may be

---

* According to an article in the *Boston Globe* in April 1973, "The Massachusetts Corrections Department has been buying hundreds of thousands of prescription drugs, from pain killers to habit-forming narcotics, for inmates at Walpole State Prison at a time when controls over their distribution has been virtually non-existent." During one two-month period in 1972, "more than 250,000 pills and capsules were delivered to the institution. These included 15,000 sleeping pills, more than 30,000 tranquilizers and more than 500 Prolixin tablets described as 'an extremely potent behavior modifier' " (*Boston Globe*, 25 April 1973). This staggering quantity of drugs had been purchased for use at an institution that housed only 650 inmates.

forced to spend in lockup. And, as Walpole's Block 10 so strikingly illustrated, even locking up a person twenty-four hours a day does not necessarily prevent antisocial actions. More fundamental, force is not effective in compelling performance of complex tasks. Nor can it be realistically relied upon for the *routine* accomplishment of even very simple tasks. Every time officers want the hundreds of inmates in their charge to enter or leave their cells they cannot pick them up and move them one-by-one like so many chessmen. But if force alone cannot accomplish such simple tasks, coercion very often can.

## Coercion

When willing compliance from inmates cannot be gained by officers through the use of authority, persuasion, inducement, or manipulation, and inmates cannot be forced to accede to the officers' will, then an attempt can still be made to coerce them into obedience through the use or threat of sanctions.

Penologists in recent decades have rightly attempted to debunk the stereotype of the "brutal screw": they hold coercion to be a minor and largely ineffective means of securing control. Sykes (1958, p. 50) maintained that "coercive tactics may have some utility in checking blatant disobedience—if only a few men disobey. But if the great mass of criminals in prison are to be brought into the habit of conformity, it must be on other grounds." But as the history of slavery and of some of the more extreme forms of imprisonment suggests, sustained compliance on the part of large groups of people *can* be secured principally through coercion. In Nazi concentration camps, where "the threat of punishment took the place of all normal incentives" (Bettelheim, 1960, p. 110), millions were not only incarcerated but compelled to perform complex tasks for detested masters. The barbarity and capriciousness of sanctions may set the SS and their camps apart in the history of incarceration and control, but coercion in modern American prisons is not a matter to be lightly dismissed.

Of course, coercion in prisons (as elsewhere) need not conjure up the image of black-booted SS guards in Nazi concentration camps. At Walpole, as at other prisons, established and reasonable procedures existed for dealing with disobedience. But informal and violent means were used as well. I will consider first lawfully prescribed procedures and sanctions and then informal sanctions, nonviolent and violent.

*Formal sanctions.* Serious inmate offenses—murder, rape, assault, drug dealing, escape—are theoretically the province of prosecutors and courts. Officials at some penal institutions make frequent recourse to courts for offenses committed within their institutions, particularly offenses against officers. But by and large prosecutions of inmates for offenses committed inside prisons are rare, convictions rarer still, and consecutive sentencing (as opposed to concurrent sentencing with the time the inmate is already serving) almost unheard of. As officers see it, an inmate "stabs somebody out in [the inmate] population. Now what in hell are you going to do with the guy? The court's not going to do anything. Nothing. Nothing!" As a result, prison officials have come to rely on internal systems of sanctions.

A formal disciplinary procedure existed at all Massachusetts state prisons which consisted in essence of the following. When an inmate broke a rule, the officer in charge could "write up" the incident in a Disciplinary Report ("D-Report" or "ticket"). The case would then be heard by the prison Disciplinary Board ("D-Board"). If the inmate was found guilty, the Disciplinary Board was empowered to impose sanctions.

Two problems undermined this system. First, frequent recourse by an officer to writing D-Reports was not deemed an acceptable means of maintaining control. Although a few officers "didn't let a sneeze go by without writing a ticket," such behavior typically led to derision from fellow officers, threats of reprisal from inmates, and routine reversal of tickets by the D-Board. (A Norfolk officer who resorted too often to writing tickets was reportedly pulled from the yard by his supervisors and placed for months in the towers.) "They lose respect when a person writes a lot of tickets," for he indicates thereby that he cannot otherwise maintain control. In the interviews, most officers reported that they rarely, if ever, resorted to ticket writing except for obvious and major transgressions: stabbings, contraband found during a major shakedown, and the like. "Why should I bother?" asked one Walpole officer. "There are more than disciplinary reports as a way to get back at the guy."

Second, the sanctions the D-Board could impose were few in number and, as Sykes (1958, p. 50) found at Trenton Prison, "do not represent a profound difference from the prisoner's usual status." At Walpole, an inmate could lose "good time" (thereby making his stay in prison longer); he could be locked in his own cell for a few days or weeks ("isolation time" or "ice time"); he could be removed from the minimum end to the more restrictive maximum end or from either minimum or maximum end to Block 10; within Block 10 he could be placed in a "box car" cell or, at least until 1979, in one of the punishment cells or "blue rooms." Each step involved more of the same: more restraint, more isolation, more deprivation.

The infamous blue rooms were seen as a substantial punishment and thus as effective deterrents to future transgressions. They were, as one officer put it, places that "would scare anyone." But after considerable public pressure and a finding by the state attorney general's office that the blue rooms violated the Eighth Amendment's prohibition on cruel and unusual punishment, the Department of Correction ordered in 1978 that they be converted to more conventional cells. It was a move many officers opposed and regretted.

Once the blue rooms had been abolished, the worst punishment that could be formally inflicted on an inmate at Walpole was placement in Block 10 and that was often not viewed as punishment at all. Despite confinement to one's cell twenty-three hours a day or more in squalid conditions, in the upside-down world of Walpole many inmates *preferred* to be in Block 10. It was often safer than the maximum or minimum blocks, had natural light and fresh air, which the "max" blocks did not have, and the inmates were usually permitted the same assortment of personal belongings in their cells that they had had out in population. Indeed, some inmates were there at their own initiative. By committing an obvious offense (preferably assault on an officer) and being "sentenced" to Block 10, an inmate could effect his withdrawal from the prison population without losing his standing among fellow inmates. An appreciation of the inmates' dilemma led a few officers to be tolerant of some inmate assaults on officers. "A lot of inmates for some reason or another, they're not getting along in their block or whatever and they want to get out of their block. And it's very hard to just move . . . So a lot of times I used to feel that an attack against an officer, especially when the officer was never touched, was just a move to maybe go to Block 10."

Officers at institutions other than Walpole also complained about the failings of the official system of sanctions within their respective institutions. Their grievances were directed at the lack of support administrators gave to D-Reports and at the trivial nature of many of the sanctions imposed (for example, "early bed," "suspended sentence") when inmates were found guilty of rule infractions. But hanging over the heads of most inmates outside of Walpole was the prospect of being "escorted back to Walpole" if their offenses were sufficiently serious or frequent. This threat, coupled with the realistic hope most non-Walpole inmates had of furlough, transfer to a less secure institution, and ultimate parole, was considered a major deterrent. Norfolk officers, in particular, attributed the relative tranquility of their institution in large measure to the fact that "most of the inmates are trying to get a good name for themselves so they can go somewhere" other than back to Walpole. "Most of these guys worked hard to get to Norfolk and they were working hard to get out of Norfolk." While the threat of transfer to Walpole may have been an effective deterrent for inmates in *other* institutions, inmates still in Walpole knew they could fall no further.

Even before the blue rooms were banned, sanctions officially available for use against inmates at Walpole were deemed inadequate to the task of coercing compliance. "You can write all the D-Reports—there's no further they can go. You can lock them up but that's not going to do any good because they're locked up *anyways*." Something more was required. "They don't care [about] lockup. It's like a game. It's fun. But there's a different way of punishing them. And that's the way it should be done."

*Informal, nonviolent sanctions.* "The way it should be done" involved the use of informal sanctions, nonviolent and violent, applied by officers acting in concert or alone. In their study of a British prison, Pentonville, Terence Morris and Pauline Morris (1963, p. 267) noted the maxim that "if a screw wants to get you, he will get you." There were a multitude of ways by which an officer could "get" an inmate, for if the supply of official punishments (and official and unofficial rewards) was meager, that of unofficial punishments was not.

Officers had at their disposal sanctions that mimicked those of the D-Board but which carried none of the stigma of writing D-Reports. "Tickets—it's a waste of time. It really is, because fifteen days isolation is nothing to them. It makes them think less of you. If you give them your own type of punishment they'll think more. Like I kept my own punishment my own way." In the first instance at Walpole, an officer could simply lock inmates in their cells "without giving them a ticket." One officer recalled asking an inmate several times to get back into line, but the inmate would just respond, "That's cool." Later that day when it came time to unlock all the cells, that inmate's cell stayed locked. When other inmates came running to the officer to say that the inmate wanted to come out, the officer asked them to relay the message, "That's cool." The inmate stayed locked until the next day and now "the inmate doesn't skip out of line anymore." (Informally locking up an inmate was particularly effective on Friday nights, this officer explained, for the inmate might have to wait in his cell until Monday morning before he could see the deputy superintendent. An inmate could also be transferred to Block 10—and before 1979, to the blue rooms—and be kept there until his case had been considered by the administration. Even if the D-Report did not stick, the inmate might have spent days in Block 10 waiting for the case to be dismissed.)

But officers had more effective ways of dealing with inmates than informally turning the key. Jerry Sousa, for years an inmate leader in Block 10, recalled time he spent in the blue rooms where there was nowhere to sit but on the floor. Officers would "flush the toilet back into the cell to get back at you. They'd laugh at me standing ankle deep" (*Boston Globe*, 7 March 1980). An older officer labeled this type of behavior on the part of younger colleagues "kid shit." "It's ridiculous. They act like kids. They're not grown up . . . They run around and tear up a guy's room and throw stuff in the toilet and get him aggravated and egg him on and hope he does something." A colleague recalled, "They'd shut the electricity off for the whole tier and the guys would start screaming and yelling. Aggravation! Or turn the hot water off or go behind the guy's cell . . . and turn off his plumbing or something like that." The means of aggravation were endless. They included withholding toilet paper or matches, even food.

> The food that we used to dump away, just throw it away, perfectly good food, instead of giving it to them . . . There'd be a big piece of roast beef that they'd slice up into steaks. These guys would throw it away, maybe thirty, forty pieces of it, just dump it into the garbage barrel! . . . Not save it or send it back to the kitchen. They'd dump it sometimes right in front of some of the inmates' faces.

Nor was it necessary to stop up a man's toilet or deprive him of food to aggravate him. "In one way or another they'll get . . . to them, maybe not physically, but mentally they'll get to them." "During summer it's like 110 degrees down there. Guys are yelling it's hot and [an officer] . . . would yell down, 'Nobody said it was going to be easy' or something like that and the guys would flip out." One officer who was not in Block 10 settled on a device that caused an inmate who had verbally abused him particular aggravation. He passed on a "tip" to a fellow officer who loved shaking down cells that the inmate in question had contraband hidden in his room. After the inmate's cell had been torn apart in a futile search for the forbidden items, the officer was able to shrug off his "misinformation" to his fellow officer ("you get some good tips and some bad tips") and happily concluded, "The officer got his jollies off shaking the room down and I've gotten my satisfaction."

At institutions other than Walpole and the Bridgewater State Hospital, methods used were often indirect and surreptitious. An officer at one of the other facilities asserted, "A write-up don't do any good. So you just burn him in your own way . . . And I have the time. It may take me six months." A colleague who was a self-acknowledged master at playing "head games" with the inmates provided specific examples.

> Guy wants to make a phone call? You can make him wait ten, twenty minutes. Guy wants some writing paper? Tell him you don't have any. Guy wants some matches? You can have a drawer full of matches, "I don't have any matches," you tell him. Just things like that. And they know . . . And there's the ways that you can screw around with his property when he's not around . . . One inmate . . . he gave another officer a hard time . . . This particular inmate loves plants . . . And he had about . . . two dozen plants . . . He woke up the next morning and every one of them plants was dead . . . Say a guy works . . . with the woodworking stuff. Just put a scratch in his furniture or something. He knows how it got there. He knows why it was put there. But there's nothing he can do about it . . . There's so many ways you can get these guys.

At institutions where physical reprisals by officers could get them in trouble with the administration, "the indirect way is used the most because the direct way you get yourself in more shit." But at least at Walpole and Bridgewater State Hospital, officers did not have to concern themselves with such subtleties.

*Informal, violent sanctions.* "Legalized cruelty and not infrequent torture" (Lewis, 1967, p. 114) characterized many (perhaps most) American prisons in the nineteenth century. The situation had improved by the early twentieth century, but "there is simply no question that prisons were places of pervasive brutality . . . the capriciousness and cruelty of prison discipline was a thing unto itself" (Rothman, 1980, pp. 152, 148). The use of physical coercion in prisons apparently declined considerably in the United States over the first half of the twentieth century. In 1958, Sykes concluded, "it is true that isolated acts of brutality on the part of the guards still occur. But the gross sadism and systematic neglect . . . have largely disappeared in the United States today with a few notable exceptions" (p. 32). Throughout the 1970s, however, the Massachusetts prison system, especially Walpole and the Bridgewater State Hospital, remained among the "notable exceptions." While the vast majority of violent acts, at least within Walpole, were inflicted by inmates on inmates, the officers, too, were involved in the violence as perpetrators and victims of assault. By their own accounts, violence was used by officers at Walpole and, to a lesser extent, Bridgewater State Hospital as a primary means of maintaining control within their institutions. Officer violence against inmates will be discussed at length in the chapter on prison violence. Here I shall focus on advantages and disadvantages to officers, especially at Walpole, of using physical violence as a means of coercing the inmate population into submission.

Officers at a prison like Walpole are dealing with hundreds of men convicted of violent crimes, some of whom are insane, some sadistic, some serving multiple life sentences who, at least in the absence of capital punishment, have nothing further to lose—except their bodily well-being at the hands of officers or fellow inmates.

> Some of these guys are just so far gone that they're burnt out and that's it. I mean, they don't know and they don't care. And a lot of these guys are just so institutionalized that this is the only life they know. It's the only life they *want* to know. And they just don't care. There they are anyway, so what does it matter?

Under the circumstances, it is not surprising that some officers conclude that the "only way to deal with that type is to meet violence with violence."

From the officers' perspective, too many inmates have spent their entire lives—incarcerated or "free"—in environments where force, not discourse, determines action. Observed one officer who felt he could reason with most inmates and endeavored to do so, "Some of them have just gone off the deep end and you just cannot talk to them rationally. So you have to use force, okay, when the situation calls for it. There is no getting around it." A colleague concurred, "In handling a maximum-security setting like that you have to go in with some kind of force because these guys, that's all they know. You have to maintain that edge, and you have to maintain that kind of discipline, that threat, in order to mold them into following rules and regulations."

Officers who were serious about running a good block—reasonably orderly, at least superficially clean, with a minimum of inmate-on-inmate aggression—often felt the necessity to crack a few heads, at least at first, to gain control.

> It takes you a long time to get a block exactly the way you want it. Sometimes you have to bang heads against guys until you finally get it through their thick noggin that . . . you're there to do it the way you want it done and it's going to be the way you want it. Otherwise, if you can't control your own block, there's no point in your really even coming in the next day.

> *What would happen if the officers . . . just stopped beating [the inmates], never used force beyond simple restraint? . . .*
> They would be running the place. They'd be doing whatever they wanted to do.

Walpole was not the only Massachusetts institution in which officers deemed physical coercion to be necessary for control. Despite use of drugs at Bridgewater State Hospital to help control aggression, many inmates were still capable of considerable violence. A heavy hand was seen as an important aid in maintaining control in units for more intractable inmates. An officer who opposed most of the violence at the State Hospital as unnecessary nevertheless concluded that some was inevitable because "that's the only way they understand . . . You're working with a hard clientele." He admired a senior officer in one of the more difficult units who maintained control along with "a reputation for beating people up."

> He was definitely fair. But if a guy gave him any trouble, the first thing he'd do, put him in his room. If he got any other back talk, that was it. He grabbed him, threw him right down on the bed or just manhandled them. He handled them. He did. He had to because, if he didn't, they'd handle him . . . I thought he was

right. He was fair, but he wasn't too lenient . . . He ran a good
ward. It was always clean. The place smelled good . . . Everything was the way it was supposed to be. He ran a good tight
unit . . . You knew he was in control and that's the way it is.
You have to have control and he had control.

Physical coercion was deemed less practical and less appropriate
at Norfolk and Concord. Inmates there generally proved more trac-
table, especially because they were able to appreciate the threat of
being shipped to Walpole.

*Why coercion fails.* Terence and Pauline Morris (1963, p. 271)
observed of Pentonville Prison, "In many situations crude coercion
and physical force are remarkably effective in obtaining at least
temporary compliance." And so they were at Walpole and Bridgewater State Hospital. But for a number of reasons coercion—both
official and unofficial—failed as a *primary* means of securing and
maintaining control at Walpole, as it does at most other prisons.

Coercion failed in part because officers at Walpole and the other
Massachusetts prisons were unable and, for the most part, unwilling
to use the extreme measures that, for example, allowed the Nazis to
maintain mastery over their prisoners in concentration camps.
Other modern American prison systems are apparently less constrained in their use of sanctions. The Texas penal system with its
rigid discipline and harsh sanctions may have roots more in Southern slavery than in the emergent penitentiary. Defenders of the
Texas Department of Correction point out that it has one of the
lowest death rates among inmates of any major American prison
system and that its "plantation" economy makes it a financial success. But such open and systematic exploitation of inmates would be
less well tolerated in liberal Massachusetts. And, as will be discussed later, many Massachusetts officers (including Walpole officers) opposed the brutal excesses that would have permitted an
informal system of sanctions to cow the inmate population.

Coercion failed, too, because conformity that is secured through
sanctions in a prison is in large part conformity won individual by
individual and is not generalizable to the group. For example, unlike
the internees of concentration camps where "successful escapes
drew such savage punishment upon the entire camp . . . that the
political prisoners renounced even the attempt until the final
months" (Kogon, 1960, p. 84), inmates at a prison like Walpole are
not usually deterred from escaping by concern for those they leave

behind. As Charles E. Lindblom (1977, p. 22) has pointed out, "Governmental control through ad hoc deployment of rewards and penalties—say, a bargain struck with each individual citizen on each of repeated occasions—is hopelessly expensive and time consuming for the vast tasks of government." What is true of society as a whole is true of the prison society as well.

Coercion also failed because rather than dampening the spirit of rebellion and the anger and hatred that provoke it, coercion fuels it. What is more, the danger always exists that when the opportunity arises the coerced may become the coercer. "Really, what good does it do? It makes it worse. It's like you've got a dog. It does something wrong and you keep beating it and beating it and beating it. You're going to make the dog worse. And a human being is the same way. You push a human being so long and he's going to snap." At Walpole the bite of the dog might be a long time in coming but devastating when it did. Reasoned an officer,

> An inmate, any time he gets upset he can take out the officer; any time he feels like it. And it could be any inmate in the prison. And so just because you get one inmate and beat him that's not going to stop another inmate from jumping an officer if he just feels like doing it . . . It might stop that particular inmate from doing it again. But . . . if he's crazy enough, he's just liable to kill the next officer.

Coercion failed as well because it requires constant escalation in severity and frequency of sanctions if they are to be used as long-term measures of control. Sanctions overused lose effect. The problem is multiplied when no sanctions exist that are more severe than those routinely used. Rather than enhance control, this debasement of sanctions eventually undermines control.

> They see it over and over and over again. They become accustomed to it. "Come on, what are you going to do? Come on, give me a couple of bumps on the head. So what, I don't care. I can take that . . . So I get a headache for two or three days." . . . The thing that they're afraid of, it doesn't become quite as fearful anymore {if you constantly use it}.

Finally, coercion failed because it does not provide resolution to conflict for either the coerced or the coercer, or for the system of which they are a part. Understanding this point, a Walpole officer elaborated a thoughtful critique of the entire Walpole system.

You can only take so much away from an inmate. I mean, at a place like Walpole he hasn't got a hell of a lot to start with, all right? He's locked up for a long period of time. You say, "Okay, you've been bad, I'm taking you out of the minimum end, put you in the maximum end. Okay, you've been bad in the maximum end, I'm going to take you out of the maximum end and put you in segregation unit, Block 10." . . . And now he's bad and he says, "What are you going to do to me now, boss?" How far can you take it? It's better to get them moving forward than it is to have them back because then *you* get your back up against the wall and they realize it. Now they say, "All right, now I'm going to rip out my hopper [toilet] and there is nothing you can do about it. You can't do anything to me. I've won! I beat you! You can't do nothing. You can come in here and beat me over the head, and you did it before, and you can do it again, but I've won! You can't do nothing with me." And I would think that the system would want to be moving forward for him to say, "Okay, I respect you. I want to get into programs, or I want to get into the community. I just want to get out of here and I want you to show me how to get out of here. I don't want you to show me how I can get to the bottom of the pit and stay there and that's my only way of victory."

## Inmate Power

Each of the forms of power discussed here offers officers leverage over inmates, with authority and coercion perhaps offering most. Each has its failings; none by itself is sufficient to overcome all resistance to intrusions into individual autonomy. More important, these forms of power collectively fail to provide officers adequate means for controlling prisons such as Walpole largely because officers must compete with another group of power-wielders within such prisons—those inmates who seek not just to maintain personal autonomy but to dominate their prison world themselves.

*Inmate power over officers.* Inmates' attempts to dominate include, of course, efforts to control officers directly. In doing so, they have access to the same *forms* of power that officers attempt to use over them.

The 1960s and 1970s witnessed a sudden upsurge in prison litigation. Spurred by several major court victories, prisoners across the nation brought and threatened thousands of suits over prison con-

ditions and the conduct of officers and administrators. Although
only a fraction of suits succeeded (including one against several
officers and the superintendent at Walpole for a beating that took
place in the early 1970s), officer-inmate relations were widely affected. The scope of officers' authority was diminished as constraints were placed on what they might lawfully do, and their
status as authority figures was undermined as they faced censure,
individually and collectively, in courts across the nation. At the
same time, inmate "jailhouse lawyers" achieved status as alternate
sources of authority within the cell block. "They can go right to a
book and quote it to you, 'You can't do this and here's why you can't
do it. I'm telling you you can't.' " Often seeing themselves personally empowered by the courts, jailhouse lawyers assumed a much
applauded role of telling the *officers* what to do. Only at Bridgewater
State Hospital were officers largely immune from the threat of lawsuits. As a Bridgewater officer pointed out, "A lot of the [inmates] at
Walpole are smarter, like they know what they can get away with
and they know what they can't get away with, and they know what
the guards can get away with and what the guards can't get away
with." But not so at Bridgewater, where most inmates are "walking
around in a circle . . . They don't know anything." (As will be discussed in Chapter 6, this difference may have had an important
bearing on the types of violence within the two institutions.)

Inmates can also seek to influence their environment by trying to
persuade their captors to adopt a preferred course of action or style
of interaction. In many prisons, inmate "trustees" still play a semi-
official role of breaking in new officers and some no doubt heavily
influence their "pupils." Several Walpole officers on reasonable
terms with inmates reported instances when inmates persuaded
*them* to persuade less reasonable officers to moderate their methods
of handling inmates.* As already mentioned, inmates are often very
successful in inducing and manipulating compliance on the part of
officers. Nor do officers always monopolize force vis-à-vis inmates.
Hostage taking became almost commonplace in American prisons
during the 1970s, and officers are acutely aware that they may

---

* Even in the extreme case of Nazi concentration camps, prisoners met occasional
success in their "efforts to make higher SS officers subservient to the purposes of the
prisoners, not merely by corruption but by direct political influence" (Kogon, 1960, p.
260). At Buchenwald, for example, the hated SS doctor, Ding-Schuler, who had been
involved in human experimentation, at times aided the prisoner underground during
the last years of the war (Kogon, pp. 260–262).

someday become the prisoners and the inmates become their guards.

Most important, inmates at prisons like Walpole seek to control their captors by coercion, principally the threat and use of violent sanctions. Inmate violence against officers will be discussed in Chapter 6. Suffice it here to say that officers at Walpole, and to a lesser extent Concord and Norfolk, had good reason to take heed of that threat. (At Bridgewater, officers were often attacked by inmates but these attacks were more random acts of violence than they were calculated efforts to control officers or modify their behavior. At Norfolk, the ability of inmates to coerce officers into compliance was apparently greatest in the mafia-dominated house. Officers dealing with inmates in that house perceived that they would receive only limited backing from the administration and thus felt more vulnerable.)

A Walpole officer conceded,

> The balance has tipped out of our favor. We've got very little to hold over a man, over the inmates, that commands just the respect of everyday dealings that we used to. They're no longer afraid of us. Let's face it, the fear is on our part now, not on theirs. The cons always used to do it out of fear. Now we're the ones that are afraid.

*Inmate power over other inmates.* Inmates undermine officer power less by direct efforts to control officers than by competing with officers for control over the inmate population itself. Some inmates may seek to control fellow inmates by authority (as in the case of gang leaders or Black Muslim ministers), persuasion, inducement, or manipulation. But once again, far more important than any of these forms of power for the life of an institution like Walpole are inmate attempts to gain mastery over fellow inmates through coercion and force.

Inmate victimization of other inmates is a major problem in American prisons. At Walpole during the 1970s it was constant, bloody, remorseless. During the decade at least twenty-one inmates were murdered at Walpole. Many of the murders were, in the words of the district attorney, of "the most heinous nature" (Delahunt, 1978, p. 38). They were only the most obvious and dramatic events at an institution where violence was routinely used to resolve even trivial differences. Inmates at Walpole were, according to the Governor's Advisory Committee on Corrections (1978, p. 29), "constantly at risk of physical assault, rape and murder." So common, in fact, were assaults that the prison administration did not bother to keep records of them.

Inmate coercion of inmates at Walpole was not limited to vengeance or territorial disputes, but extended to the minutiae of prison existence. "Inmates stab other inmates over card games, a carton of cigarettes." They were raped if they were young and meek, robbed if they were weak and unallied, murdered if they were in debt or a rat or simply in the way. Examples of inmate tyranny over inmates were legion. Take for instance the situation in Block 10 regarding exercise. In theory each inmate in Block 10 was entitled to one hour out of his cell each day for exercise and a shower. But the situation was very different in practice.

> Usually there's one [inmate] on the tier that's in charge and runs the tier. If he wants to stay out all day he says he's staying out all day and he stays out all day . . . Some guys never come out . . . because they're not strong enough to stand up to the [inmate] who is in charge and say, "I'm coming out next." "Huh! You are *not* coming out!"

Nor were the officers strong enough to stand up to them.

> *When you were in charge of the tier, did you let everybody out?*
> I let out who wanted to come out, who said they were coming out.

No inmate was immune from the violence at Walpole, but some dealt out a great deal more of it than others. It is no wonder that the bulk of inmates obeyed. It is also no wonder that they adopted a facade of indifference to events around them and of hostility to officers' efforts to make them respond to officers' initiatives or comply with officers' directives when doing so might bring reprisal from fellow inmates. A telling measure of the extent to which Walpole inmates feared for their lives if they remained in contact with fellow inmates was the extraordinarily high percentage of inmates who were in protective custody.

Inmate coercion of inmates was less of a problem at the other Massachusetts institutions studied. Homicides among inmates at Concord were rare, but officers at that severely crowded facility asserted that rapes and beatings were commonplace. The protective-custody section at Concord was always jammed. Inmates regularly settled scores by burning each other's rooms out. Gangs extorted goods. "For a time there every guy that was under six feet tall had a black eye [who] wasn't in with a gang." An officer assessed the fear with which many Concord inmates lived and their need at times to escape it.

> Inside here, the inmates are more afraid of each other than they are of the officers, ten to one . . . Most people when they escape don't escape to go someplace. They're trying to escape from something. They were very afraid of something. They were afraid of getting killed or getting a bad beating . . . Ninety-nine and nine-tenths percent of the escapes up there were somebody running from somebody and not to someone.

At Norfolk, inmate coercion tended to be much more subtle, though perhaps no less effective. For example, if inmates in a unit

> don't want somebody in the unit, or if they know there's a unit transfer coming in, they'll wreck the room that he's supposed to go into or whatever, and that should be enough of a hint to the man, don't go in that unit. And if he doesn't take that hint and somebody doesn't want him bad enough, they'll burn him out. They seem to stay away from actual fight[ing] and physical contact because they know that {they're} locked up for that. But [if] they can burn a guy out, well, they can get rid of him that way.

But unlike Walpole, where an inmate's cell might be burned out with the inmate still locked in it, at Norfolk "they'll usually make sure the guy is out of the room. They don't seem to want to hurt the man, they just want him to get the message to stay out and that's it." These were messages rarely ignored.

Officers believed that the amount of space provided for inmates in an institution was a critical factor in determining the amount and the severity of violence. A Norfolk officer observed, "Guys who have enemy situations at Walpole—close quarters—can do fine here at Norfolk with their enemies if they're kept in different units. They can avoid each other. There's room, there's space to do it." But at Walpole "you cannot claim a space." It was this inability to avoid enemies that led not only to confrontation, but also to murder over seemingly trivial matters. A Concord officer observed of Walpole, "You can't just expect to beat somebody up and expect to be forgotten because then you turn your back, it's going to be you. Especially if you're down for murder, why are you going to hesitate? You're thirty years old, you're down for murder, you got twenty years, you'll probably never get out of there alive. What's going to stop you from offing somebody? So minor things become very serious."

Only at Bridgewater was inmate coercion of fellow inmates not a major factor in control. Inmates were prone to sudden, random attacks on other inmates and staff, but few were capable of systematic coercion. The greater security offered at Bridgewater led numerous inmates in other prisons to fake suicide attempts in the hopes of serving part of their sentences in the State Hospital.

## Inmate Coercion versus Officer Coercion

In this chapter, I have discussed reasons why different forms of power—including coercion and force—fail officers in their quest for control. Coercion and force also to some extent fail those inmates who seek to dominate fellow inmates. Thus, as was true for officers, dominance achieved by one inmate over another at a particular moment through coercion or force is usually not generalizable to other inmates or over time. More important, inmates usually constitute a far less unified group in their quest for control than do officers. Thus, to a large extent, inmate efforts to dominate are consumed by bloody conflicts *between* competing inmate factions or individual inmate "heavies."

But when coercion and force—especially violent coercion and force—become the currency of control in a contemporary American prison, as they did at Walpole in the 1970s, the advantage as often as not goes to the inmates. This is true for a number of reasons.

First, sanctions imposed by inmates on fellow inmates are potentially far more severe and less susceptible to constraint than sanctions imposed by officers. For all the brutality that Walpole officers reportedly inflicted on inmates in the 1970s, they apparently did not kill them, stab them, or rape them. As already mentioned, inmate assaults on fellow inmates during the same period were routine and vicious; the murders they committed were of the foulest sort. Not content merely to eliminate opponents, they went out of their way to make them suffer.

Many inmates, of course, abhorred the violence—they were, after all, its chief victims—but whatever internal constraints they might have had in regard to violence were diminished by the necessity for *all* inmates to use, or demonstrate a willingness to use, violence against their peers. Officers who opposed violence—and there were many—felt considerable pressure to use it as well, but they were better situated to heed their own internal constraints against involvement in it than were inmates. Their opposition also served at times to constrain violence committed by fellow officers. Thus, some officers reportedly halted or tempered the violence of other officers. Furthermore, some officers declared in the interviews their willingness to testify against fellow officers if those officers were actually to kill an inmate (see Chapter 5). An inmate, on the other hand, dared intervene in the violence of fellow inmates only at the very risk of his life, and there was almost no cause for inmates who perpetrated violence to fear a public breach of the code of silence. *

Inmates are not only less constrained in their use of violence, they also possess more formidable weapons in carrying it out. Notwithstanding periodic discoveries during the 1970s of handguns and explosives in the possession of inmates at Walpole and Norfolk, officers usually monopolize the use of firepower in prisons. But guns in the possession of officers are permanently consigned to the perimeters of the prison and are never brought inside. At least in small-scale conflicts, officers are limited to the use of batons. (In large-scale conflicts they may use tear gas or even dogs.) Alone in the cell blocks, an officer carries nothing but keys. Nearly all inmates, meanwhile, carry or have ready access to a knife, lead pipe, or other lethal weapon.

Thus, the terror under which most Walpole inmates lived was terror inspired principally by the actions of inmates, not officers. To the extent that obedience in the prison was motivated by fear, an inmate intent on surviving heeded fellow inmates long before he heeded officers.

The second reason that inmates have the advantage when coercion is relied upon is that inmates have numbers on their side. Coercion and force are manpower-intensive forms of power (assuming, of course, that weapons of mass destruction are ruled out, which they effectively are in prisons). Thus, even if Walpole officers had been willing to match the ferocity and frequency of inmate

---

* Murders of inmates by inmates rarely result in convictions unless an officer or outsider witnesses the slaying, which is, of course, uncommon. According to the Norfolk County District Attorney's office, of the approximately twenty-two murders at Walpole in the 1970s, only one yielded a conviction. This was the case of Robert A. Perrotta, who was castrated and strangled with his penis shoved down his throat. The district attorney reported that the " 'animalistic mutilation' of Perrotta before his death shocked even the inmates and resulted in the finding of two witnesses to the murder willing to testify" (*Boston Globe*, 24 November 1977).

violence, they would still have lacked the necessary manpower to maintain control. It was precisely the officers' reliance on coercion and force at Walpole that rendered the shortage of officers there so critical.

Nor was the problem of manpower confined to Walpole. According to Ben M. Crouch (1980, p. 223), the ratio of officers to inmates was also important in a "highly controlled, efficient" Southern prison. A rapid increase in the inmate population that was unmatched by an increase in officers apparently led to a "marked decrease in control" in the 1970s. Even in Nazi concentration camps, where the violence was extreme and the SS sophisticated in its use, the ratio of guards to inmates was still important. Eugen Kogon (1960) reported that at Buchenwald the SS was utterly dependent upon prisoners for drawing up lists of the all-important work details and human shipments (p. 263). By the end of the war, when the camps were swollen with inmates and the SS ranks depleted, at night "the SS dared enter the camp only under heavy arms" (p. 280).

Officers at Walpole (and elsewhere) attempted to compensate for their numerical disadvantage by timing their use of violence so as to reverse the ratio of officers to inmates, as when the inmate population was locked for the night or a group of officers were alone in a corridor with an inmate. But officers are too few in number and strength to coerce many inmates even some of the time in this fashion. Only the forceful restraints offered by a prison-wide system of solitary confinement or the psychological isolation offered by pharmaceutical means of control make domination by force and coercion truly practical. At most prisons, however, only a small proportion of inmates can be held for long in the solitude of their cells or their minds. With most inmates free in the blocks for most of the time, officers working singly or in pairs, only intermittently backed by more officers, cannot hope to maintain control in a block by force and coercion alone. Inmate factions within a cell block are not similarly disadvantaged. Thus inmates who seek to control other inmates may not only be more dangerous, the threat they pose is also more credible.

Third, officers lack sufficient knowledge of their captives' activities to rule effectively by coercion and force. That control which is offered by coercion and (with some exceptions) force can only be sustained if the controller knows what his subjects are doing. Orwell's Oceania in *1984* was an all-encompassing prison where "you had to live . . . in the assumption that every sound you made was overheard, and, except in darkness, every movement scrutinized" (1974, p. 7). One might assume that as in Oceania the power of knowledge in a prison would advantage the official regime. Thus Richard McCleery (1961b, p. 161) reported in his analysis of the maximum-security prison in Hawaii that "the principal foundation of custodial order was the custodians' monopoly on information." But that was certainly not true of the Massachusetts prisons in this study. Officers might, if they were lucky, monopolize information about official directives but they were almost always woefully ill informed about what was happening among the inmates. They lacked adequate knowledge because they were few and the inmates many, because they were socially distant from the inmates, because their individual involvement with the prison was only intermittent while that of inmates was continuous, and (especially at Walpole and Concord) because of construction flaws in the prison itself (see Chapter 3). Inmates, meanwhile, have ample opportunity to become and remain well informed about their captors *and* their fellow captives. Thus actions to which sanctions might apply are far more likely to come to the attention of those inmates who seek to assert control than to officers, further enhancing the credibility of the inmate threat.

Fourth, and most important, use of coercion and force does not disadvantage *inmates* by undermining other forms of power they might use, but reliance on coercion and force, especially violent sanctions, as a means of control does seriously disadvantage *officers* by undermining the most important form of power available to them: power based on authority.

The use of coercion and force appeals because it offers an immediate, often substantial, increase in power: If an inmate refuses to go into his cell, don't stand there arguing, toss him in. If he throws excrement at officers, a beating may cow him (and if not him, then others) from doing it again. If he is a constant source of trouble, a spell in the "blue room" may break him physically or mentally, or at the very least keep him out of the way for a while. But the momentary upsurge in power offered by the use of force and coercion costs the officers dearly over time. Although it may increase their total power on a temporary basis, it decreases their authority on a long-term basis by undermining the legitimacy of the officers' rule.

Diminution in their authority is disastrous for the officers. Coercion and force are forms of power to which both inmates and officers have easy access but, with rare exception, only officers can make claim to institution-wide authority and the advantages that authority confers. Unlike coercion and force, the power offered by authority is continuous and long-term. It does not require a high ratio of controllers to subjects because authority is a manpower-efficient form of control. It overcomes deficiencies in knowledge because obedience to authority is internalized and automatic and thus does not require constant surveillance of those who are to obey. The *disadvantage* of authority is that once lost it is much more difficult to restore than is the power conferred by coercion and force (which may be asserted or reasserted in a single confrontation). As authority declines, coercion and force become more attractive and so the cycle continues, not easily broken or reversed even by good officers and wise administrators.

If the net increase in officers' power offered by coercion and force could be sustained, it might be worth the diminution in their authority. But use of coercion and force by officers serves to stimulate, and to justify, inmate use of coercion and force against officers and inmates, thereby neutralizing the initial advantage gained by the officers. What is more, violence between officers and inmates is likely to contribute over time to an atmosphere within a prison in which differences between any parties are routinely resolved by violence. In addition to diminishing the officers' authority, use of force and coercion may also undermine other forms of power at their disposal that involve willing compliance, such as persuasion and inducement. An officer who routinely relies on coercion and force to make inmates do certain things may find himself less able to persuade them—without reference, direct or implied, to negative sanctions—to do other things. Thus, as Walpole so strikingly illustrates, reliance on coercion and force eventually leads to a decline in the officers' power. If officers are losers in this situation, by no means are all, or even many, inmates winners.

## The Garbage Problem

To help draw together the strands of the discussion in this chapter, I shall conclude with an illustration of the limitations on officers' power at Walpole.

Proper disposal of garbage and human waste is usually considered a prerequisite for congregate living. As such, one of the more basic tasks of governance is to oversee and enforce a sanitation system.

Yet even this basic task was beyond the scope of the official regime at Walpole during the 1970s. As described in Chapter 3, Walpole was infested with rats and roaches, its walls caked with excrement, its floors covered with trash.

When the Department of Public Health declared in 1978 that parts of Walpole were "unfit for human habitation" (citing a worsening of problems reported in previous years), prison administrators responded characteristically. They asserted that the situation was not actually as bad as inmates, the Public Health Department, and journalists claimed, and even if it were, it was the fault of the inmates and thus not the responsibility of the administration. Officials of the Department of Correction disingenuously suggested that the public health inspector had come on a bad day. A department spokesman said in words that parodied the real situation, "If [the inmates] dump garbage on the floor, the inspector may see this before a guard can clean it up. I think the inmates, the prison and the public would be better served if [the public health inspectors] work with the department" (Lowell *Sunday Sun*, 12 November 1978). But rats do not infest a building, nor roaches blacken its walls, overnight. The problem was long-term and pervasive.

Officers were willing to call a spade a spade. They recognized Walpole for the "rats' nest, garbage hole" that it was. They had to work daily in the filth, and they hated it.

> They get mad about something and they decide they don't want to eat and they just take the food and throw it against the wall and smash it, knowing all the time that they have to live in that. And I can't stand that filth, okay? You've got to walk {along} the block, and you've got to walk through papers and food and stuff that's been down for two or three days. That is really depressing to me because I really cannot stand filth . . . I feel the most depressing thing of all working out there is the filth that they live in.

Officers at other prisons do not work in filth. Norfolk was reasonably clean, and parts of the prison in which I worked were spotless. Why could Walpole officers not do something about the garbage problem? In responding to this question, I shall briefly consider the six forms of power that they might have used to accomplish this end.

The problem was not whether most inmates saw sanitation as a proper and rightful facet of prison life over which the officers might exercise *authority*. Nor was it a question of whether most inmates would have disputed that a cleaner institution would have been in their self-interest. Judging from complaints by inmates in letters, newspapers, lawsuits, legislative hearings, and private conversations with officers, as well as one's own common sense that, as a *Boston Globe* editorial put it, "not even dogs choose to live near their own excrement" (7 May 1979), most inmates hated the filth, too. But all too often *obeying* an official command to clean up *would* have been counter to an inmate's self-interest.

> You'd have ten guys on the tier that wouldn't want the garbage around. You'd have three or four guys on the tier that would figure if you give in to [the officers] what are they going to ask for next? And the ringleaders would tell [the other inmates], "You don't want it either guys." They've got guys on the tiers that are running the tiers.

What would happen to an inmate who cleaned up against the ring-leaders' will? "The other guys would kill him." With stakes that high, it is little wonder that cleaning up was not something an inmate did simply on an officer's command or request. Some blocks were clean—those inhabited principally by Black Muslims. But they were clean by virtue of authority exercised by inmate Muslim leaders, not officers.

Occasionally inmates could be *persuaded* to pick up a bit:

> You could get some guys that you could talk to. "Man, I mean you guys shouldn't live with a mess like this. You should clean it up." You find guys that will volunteer to come out [of] their cell . . . and just take a broom—they won't get it up off the floor, but they'll take the broom and push it all back to the back side. And then maybe you find a guy that every now and then that would get it up and put it in a trash can. But then if they get mad again, you get a guy that's going to take it and throw it right back over the floor again.

A little bit of bribery was also occasionally successful in *inducing* a single inmate to cooperate. (" 'Hey, why don't you get the block cleaned up and I will get you a milk when the cart comes by.' ") More commonly, deals could be struck with inmate leaders to allow the block to be cleaned:

> There was a lot of deals between certain cons and the admin-istration that we were involved in. I remember when they tried

to clean up 10 Block and we had to make deals. Imagine having to make a deal to clean up the block! All this time that the cons were {crabbing} about "We're living in bad conditions" and all this. When we tried to clean up they wouldn't let us. Then we had to make deals . . . [Inmates] from upstairs would talk to [inmates] from downstairs in the visiting room to get their ideas on whether they should clean up or not. That was ridiculous.

In trying to command, persuade, or induce the inmates to clean up, an officer tipped his hand that he cared about the mess. That was a major tactical error in the eyes of some officers. They tried to *manipulate* the inmates to clean up by affecting the same nonchalance regarding the filth that the inmates did. Explained an officer who admitted in the interview that he did care about the filth,

I told them, "Hey, listen, I'm not living here, you are. This is the filth you're eating, not me. I go home every day." I made sense in that way because I made them know that that was hurting them more than it was hurting me. And they became cleaner because they knew that it wasn't bothering me any. Once they got to know that it didn't bother me, then they did something about it because it was bothering them . . . A lot of officers make it look like . . . it's bothering them . . . But I knew enough not to let it bother me—not to *show* it at least. I was able to con them instead of them conning me.

But conning the cons did not result in appreciably cleaner blocks. If anything, the officers' pose of indifference may have reinforced in the eyes of some inmates the wisdom of also affecting such a stance.

Nor were *force* and *coercion* particularly effective. When I asked one officer, "Isn't there some way of forcing the inmates to [clean up]?" he sensibly replied, "How?" Officers could not put brooms in the inmates' hands and physically propel them down the block. Many of the principal perpetrators were already in punishment cells and had experienced severe physical reprisals for transgressions far more serious than throwing excrement. Nor could they be disarmed. Their weapons were food and feces. Short of starving them to death, the inmates had to be fed, and the supply of excrement was continuous and inevitable—such is its value to the completely dispossessed.

Authority, persuasion, inducement, manipulation, force, and coercion, singly or in combination, failed to alter the equation. Inmates who were rebellious or angry or frustrated or crazy or simply indifferent threw the refuse down. Inmates who did not like it were scared for their lives to pick it up. Officers, meanwhile, were unwilling to play the role of janitor themselves even if that would have helped—which it would not have. And they were powerless to ensure that someone else did. And so, life went on amidst the muck with only the rodents and roaches clearly in control.

The "garbage problem" at Walpole was only one of the more obvious failures of the official regime to control the prison. Officers in this study did not describe their relationship with inmates in terms of the commanders, leaders, or managers of men that many would have liked to have been. Rather, the metaphors they used were those of combatants, zoo keepers, and warehousers of men. They controlled what little they were able of the life of the institution, contested—often violently—what they felt they must and could, and conceded the rest to the control of inmate "heavies," themselves usually in bloody dispute.

# 5

# The Officer Code

The existence of an inmate subculture within prisons has long been recognized. In fact, much of the research conducted on prisons over the past half century has concentrated on the unique features of that subculture: the beliefs, values, and "code" of behavior that characterize it. The inmate subculture has captured the popular—as well as academic—imagination in large part because of its "code" and the deadly consequences for those who violate it. Basic norms of the inmate code are: don't "rat out" a fellow inmate, don't cooperate or fraternize with prison officials, maintain an outward solidarity, and be loyal to one's mates. While other groups may share some or all of these principles of solidarity, the degree to which inmates must adhere to them is greatly magnified by their inability to escape membership in the inmate society, by their perceived reliance on one another against a common enemy, and by their realization that, within their closed world, retaliation is likely to be swift and may be lethal.

Officers also possess a distinct subculture within prisons. Their own beliefs and code of conduct set them apart from administrators, social workers, and, of course, inmates. The central norms of the officer subculture are the subject of this chapter.

The norms of a group are *"ideas in the minds* of members [of that group] about what should and should not be done by a specific member under specified circumstances" (Mills, 1967, p. 74, emphasis added). Thus, the norms of the officer subculture cannot be defined simply by observing the behavior of officers but depend instead upon the meaning that officers ascribe to specific behaviors. The account of officer norms presented here is based on the attitudes that officers expressed about certain types of behavior and their expectations regarding the likely consequences within the officer group of engaging in such behavior. Most of the discussion of norms in the interviews was spontaneous on the part of officers. These norms were, after all, central to their lives as officers. They readily identified them and identified *with* them. To introduce some uniformity to the analysis, I asked every officer, "What is the worst thing you could do in your own eyes as an officer?" and "What is the worst thing you could do in the eyes of the other officers?"

The nine norms discussed are presented in order of their strength and acceptance among officers. The strength of a norm was gauged by the degree of unanimity with which the officers espoused the norm in the interviews, by the extent to which they reported that the norm was upheld in practice by themselves and by their fellow officers, and by the extent to which violations of the norm were deemed likely to lead to disapproval and negative sanctions by other officers. In general, these different indicators of the strength of a norm coincided.

Because the norms were in sharpest relief at Walpole, the discussion will center on that prison. Brief comparisons with the officer subcultures at Norfolk, Concord, and Bridgewater are made at the end of the chapter (for more extensive commentaries on the norms at the other three prisons, see Kauffman, 1985, chap. 5).

## Norm 1: Always Go to the Aid of an Officer in Distress

The obligation to go to the aid of a fellow officer is the most important positive responsibility of any officer. It is the norm on which officer solidarity is based, the foundation of their sense of brotherhood. It is a command that in theory applies to any officer in distress and an obligation that, if consistently discharged, permits considerable latitude in upholding other norms.

At Walpole the imperative "Always go to the aid of an officer in distress" took the specific form "Always respond to a 'slam.' " When the heavy metal door to a cell block in Walpole was slammed shut the noise reverberated throughout the institution. The sound was universally recognized as the signal of trouble in a block. It was in theory the responsibility of every available officer throughout the institution, including block officers (who were supposed to lock their own blocks before coming), to respond to each and every slam. "When somebody drops the coin in the juke box and plays that little number, everybody comes and dances . . . From the smallest and meekest and weakest to the biggest and tallest and biggest loud mouth, I know they're all going to be there. If I need help, it's coming."

When a "slam" took place the way it was supposed to, a dozen or more officers arrived on the scene of trouble within a minute or two. The immediacy and size of the response not only protected the particular officer in trouble, but also served notice on the inmates that the officers would immediately back each other whenever there was trouble. Perhaps equally important, a good response to a slam was an unparalleled source of good feeling and camaraderie among officers. Walpole may have been dangerous and the officers' job taxing, but at least the officers were in it *together*, willing to share the dangers and dedicated to upholding their common good. An officer described his feelings about one incident:

We were sitting in the staff kitchen, the officers. There was a good fifteen, twenty guards there. And the phone rang. And I don't know why—it was strange—I remember clearly, everybody stopped eating. The phone rings—the phone rings in there five, six times a day. Everybody put down their forks and knives . . . The guy picked up the phone, he didn't even hang it up, he dropped it and he says, "Trouble in Block 10!" Oh, Kelsey, incredible! We were running each other over to get down to 10 Block. "Get down to 10 Block!" Oh, I still get goose bumps with that. We flew down there. If we didn't have thirty guys down there in a matter of sixty seconds—I mean this is from Block 9, that's a good long run from 9 Block all the way down to 10. And it was over some little thing too . . . [The inmates] got a pretty good idea that . . . if they're going to do something, if it's going to be something serious, they can expect that we're going to {round} up the {full} guys and that they'll be down here very, very determined to put an end to this problem, within sixty seconds . . . And we're {ready} to do business. And I think that works.

The strength of this norm lay in the very real sense that an officer alone "can't last in a place like that a long time." As will be discussed later, the ultimate sanction that could be imposed upon an officer was that of being cast adrift within the institution. Yet barring that extreme sanction, officers agreed that any officer in distress should be helped regardless of his own record in responding to slams or his general standing in the eyes of other officers.

No matter how much of a jerk the guy is, whether he is black or white, he is still a correction officer. He's still wearing this uniform and everybody is going to be willing to help him out. All of those other things are put aside and the concern for his safety is foremost. There is no question about that. Because we have to work together and our main concern is going home at night . . . safely. That is the main concern. And it has to be in this type of an atmosphere where it's so tense.

More than anything else, a new officer was judged by his willingness to uphold this norm. "That is a major thing [in] how you're accepted, if they know you're going to be there when there's trouble. Then at least they know they can depend on you, and depending on you in a place like that is crucial. You've got to depend on somebody if something happens. You're useless if you're not." "At least you show up. You bring your body to the scene . . . even if you don't do anything."

So important was this norm that once an officer had proved himself, and as long as he remained steadfast in his support of fellow officers in trouble, he could be pardoned for a multitude of other sins. An officer who consistently violated norms mandating a hard line toward inmates recalled:

A lot of times [the officers] told me, "You're no good. You're a pushover. You're this or that." I said, "Well, that's too bad. You don't have to like it. But I'm going to do what I want to do." . . . They'd say, "Well, we're all supposed to stick together. We're all supposed to be one." And I'd say, "Well, I think you guys are wrong and I'm going to do what I think is right and if you don't like it, that's too bad."

*Didn't they worry, wondering whether you were sticking with the officers?*

No, because whenever there was trouble I was always right there. A lot of times maybe the first one there.

*And that's what makes the difference?*

Yes.

The sanctions that came to bear on those who violated this norm at Walpole appeared to depend on a number of factors: whether the officer was a rookie, what shift he worked, and the frequency of the violation. A rookie working the 3–11 shift who consistently failed to show up for a slam when he was in a position to do so was likely to be ostracized by his fellow officers.

> They'd ignore you . . . When you sat down at the table, they'd all get up and move. Or somebody would take the chair away when you went to sit down or something. They'd let you know that you're not wanted. They wouldn't come right out and say it, but they might as well come right out and tell you, "Just get out of here."

If the pattern persisted on the 3–11 and the officer did not resign, he would almost certainly be moved to the 11–7 or 7–3 shift. On the 11–7, with the inmates locked, crises rarely occurred. On the 7–3, an officer who failed to respond to a slam at least had ample company with others too scared or burnt out to appear. A new officer who consistently failed to appear on the 7–3 might be subjected to mild harassment and open criticism, but not much else. An older officer's absence would hardly be noticed.

The degree to which the injunction to come to the aid of an officer in distress was observed had direct bearing on officer morale. Strict adherence to it was one of the hallmarks of the 3–11 shift. The resulting sense of security and esprit de corps were among the things that made that shift what it was. The norm was central to each man's sense of identity as an officer. One measure of its strength on the 3–11 shift was the derision with which the 7–3 shift was treated for the frequent failure of officers to respond to a slam.

> If there was a slam everybody [on the 3–11] came. Not like the day shift. If there was a slam [on the day shift], two or three guys will come. The other guys would screw off. Nobody would have shown up. Imagine that! Imagine thinking, working in a max block, slam the door, and have nobody come!
> *Why?*
> Either you couldn't find them because they had disappeared, or because they were too scared and they locked themselves up in their own blocks . . .
> *Why didn't the officers put pressure on the other officers who didn't show?*
> They do. They do.
> *And what can they do?*
> Well, they can threaten them. They can do a million things to

them. It doesn't mean they're going to come the next time. They're too scared. They're scared. Can't blame them.

All but one of the younger Walpole officers I interviewed—most of whom worked the 3–11—said they responded to a slam whenever possible. (The single exception, an officer on the 7–3, claimed he responded only in his section of the institution.) But older officers on the 7–3 shift made clear in the interviews that they saw slams as the responsibility of younger men who had not yet put in their years and run the risks they already had. A younger officer observed of his older colleagues, "A lot of guys . . . they just [don't] have the ambition anymore and just don't want to put up with the hassles. They don't care about it; let things slide. They've put in their time. They're a little bit burnt out and they're waiting to get out of there." In any case, such officers usually had sufficient seniority to bid onto positions that were removed from inmate contact, and were remote from the need to respond to others *and* for others to respond to them. They were shielded from sanctions by their own longevity and the number of like-minded officers on their shift.

Apathy and fear—fear heightened on the 7–3 shift by foreboding that you might be not one of twelve but one of only two officers responding to a crisis—these were the main incentives for violating this norm. When an officer who had worked the 3–11 for a number of years was asked what was the worst thing he could do in his own eyes as an officer, he responded, "I won't even insult you or myself by saying, 'not going to another man's aid,' because that isn't even in my dictionary." That it *was* in the dictionary of many 7–3 officers had considerable bearing on the socialization of new officers, as will be discussed in Chapter 8.

## Norm 2: Don't "Lug" Drugs

No norm of the officer subculture received more spontaneous endorsement than that against "lugging" drugs, that is, bringing drugs into the prison for inmate use. Officers did not view "lugging" as an unpardonable offense because of personal revulsion against the use of drugs per se. Indeed, some officers reported that they used illicit drugs themselves or knew of officers who did (and nearly all used alcohol). Nor was this norm merely part of a general prohibition against bringing things for inmates into prison. Such practices were covered by weaker norms against positive association with inmates. Rather, the strength of the norm against lugging lay in the potential danger to fellow officers presented by inmates on drugs or under the influence of alcohol. "I'm figuring that someone's selling my safety and everyone else's safety for a buck. You got to be down crawling on the ground. That's like a snake."*

The seriousness of the prohibition against lugging was underscored by the sanctions for violating it, principally removal from the officer corps and/or physical reprisal. Many officers stated that if they believed a fellow officer were lugging they would, under that circumstance alone, violate the norm against ratting on an officer (Norm 3). What is more, almost all officers indicated that any officer who did rat out a fellow officer for lugging would receive support, not condemnation, for doing so even though the accused officer would face dismissal were the allegations substantiated. If the offending officer was not reported and officially dismissed, officers would ensure by other means that he left the prison.

> If another officer lugged, he would be definitely blackballed. Whether they would go to the front office [administration] and tell—what they'd more and likely do first would be get him out in the parking lot, put a beating on up and say, "We know. You either resign or we are going to rat you out."

And yet even an officer caught lugging drugs would still benefit from a sense of brotherhood among officers.

> I'm sure they'd confront him with it first. They'd give him more opportunities than they'd give someone else . . . That's like the unwritten code. He gets a break; you give him one shot—to leave. There's no respect, no real feeling other than, "You're lucky you're wearing the uniform or else we'd hang your ass."

Given the strength of officer feeling about lugging and the sanctions for engaging in it, it is not surprising that its incidence as reported in the interviews was low. Only one of the sixty officers I interviewed indicated that he had brought drugs into his institution for inmate use and that one individual was not a Walpole officer. (He

---

* Bringing an inmate a weapon, especially a firearm, would, of course, be viewed as more dangerous to fellow officers and thus as a more serious offense than lugging drugs. But sanctions against smuggling a weapon into a prison that would be imposed by authorities beyond the officer society are potentially so severe, and the incentives for doing so are correspondingly so small (and in any case the reported incidence nationwide of such offenses so low), that the officer society did not need to espouse and enforce a norm against such behavior.

claimed to have brought in marijuana not for sale but for sociability's sake.) Many Walpole officers made clear in the interviews that, whatever else they had done as officers, they had never, and would never, have brought in drugs for inmates.

Several Walpole officers reported that, although they did not bring drugs into the prison themselves, they took a tolerant attitude toward the presence of marijuana and home brew in the institution. Some tolerated moderate use of drugs and alcohol in their blocks, others said they would flush them down an inmate's toilet if they found them on searching an inmate's cell. To some extent such tolerance was a form of ingratiation with inmates. ("Those kinds of things got me through a little bit," reported one officer.) More often, however, officers who permitted moderate drug use among inmates seemed motivated by a sense of empathy for men deprived of the pleasures of life. Remarked one Walpole block officer,

> I don't get upset over home brew and marijuana, small amounts
> . . . He can have a high if he wants it . . . "You want to do a
> couple of pints of booze one night, get a little {high}? Fine. You
> keep it, do it like a man, don't start any trouble, and don't put
> the heat on me, and I'll let you do it."

A clear distinction was made between tolerance for the use of intoxicants in an officer's own cell block and lugging drugs into the prison. Although pressure might be put on an officer for the former, especially if the inmates involved got out of hand, he was not likely to suffer the stiff sanctions imposed on the officer who lugged.

The vehemence of officer opposition to lugging will be treated with skepticism from some quarters. Walpole, like so many other American prisons, had a staggering quantity of illegal drugs available to inmates within its walls. Officers at Walpole (and elsewhere) were often accused of being the principal source of those drugs. As their accusers pointed out, officers, unlike inmates and their visitors, were not subject to search on entering the prison. (In fact, most visitors in the 1970s were not searched either but were merely obligated to pass through the same metal detector through which the officers passed, a detector, of course, that did not signal the presence of drugs. Nevertheless, some officers advocated that all officers be subject to random searches of themselves and their lockers to catch offenders and minimize suspicions about the majority of officers who did not lug.) The financial incentives for an officer to lug are high. Even officers believed that some among them must be participating in the trade. Their suspicions were the source of constant vigilance and discussion among officers. "That's the big gossip inside there. 'You know what so-and-so, the inmate, told [me]? That this is the guy bringing in the dope.' And then it would be like a vicious rumor and people would be very cautious of this guy and watching." Fear of arousing suspicions regarding lugging helped to reinforce the norm not to fraternize with inmates (Norm 7). Too close the association, too great the cooperation on the part of inmates with a particular officer caused "everybody [to jump] . . . to that conclusion that, 'How come this guy likes you so much? What are you giving him? What are you bringing him? What are you doing for him? How come he's so friendly with you?' "

The officer who lugs is popularly portrayed as motivated by greed, but like so many other caricatures of officers, this one provides a distorted image of life inside a prison like Walpole. For many officers, the incentive for lugging is not money but rather peace and the hope of at least momentary release from fear and the threat of violence. A seasoned officer described the fears he faced not only from the inmates but also from within himself, the fear that he might betray his fellow officers:

> Fear is the biggest enemy we have up there . . . It doesn't have to be fear of physical violence. It can be a fear that you're not going to be able to say "no" to a guy that asked you to lug something in for him. And now you're compromising your own beliefs and your own true feelings. I don't believe it's right to bring something in—contraband. And yet, you don't have the nerve to say "no" to the guy. That's another kind of fear, aside from the fear or the threat of physical violence.

The pressures to lug were often greatest for those officers who came from the same communities as inmates or knew those inmates and their families and friends outside the prison. It is a measure of the strength of the norm against lugging at Walpole that despite the incentives and pressures to violate it, interviewees who accused fellow officers of much else steadfastly believed that few among them succumbed to the temptations of lugging.

## Norm 3: Don't Rat

The injunction "Don't rat" is fundamental to most codes of solidarity. The nature of the injunction and the sanctions for violating it

varied considerably at Walpole according to which officer was being
ratted out, to whom, and for what. An experienced officer watching
a rookie officer could pass on impressions to a supervisor without
fear of being labeled a rat. And, as already discussed, informing on an
officer who lugged drugs would have been widely applauded. But the
rookie officer had not yet been accorded full membership in the
officer society, and the officer who lugged had effectively forfeited
his claim to membership in it.

The prohibition against ratting took on special significance for the
officer corps in two related injunctions: (1) Never rat out an officer
*to an inmate*, and (2) Never cooperate in an investigation or, worse
yet, testify against a fellow officer in regard to that officer's treatment of inmates. To do either was to commit a fundamental sin, in
essence to betray one's own group to the enemy.

*Never rat out an officer to an inmate.* In a prison like Walpole,
where violent retaliation is commonplace, remaining anonymous is
deemed in many circumstances to be synonymous with remaining
healthy and alive. The identity of the officer who signed the report
that resulted in an inmate's transfer to Block 10, or of the officers
who were involved in a beating or in the quelling of a block disturbance with tear gas and force, was not always known. Betrayal of a
fellow officer to inmates was, as one officer put it, the "sin of sins,"
because doing so might jeopardize the other officer's safety.

> I seen things that I didn't like and it's a sin that I didn't do
> anything. I didn't participate, but I didn't do anything to stop it
> other than voice your opinion later on to the officers. But it was
> like an unwritten code that . . . the sin of sins would be to rat out
> an officer or something like that. So you could even go so far as
> telling the inmates, "Say, I really thought that was a bummer
> what happened. I just want you to know that I had no hand in
> that." And they'd say, "I know,——," and stuff like that. But they
> understood, just like you understood, that if I asked one of them
> to rat on their friend, "Who hit Officer Jones?" or . . . "Who put
> the crap in his desk drawer?" he's going to say, "——, you know
> you're wearing a brown shirt and I'm wearing a white and we rap
> and we have good communication, but don't ask me to be a rat."
> So on the other hand it was the same thing.

No doubt related to this taboo was another injunction: never
discuss a fellow officer (nor much about oneself) with inmates. It
was best that inmates knew as little as possible about the identities,

characters, and peer group standings of the officers. On the other hand, officers could and often did entertain inmate complaints about other officers. As long as communication about an officer went *one way*—inmate to officer—then it was not likely to be considered a breach of this norm. For example, a white officer related an incident when a black inmate complained to him about a black officer.

> [The inmate] comes over to me, "I am going to kill that motherfucking nigger." I said, "What is the matter?" He says, "He's too hard. He's too hard on the block." . . . And from my observations this guy is a little hard. He will come in and act like a drill instructor down at Parris Island . . . So I got him out in the corridor and I talked to him and tried to get through to him in the most tactful way that I can . . . "Maybe you ought to just be a little bit more flexible, try to adjust your approach a little bit."

The nature and extent of sanctions for ratting on an officer to an inmate depended, of course, on the seriousness of the breach and the certainty that the breach had occurred (inmate informants were not necessarily to be relied on, it being perceived to be in the inmates' interest to sow dissension among officers). In a single known instance, the offending officer would presumably face the wrath of the officer ratted out. A *pattern* of ratting to inmates would likely result in ostracism by the rest of the officers and perhaps time "on the walls," where no further harm could be done. In any case the penalty was certain to fall short of that accorded to an inmate rat by his peers: death.

The incidence of ratting among officers is hard to gauge. None of the Walpole officers I interviewed suggested that he had ever ratted on another officer to an inmate, nor could any cite incidents that had occurred among fellow officers. At the very least, then, it does not seem to have been a common occurrence at Walpole. In that sense, Walpole officers appeared to have been truer to their code than inmates were to theirs.

*Never testify against a fellow officer.* This prohibition was significant not for the frequency of its violation nor for the temptations that might have existed to violate it, but rather for the severity of sanctions that would have been imposed on an officer who did violate it. During the 1970s, Walpole officers were the subjects of several state and federal investigations and were charged with brutality and mistreatment in numerous lawsuits brought by inmates.

In all but one of the suits and in each of the investigatons the officers were exonerated. The questions I posed to interviewees were hypothetical: (1) If the interviewee were asked to testify against a fellow officer(s) regarding the beating or killing of an inmate which he had witnessed, would he violate one of the central tenets of the officer code by testifying about what he knew to be true, or would he maintain that code and in the process perjure himself? (2) If he did testify, what would be the consequences of doing so?

When interviewees were asked what they thought *would* happen in the event of an inmate death and official inquiry they agreed. "The code [that] protects the officers would more than likely hold up in that they would find fourteen signatures [signatories] who said they saw it and the guy was attacking me or anybody else with a knife."*

But when interviewees were asked what *they* would or should do in that circumstance their answers were more complex. Some felt that what they would do would depend on the circumstances of the death and the identity of those involved. One officer who had witnessed a fellow officer "flip out" and make an inmate "beg for his life" said in that circumstance at least he would have testified against his fellow officer if the threat of death had been carried out. To another officer,

> It would depend on the inmate. If it was this one particular person who I think should be executed, or a few people in there that I think should be executed, I'd say I didn't see a thing. If it was somebody in there just stealing or something that wasn't— none of it is nickel and dime, I mean they're in *Walpole*—but there are some things that just cannot be tolerated. I think that I would probably step forward and tell them what happened and hopefully remain anonymous. As a matter of fact, that's what I would definitely do.

Others focused neither on the circumstances of the death nor on the identity of the inmate victim but rather on their own relationship with fellow officers and on their desire to remain employed. For

---

* I once attended a court hearing (not in New England) regarding allegations of officer brutality in which the officers one by one perjured themselves to protect their colleagues. How I came to know that the officers lied provides another insight into the workings of the officer code. The officers freely volunteered to me that they had perjured themselves at no guarantee of silence from me but solely because I had introduced myself as a former prison officer.

an officer to testify against his fellow officers meant betraying men about whom he cared deeply, with whom he had suffered, and to whom he often in the past owed his own safety. To do so would also mean he could never again work in Walpole.

For an officer who opposed violence, yet felt loyalty and affection for his fellow officers, and who wanted to remain employed as a prison officer, there were few more troubling dilemmas than this one. In the following exchange, one officer captured the force of the dilemma, the ambivalence about testifying, the feared consequences of doing so, and the relation between such an act and the code and culture it would have violated:

*Let's say that one of the inmates were killed and you were there, you witnessed it . . . What would you do in that situation?*

. . . If somebody would have died and I thought I should have done something, I'm sure—hopefully—I don't know. I don't know right now today what I'd do. Hopefully I would like to think that I would come forward as much as it would mean that I'd never be able to work in Walpole again.

*How many other officers do you think would do that?*

. . . To that degree, probably very few . . .

*. . . What would happen if you continued working there?*

I think it would be unbearable as far as the pressure you'd take . . . I think you'd lose any chance. It would be as if . . . they all stayed stone. No matter what I did they all stayed stone. Because it's like a valve. They just turn you off. They'd think they'd have to because you were no longer trusted. And above all else they did think that they could trust you . . .

*You said that you didn't think that more than a handful of people would actually turn the guy in.*

I don't know if I could either. I said I hoped I would.

*But there are probably some who wouldn't be willing but who—*

Wished they would have?

*Or, yes, or would respect somebody else for doing it. What percent would you say? One out of every ten? Or one out of every hundred? Or—*

I don't know. A lot of guys put on a good front. I'm sure that I'd probably give a low figure, but I'm sure there'd be more. But even if they did respect you, they wouldn't be able to show that they respected you. So it would be hard to measure it. Maybe they'd say afterwards, after you were fired or after you finally left and everything, they'd say, "You know,——, I really want you to know that I didn't hold anything against you them days," or something like that. Which would do me no good at that time. I wanted your help then or something. But they'd probably feel something for you. But I don't think—they *couldn't* show it. If nothing else, you do believe that you need, you *know* you need the rest of the officers in order to perform. And if you're alone, you can't last in a place like that a long time.

*Of those you think that might be secretly sympathetic to you, how many do you think there would be? Ten in the whole prison?*

No, I think it'd be a lot that would feel something for you. To what degree I haven't the slightest. But I would like to think that it would be a lot. It could be the whole group. But no one's willing to make the first move. No one's willing to make the first step because of that unwritten code that says that I violated them or I violated their code and I'm a *correctional officer*.

"That unwritten code that says I violated them or I violated their code and I'm a *correctional officer*": That is the offense. "If nothing else you do believe that you need, you *know* that you need the rest of the officers in order to perform. And if you're alone you can't last in a place like that a long time": That is the sanction. In these two statements lies the heart of the officer code and beyond that the officer society at Walpole. To transgress central norms of the subculture was to *violate* your fellow officers and the trust and comradeship in which they held you. It was a betrayal the penalty for which was being cut adrift, set apart from the officer community—a sanction that at least at Walpole could not be borne. To cast the dilemma any other way is to grossly underestimate its force.

One of the principal problems presented by prison violence lies in the unwillingness of both officers and inmates to testify against members of their own group. On both sides the resistance to testifying lies not so much in the conviction that the accused is right or justified in what he did nor in the moral value of silence per se, but rather in commitment to the group and palpable fears as to what the consequences would be of violating the group's code. While officers may be motivated more by commitment to the group and inmates more by the consequences of betrayal (the consequences in any case being much more severe for inmates, who, after all, do not have the option of quitting the institution), loyalty and fear are important motivations for members of each group.

## Norm 4: Never Make a Fellow Officer Look Bad in Front of Inmates

The first three tenets of the officer code have dealt with extreme situations: an officer in distress, or caught lugging drugs, or called upon to testify against fellow officers. The remainder of the norms discussed in this chapter concern everyday conduct of officers, the routine behavior expected of them vis-à-vis one another, the inmates, and the world beyond.

An officer should never be made to look bad or be in any way embarrassed or criticized in front of inmates regardless of whether the officer in question is behaving correctly. "If an officer does something, even if it's totally wrong, you can't make him look bad. It's about the lowest thing you can do . . . It makes the officer look bad and makes the inmate think he can push for more." Violations of this norm were taken seriously. They not only jeopardized the effectiveness of the officer criticized, but also undercut the appearance of officer solidarity and thus increased the vulnerability of the officers as a group.

*What do you think would be the worst thing you could do in the eyes of the other officers? . . .*

I assume more or less the worst thing you can do is, an officer is confronting another inmate, telling him off about something, and then you sides up to him and tell him right in front of the inmate, "No, you're wrong. You shouldn't do it this way. The book say that you should do it this way. You shouldn't be messing with this man about this and that." I figure that's more or less the worst thing you can do, because that's belittling the other officer in front of the inmate and then he's going to label him as a no-good so-and-so, simply because you've proved him wrong in front of the inmate. If an officer's wrong about something, you let him finish what he's saying, get him outside, to the side, and then explain it to him. And then it's up to him to go back and straighten things out or whatever . . . You want [the inmates to] have the impression that the officers are together, they know what they [are] talking about.

The injunction "never make an officer look bad in front of inmates" applied to behavior of which another officer *may have personally disapproved*. It was not limited to whether an inmate should or should not go to his cell or whether he could or could not make a phone call. It embraced as well such matters as whether an inmate should or should not be harassed or beaten. As will be discussed in Chapter 6, many officers were privately disturbed by the level of officer violence at Walpole, but few felt willing or able to do anything to stop their fellow officers at least while a beating was in progress.

> Say we had four officers lugging an inmate down in Block 10 and one officer had maybe a stick and was beating him with it. At the time I probably wouldn't have said anything. And then after I would have got that officer by myself and probably I would have told him that I didn't think the beating was right. I wouldn't confront him probably in front of the other officers and the inmate.

(For more on this issue, see the discussion below of Norm 6.)

To some extent, officers were deterred from interfering with one another by notions of reciprocity. ("I wouldn't appreciate it if I were doing something and someone else butted in. Even if it was the wrong thing to do, still you shouldn't interfere.") Those not concerned by reciprocity still had to contend with the officer they had embarrassed. An officer related an incident when, as a rookie, he asked a senior officer for advice on how to handle an inmate's request. The officer, who had been reading a magazine,

> threw it off the wall and said, "Do I have to teach you how to become a good fucking officer?" He says, "I'll handle this." And he went on to really lambast me with a few adjectives. And there were inmates nearby. So I almost blew my cool, but with inmates nearby I tried to remain calm about the whole thing . . . He came back and I closed the door and I told him if he ever opened his mouth like that to me again he'd have it . . . I don't care if they're senior or anybody, the deputy or nothing. And so I said, "If you don't like it, we'll straighten it out between each other."

Such strong words from a rookie to a senior officer would have been unusual, but in this case, according to the officer, the senior backed down with an apology.

Any officer who made a habit of putting down fellow officers in front of inmates would face more serious sanctions than a threatened fight. As "word got around," he would encounter stiff social disapproval, perhaps ostracism. Depending on his shift and assignment, his behavior might be brought to the attention of his supervisor, who in turn might take official action such as moving him to a different shift or assignment or, in extreme cases, pressing for his dismissal.

Officers, like the one quoted above, invariably had a story to tell about how when they were rookies a more senior officer had humiliated them in front of an inmate. Once an officer had gained some seniority, however, the incidence seemed rare. Although "there are officers who do that kind of thing," open violation of this norm did not appear to be frequent. One reason for low incidence of violation may have been the slight incentives for doing so. Another may have been that breaches of this norm are, by definition, openly performed with an identifiable officer "victim." (Secretively making an officer look bad to inmates takes on the color of ratting, a violation that, like lugging, is more serious but harder to prove.) Of the norms most easily monitored, compliance with this one was taken very seriously.

### Norm 5: Always Support an Officer in a Dispute with an Inmate

Norm 5 is the positive counterpart of Norm 4, "Never make an officer look bad in front of an inmate." The objective served by both norms is to maintain officer solidarity, in appearance and fact, before inmates.

> I've walked around ... just walking by another officer and picked up a little of the conversation and then I realized that he was having an argument with this inmate. Turn right around and just stand behind my fellow officer. I don't have to say a word and that guy knows, "Go ahead, start something and I'm here to help him."

An officer was not supposed to be an independent arbiter of disputes between inmates and fellow officers. He was there, instead, to provide unquestioning support for officers—just as an inmate was expected to provide unquestioning support for fellow inmates. As one officer trainee prophesied on the eve of entering prison service, "I think you'll find yourself on the side of the guards always." With inmates invariably allied against them and support from the administration unreliable, Walpole officers perceived that their situation would have been intolerable had it not been for this unquestioning solidarity. So important were expectations of support that even defending an inmate in a *private* conversation with fellow officers was frowned upon. One hard-line officer declared that any officer who stood up for an inmate "was a shit-head. The word would get around and the other officers would think that too."

Officers justified their automatic support for each other by their belief that any inmate in a dispute with an officer must be in the wrong, if not in the particular situation, then at least in events that preceded it. As a trainee saw it, "I believe the inmates are wrong {with} the officers almost all the time, or 95 percent of the time anyway ... I know that [the officers] just go around writing out D-Reports if they want to get a guy, but I believe that the guy is asking for it in an indirect way." So strong was this attitude that inmates were inevitably wrong and that one officer should always support another in any dispute with an inmate that some officers willingly signed D-Reports as witnesses to events that they had not in fact observed. For example, one officer would say to another, " 'I seen Joe Blow lighting fires but I was the only one there. I want you to be my witness.' ... And [the other officer] would say, 'Sure, I'll sign it. I never liked the maggot anyhow.' And they'd sign it."

As with other norms calling for positive action, sanctions for violating this norm were not as severe nor as definite as they were for norms that prohibited behavior (don't lug, don't rat, don't make an officer look bad). Although an officer ran the risk of being considered a "shit-head" for supporting an inmate's version of events in the privacy of officer discussion, or for refusing to sign a D-Report for a violation he had not actually observed, these were behaviors in which he could have engaged without undue repercussion *if* the officer had proved himself loyal in other ways.

> I'd say, "Jesus, I didn't see it." And they'd say, "Well, so what? Just be my witness. It's not going to hold up in the D-Board if I say I'm alone. He couldn't see us anyhow." And I'd say, "Well, Jesus, I just don't do that. If I see it, I'll gladly sign it. If I don't see it, I don't like to sign it." And at first you're kind of {shaky} for that. But after a while they'd say, "Oh, okay, uh, Harry,

would you sign it?" . . . And to me that was like, that's not fair. You play fair. If he gets caught, he gets caught. If he don't get caught, he don't get caught.

*That's interesting that you could do that. Did you receive an enormous amount of heat for doing that?*

Not an enormous amount of heat. At first you probably would. They would say, "Well, that's what they told us about you anyhow. Tomorrow you'll find yourself in the tower." But after a period of time . . . you were accepted for what you were. They'd still ask you from time to time or hope that you would do it to protect their own can.

Another officer took a similar stance regarding D-Reports:

I wouldn't go along with that. Because I—how would you know the officer's telling the truth? [*laughter*] It sounds crazy, but it's true.

*Would you get a lot of heat for not doing that?*

No, because he'll find somebody else to sign it if they really want it. They may not like it. I don't know. I'd tell a guy if I hadn't seen it, I'm not going to say I saw something I didn't see.

"It sounds crazy," this officer said, to even suggest that a fellow officer might not be telling the truth. Given the strength of the idea that an officer was by definition right, it is not difficult to see why few officers violated norms surrounding that belief.

As already mentioned, this norm derives its importance in part from the perception—regularly reinforced by observation—that inmates will provide unquestioning support for fellow inmates, and thus that officers must do the same for each other. The rigidity of these positions breaks down at some prisons. In interviews that I conducted at a Massachusetts county jail, for example, officers complained bitterly about lack of support provided by fellow officers, and many crosscutting alliances appeared to exist between inmates and officers.

At Niantic prison I observed the breakdown of this norm for both inmates and officers in the Democratic Unit, as the following example illustrates. A meeting was called one day of all officers and inmates in the Democratic Unit to consider problems caused by two inmates who were openly lovers. The discussion initially cast the issue as one involving conflict between officers and inmates and their opposing interests and expectations. Then some of the younger staff took issue in the meeting with the rather rigid rules on homo-sexuality at the prison, sparking open debate between the older and younger officers in front of the inmates. The outcome was hardly what might have been predicted by stalwarts of officer solidarity. Rather than taking the opportunity presented by disunity among officers to advance their own—presumably hostile—interests, the inmates too proceeded to break ranks. The result was that a majority of inmates eventually voted stiffer sanctions against the couple than any of the officers felt appropriate. Among other things, the inmate who played an aggressive "butch" role in the relationship was "sen-tenced" to wear only dresses from then on—an outrageous violation of her rights in the view of some of the younger staff members, who nonetheless had to go along with the majority decree.

## Norm 6: Always Support Officer Sanctions against Inmates

To some extent Norm 6 is merely a more specific version of Norm 5, "Always support an officer in a dispute with an inmate." Obvi-ously it is part of the job of an officer to enforce official sanctions (such as loss of privileges, isolation time in one's cell, removal to a more restrictive block) levied on inmates for specific offenses. But this norm goes beyond general support of officers or enactment of official duty and involves active participation in the application of informal sanctions whose wisdom—and sometimes morality—the officer may doubt.

The cutting edge of this norm at Walpole was the issue of physical force and coercion in response to inmate violence. The norm was important not for the degree to which it was enforced (in fact, sanctions for noncompliance were relatively weak), but rather be-cause systematic reprisals as a means of curbing inmate-on-officer violence could not have been sustained without it. As will be dis-cussed in Chapter 6, many officers believed deeply that such repris-als were the only means of deterring violence directed against them. Thus, to abstain from participation involved not only failure to support officers in a particular instance, but also failure to prevent harm to officers in the future. To go beyond abstention and actually interfere with reprisals inflicted by other officers was deemed by many to undermine the safety of all.

Discrepancies existed in the degree to which Walpole officers who did not want to participate in the violence felt under pressure to do so and in the types of sanctions they experienced as a consequence of nonparticipation. One Walpole interviewee apparently felt under little pressure to participate yet believed he was accepted by fellow officers based on his adherence to more important norms.

*Why didn't you participate?*

Because I'm not really a violent type of person. I'll break up fights and stop things before they start, and stuff like that. But to hurt a man, to kick a man when he's down while somebody else is holding him, that's just not my bag. I can't get into it. I never could . . .

*Did you get any heat from the other officers for not getting involved?*

No.

*Never?*

No. Well, they know what kind of person I am. I'm basically a passive type of individual and they can understand that. They can respect that. But they know that if they're in trouble I'm going to be there to help them.

Nor did this interviewee feel that other officers were pressured to initiate or participate in beatings.

*How about if an inmate beat up an officer and another officer subdued him, just put him back in his cell when he had the opportunity to kind of teach the guy a lesson? Would the officers give him a hard time about that?*

I don't think so. Nope. But if the situation takes place where an inmate does get bundled, everything is—it's just the same way. It just happens.

*It just happens? What is just the same way?*

Well, he either gets a beating or he doesn't get a beating. If he doesn't get a beating, sure, there might be some talk, "Ah, he deserved a beating." But nobody's going to get down on the guy because he didn't give him a beating.

However, this officer was all but alone in his perception of an officer's freedom to choose on this matter. As will be discussed in Chapter 6, many officers, especially new ones, felt they had to become involved in order to be accepted. "They say, 'I have to assume this role in order to make it as a correctional officer. I *have* to do this.' " A young officer described a situation when nine officers beat up one inmate. "It is not my style, teaming up against people. But if I didn't participate, if I didn't, I'd be an outcast. I just held his arms. I made it look like I was helping but I didn't hit him." Such officers took refuge in being in "the back of the pack, in the back of the line," giving an impression of their own participation as well as a heightened sense of the number of officers embracing that course of action.

Some officers consistently declined to participate, but unlike the first officer quoted above, most of them felt the pain of rejection for taking this path.

I could see if the guy was big maybe two guys holding him down or something. But I also saw like six or seven guys pounce on one guy which—I don't know if they hated me, the guards—but I wouldn't take part in it. I'd walk right away from it. And I'd tell them, and I'd tell [Superintendent] Butterworth, too, "I'm not going to do it. You can fire me, you can let me go, you can put my name in the *Boston Globe* on the front page, I will not go." . . .

*The first few times that happened, the officers are beating up an inmate, there's a group of them, you're there and you didn't participate, what happened in those kinds of situations? Did the officers get mad at you? Did they just {ignore} you?*

It was a little bit overlooked. It wasn't like brought out. It was overlooked. Because everybody didn't just look around and see who was involved in it or anything. It was just that they'd all be down on the tier and I'd be standing at the end of the tier, or something like that, and maybe somebody would throw a wise-crack, "What's the matter, you afraid to come down?" or something like that. But it was mostly overlooked. There's a lot of backstabbing up there.

Another officer recalled a situation where he managed to subdue an inmate aggressor nonviolently despite sufficient provocation and backup for a beating to take place.

*Did the officers give you a hard time for not beating a guy in a situation like [that]?*

Yeah, they did. They said a few things, a couple guys did. They couldn't understand why. They gave another guy a harder time that wasn't involved in it. He was there. He stopped them from—I more or less just held back and if someone was going to beat him up I was just going to sit there. But I wasn't going to take part myself . . . I didn't become the aggressor. And the other guy told them to stop hitting him. And they got on him. Because I wasn't involved, I felt as though it was towards me, too.

This officer left Walpole within a year, but another officer who stayed eventually overcame the criticism and rejection.

You take a lot of static at first. Which I did. I took a lot of heat because I went on and I didn't want to give up my own personal feelings of me as a person. In other words, I wasn't going to act like someone else wanted me to act. I could accept if someone screwed up and they said, "Okay, we are going to move this guy." I could accept moving him. But I couldn't—If the guy wanted to walk, as far as I was concerned he could walk. I wasn't going to go in and start a commotion or say some wise little remark or something like that to get him fired up where he is already on the verge—where a lot of guys kind of like that . . .

If you go in and you act like everyone else and you lug a guy, "Okay, we are buddies now. We've been bumping heads and everything like that," you are accepted immediately. But if you went in and said, "Okay, now let's just cool it. If the guy wants to go, let's let him go," the officers would back off and the word would pass around, "Watch him. You don't know if you can trust {him}," or something like that. But after a period of time, a lot longer period of time, you are respected to the degree that, "Okay, he's there if you need him." If the shit went down I'd be there. But I'm not going to go look for trouble. I don't go along with the get even, judge and jury type of thing. But after a while they did respect me. A lot of guys kind of talk to you after that.

The three officers just quoted were ones who declined to participate in the violence themselves. What of officers who attempted to stop the violence? "Anybody interfere? I wouldn't advise it," commented one officer. But there apparently were a few officers, well established in the eyes of colleagues, who could and sometimes did intervene to stop beatings. Though other officers might "get pissed off for a short period of time," these officers did it and got away with it.

They'd taken a kid and they'd stripped him, all right, and they ripped his clothes off. He'd just beat up an officer . . . So when they had him down they were going to do a number on him and——just told them . . . calmly and peaceably but you got the message, he says, "Listen, I don't want anyone to do that. If I see anybody hit him, I'll break his arm." Just nice and calm and everything. And everyone just like froze and then the guy got up and went to his room and everything was fine.

Thus even at Walpole officers could, and some regularly did, contravene this norm either by noninvolvement in the violence or occasionally by active opposition to it. But the norm was sufficiently strong, the pressures to conform sufficiently great, especially on new officers and those less confident of their colleagues' acceptance, to enable systematic physical retaliation against inmates to be practiced as a principal means of control. Furthermore, it was a policy that was seen by officers and inmates as having the endorsement of the vast majority of officers.

## Norm 7: Don't Be a White Hat

Proscribed by Norm 7 is any behavior suggesting sympathy for or identification with inmates. It is the most general of the norms regulating officer-inmate relations and also the most easily and regularly violated.

As was discussed under Norm 2, officers who appeared too sympathetic or friendly with inmates were often suspected of lugging drugs. Being a "white hat" or "goody two shoes" also incurred disfavor because it was felt to jeopardize fellow officers who were not themselves as lenient or sympathetic to inmates. "It puts a strain on one officer {who says}, 'No, you're not going to do it, you can't go.' 'Well, this guy lets me!' And it makes you look like the bad guy because you're doing your job and he's the nice guy. And it makes it more difficult for you." The problem was not just one of image or of whether or not inmates *liked* a particular hard-line officer. Taking over a cell block from a "white hat" could be downright hazardous. The officer just quoted continued,

They'd say, "We want this, we want that." And [the white hat officer] was running crazy. And I said, "Bullshit. They're not going to have me running around." It was a dangerous type thing, but inside me I felt like if I went and gave in on anything to them, I wouldn't be satisfied with myself because I know I didn't do a good job. So when I used to go in there and I used to lay down the law, I used to be a little bit firm. They'd say something and I'd say, "Well, I'll let you know on it," and different things like that, not saying "no" constantly but just holding them off. And I was standing at my desk and off the third tier came like a big can of soup, down on my head. And I bent down to get something out of a drawer and it bounced off the wall behind me . . . It would have hit me if I hadn't bent to get something out of the drawer.

The officer who committed a greater sin than the mere white hat was one who "acts like an inmate." He was not just making life more difficult for his harder-line colleagues. He was denying his own identity as an officer and adopting that of the "enemy." His actions denigrated and undermined the solidarity among officers that was seen as central to their safety and continuing ability to function in the institution.

This one particular [officer] . . . he's almost like an inmate. He's just like one of the other inmates. It's unbelievable! He'll just let them do anything they want to do.
*How do the other officers feel about that?*
They don't like him.

Nearly as suspect as an officer who "acts like an inmate" was one who acts like a social worker. "There were several officers, as a matter of fact, black officers, that we didn't care for too much because of the way they were doing it, because they were really more social workers than anything else."

Before the upheavals of the early 1970s, an officer "couldn't be seen even talking to inmates," much less showing concern for their needs. Those who did "took an awful lot of heat." But by late in the decade even one of the hardest-line officers was willing to say, "You can be respectful of the inmates. You can say, 'hi,' or something small. But," he continued, "you can't find yourself in the middle of the block having a deep conversation with some of the inmates." Officers—particularly younger ones—who went much beyond that risked being labeled "Joe Nice Guy." Officers who took those risks and were friendly with inmates were often ambivalent about doing so. An officer who worked a block for a year and got to know the inmates well recalled,

You can't call them friends because in [the] situation they're, of course, the opposite—they're enemies. But I had guys in there that I would come in and we'd talk about sports and we'd talk about the weather and we'd talk about everything else and get involved in it and spend a lot of time . . . Used to bother guards that I used to talk to [inmates] like I did.

Sanctions for such behavior were generally mild, rarely extending beyond unconcealed disapproval. Perceptions of disapproval were, of course, keenly felt by those who believed and feared that "if you're nice to the inmates the guards will hate you." But as long as an officer did not go much beyond being "nice" (and doing so usually involved violation of one or more of the other norms already discussed), he was unlikely to suffer much as a consequence. For those who did go beyond that (someone who "acts like an inmate" or a social worker), less subtle pressures were brought to bear.

*What do the officers do when they get a guy in there who does the social work bit?*

Well, they let him know it. They let him know it . . . Even some of the supervisors that are behind the officers can tell and they don't get that extra privilege of going here, going there.

According to another officer who was regarded as a bit of a social worker,

If an officer didn't conform to the standards that the other correctional officers set on that particular shift, then he was like blackballed or whatever you want to say. People let him know. He got all the junk jobs. He used to do all the underneath rounds which are you take off your shirt and run through the steam lines and they have phones at the end of the tunnels underneath the institution. He used to check all those for security measures in case they were tunneling down or something like that. And you got all those jobs.

The rookie officer was under particular pressure not to adopt a sympathetic attitude or approach toward inmates, but once an officer had sufficient seniority and *as long as he did not violate other important norms regulating officer-inmate relations*, he had considerable latitude and discretion in conforming to this norm. "If you've been there a short time you take a lot of harassment," noted an experienced officer. But "if you've been there a long time and you don't get any problems [from inmates], no one says anything."

### Norm 8: Maintain Officer Solidarity versus All Outside Groups

All of the preceding norms concern officer solidarity vis-à-vis inmates. This is as would be expected because the officer subculture is basically defined by its opposition to inmates. Nevertheless, officers' relations with individuals and groups other than inmates are also of concern. Officer solidarity is expected to be maintained vis-à-vis anyone who is not an officer. I shall consider this point in relation to the administration, representatives of news media, and the officer's own family.

As was discussed in Chapter 3, the administration at Walpole was not well liked or respected by the officers despite the fact that many senior administrators (including the superintendent in the late 1970s) had come up through the ranks. There was a general feeling among officers that the "administration does not give a shit for us. So that's probably one of the things that keeps us together, too." Built on this feeling were general constraints not to "start kissing ass for different things," or to appear to be doing so. Gossip about who was getting what favors from the administration (for example, hospital duty) and why was prevalent. But such gossip was probably no more prevalent at Walpole than it is in other types of employment. Furthermore, officers who had close relations with the administration did not suffer unduly for it, especially if the administrator in question was a respected shift supervisor or if the officer was a "hard-ass" favorite of the administration and selected for something like the "SWAT Team" (intended to handle emergency situations). Such "favoritism" was likely to produce carping among fellow officers but not much else.

Stricter standards applied to officers' relations with individuals outside the prison. "One of the things you learn is never to talk about the institution to outsiders. You should only talk to the other officers." (Indeed, some officers probably would not have talked to me, and certainly not as candidly as they did, had I not previously been an officer myself.) The prohibition against talking to outsiders about the prison had its most stringent application in regard to officers' relations with representatives of news media. Reporters were seen as invariably allied with inmates and unwilling to consider, much less adopt, the perspective of officers. This was not just paranoia on the part of officers. Stereotypes are strong and pervasive about officers (or "guards," as they were invariably called in the Massachusetts press). Officers saw themselves being portrayed as "either easy and lugging or they're tough and they're beating up somebody." As a result, they almost certainly rivaled and perhaps exceeded police in their adherence to a code of silence vis-à-vis the world outside. Officers who flagrantly violated the prohibition against speaking to reporters risked incurring the same stiff sanctions that would have applied to any officer who testified against his colleagues in court. (Officers who held official positions such as union representative were, of course, largely exempt from the ban on talking to reporters.)

Many officers took the norm mandating silence to all outsiders so seriously that they even refrained from discussing the prison with their wives and with individuals who, at least in the days before they became officers, were their closest friends. To some extent, officers refrained from discussing their job in order to spare their wives and families worry and anguish about what they were experiencing daily at the prison and not because they did not trust their families. Others refrained from talking to outsiders, including family and friends, about what was happening to them inside the prison walls because they had learned the hard way that "no one understands." For whatever reason an officer maintained his silence, it had the effect of enhancing his sense of isolation and further narrowing his world to that of the prison and his fellow officers. The problems created by this closed society are discussed in Chapter 9.

## Norm 9: Show Positive Concern for Fellow Officers

A final norm, "Show positive concern for fellow officers," is worth mentioning not because it was widely obeyed or transgressions against it severely punished but rather because it represented a behavioral ideal subscribed to by most officers, at least at Walpole. The exhortation to show a positive concern for one's fellow officers covered a multitude of behaviors and situations. I shall discuss two of these by way of illustration: (1) Never leave another officer a problem, and (2) Help your fellow officer with problems outside the institution.

*Never leave another officer a problem.* "Don't leave another man a problem that is rightfully yours . . . If it's your responsibility to take care of it and settle it, you do it." An officer should neither cause problems in another man's block nor leave a problem at the end of his shift that the man on the next shift must face.

> The worst thing I could do is to leave [another officer] a problem . . . I would not just go over to two guys, "I'm going to cut your head off." Or, "I know you two guys are going to have a fight and say, listen, you guys, do me a favor, wait fifteen minutes

until I'm out of here," and then pass the key to the other guy and run like hell for the door. That to me is the worst kind of dirty trick to do to someone. I try to turn a block over to a man, "This is your count. Nothing happened today *but* look out for this, you might have something—this guy had a little beef with this other guy today, so keep an eye on those two."

While this notion of decency and fair play between officers was acknowledged in theory at Walpole, in practice it was widely violated, especially between shifts. Problems encountered on one shift were blamed on the other. An officer on the 3–11 complained,

A lot of the trouble caused on the 3-to-11 is because of things that wasn't done on the 7-to-3 shift. And it lingers over and the tension has built up by the time the 3-to-11 shift comes in and when the 3-to-11 comes in, they have to deal with it . . . All they're concerned about is their eight hours and getting off. They're not even concerned with what's going to happen later on.

Officers on the 7–3 countered that the 3–11 habitually harassed inmates after the inmates had been locked in for the night, leaving them to stew all night—and then vent their rage on the 7–3 when they were unlocked the next morning. "We used to have half our trouble with the [inmates'] medication and most of the other half was from the 3–11 shift—the stuff that they pulled. The inmates would be so mad, they'd take it out on us during the day because they didn't get out at night." Officers on the 7–3 were particularly aggrieved that they often had to bear the consequences of the aggressive tactics of the 3–11. "They'd beat up a few guys . . . But then they'd throw them in their room and lock them up and they wouldn't get out until tomorrow. When we let him out, who [were] they going to take it out on? Us." One 7–3 officer bitterly asserted of the 3–11, "They weren't doing it to the cons, they were doing it to us. And we told them that. And they didn't care because they didn't have to face it."

One of the reasons this norm was so frequently violated between, as opposed to within, shifts was that there were few sanctions that could be imposed from one shift to another. Furthermore, some officers saw their principal reference group to be their shift rather than the Walpole officer corps as a whole. These officers stated that the people about whom they really cared, and for whom they were

willing to risk a great deal, were those officers with whom they
directly worked and not necessarily officers on a different shift.
Although officers who took this position in its extreme form were in
a minority, the general attitude was sufficiently widespread to com-
plicate daily transitions between shifts.

*Help your fellow officer with problems outside the institution.*
The ideal officer not only maintained solidarity with his fellow
officers vis-à-vis inmates, administrators, reporters, and the public,
and never left another officer a problem, he also helped out when
needed with problems outside the institution. Help was neither
sought nor proffered for emotional or family problems beyond supportive stories of similar trials with the wife, the cons, or the bottle,
but the ideal officer willingly lent a hand in more concrete ways. If
an officer were injured, his fellow officers offered assistance to his
family; if he was painting his house, they were there to help him; if
he was sick and no longer on the payroll, a collection was taken in
his name to meet outstanding debts. Not surprisingly, no sanctions
were imposed for not helping a fellow officer in these ways (other
than perhaps diminution in esteem or lack of reciprocity in the
future). But Walpole stood out as an institution where officers
showed genuine concern for one another and consistently demonstrated their willingness to go the extra mile when help was needed.
Many cited this mutual concern and loyalty as their prime reason
for sticking with a job they otherwise detested. The life of a Walpole
officer was generally a miserable one. The community they formed
among themselves was one of the truly satisfying things about their
lives.

## Norms at Norfolk, Concord, and Bridgewater

The degree of solidarity within a group is in large measure determined by the threat that group perceives from outside itself and the
degree to which it sees itself as standing alone in warding off that
threat. At Walpole, the threat from inmates was obvious and constant; support from the administration or anyone else was always in
doubt. Hence the nine norms discussed here had substantial impact
on the beliefs and behaviors of Walpole officers. The perceived threat
and sense of group isolation were not as great at the other prisons
studied, however, and the norms of the officer subcultures were
correspondingly weaker.

At Norfolk, two staff members were murdered and several critically injured by inmates during the 1970s, a far greater toll than officers suffered at any other Massachusetts prison. Thus, though relations there between officers and inmates were usually cordial, officers felt strongly about their interdependence. A Norfolk interviewee on good terms with inmates explained, "If you work in there, it's not them against us. But it's a situation where you can't be divided." When officers were in conflict with inmates, "An officer's word was always taken over an inmate's no matter whether or not you knew this officer. You *had* to . . . So that would be the code: officer always over inmate." Thus, those norms most concerned with officer safety (Norms 1 through 5) were salient at Norfolk, but Norfolk officers were not expected to maintain antagonistic relations with inmates. They were under little or no pressure to participate in unlawful sanctions against inmates (Norm 6) and were permitted considerable latitude in their personal relations with them (Norm 7). A Norfolk officer with "white hat" leanings always had the option of becoming a house officer. Although relations between uniformed officers and house officers were sometimes uneasy (the former often viewing the latter as "all those liberals that are going in there living with the cons"), a live-and-let-live attitude usually prevailed between the two groups of officers. Officer solidarity at Norfolk broke down when relations with inmates were not at issue (Norms 8 and 9). A relatively stable and effective administration at the prison had permitted alliances between administrators and some officers which, in turn, led to frequent disharmony among officers as a group.

Concord officers in the 1970s often perceived their greatest threat as coming from administrators intent on breaking the decades-old control of the institution by the "forty cousins." A succession of administrators had so alienated their subordinates that even the "new breed" of officers (themselves often in conflict with the old-timers) felt hostile to the administration. As a result, officers were often measured more by their loyalty vis-à-vis the administration than by their loyalty vis-à-vis inmates (Norm 8). Officers at Concord generally perceived their situation to be less dangerous than at Norfolk (and, of course, Walpole). Accordingly, demands for immediate, unquestioning support of fellow officers appeared weaker; they were certainly put to the test and reinforced less often (Norms 1, 3, 4, 5). Pressure on officers to participate in illicit sanctions against inmates was slight (Norm 6). Indeed, interviewees there reported that only selected officers were *permitted* to participate in violent reprisals against inmates. "Most of the time when you had your worst beatings was when there were people together who know what to expect from each other, who know that they can get away with this right now." Standards of behavior were much slacker at Concord than at Norfolk—for example, officers routinely came to work unshaven and unkempt, and a more tolerant attitude toward drugs may have prevailed (Norm 2)—but officers were under greater pressure not to stray into the "white hat" camp (Norm 7). No position comparable to that of "house officer" existed at Concord, and sympathetic attitudes toward inmates were treated with disdain, or worse.

Bridgewater State Hospital was largely unaffected by upheavals in the prison system during the 1970s. The administration was entrenched, the inmates incapable of organized resistance. Many of the catalysts for officer solidarity were lacking. Officers accused one another of frequent disloyalty while currying favor with superiors (Norm 8), and charged their supervisors with deliberately creating dissension among officers by rewarding group disloyalty. Officers could generally look to one another for support in emergency situations (Norm 1), but could not always rely on other officers once an immediate crisis had passed (Norms 3, 4, 5, 9). "You had to watch [the other officers]. If something went down and it didn't go down right and they were in a position where something might happen to them, they'd ride on you in a second or set you up." In the normal course of daily events, officers had considerable leeway in their personal dealings with inmates. Those who desired to do so were fairly free to take an interest in individual inmates and participate in therapeutic programs (Norm 7). Officers who were thought to be unsympathetic to the use of violence against inmates were not assigned to those parts of the institution where it usually occurred and thus were under no pressure to participate (Norm 6). Some Bridgewater officers, especially rookies assigned to the more violence-prone parts of the institution, did feel pressure to conform. Yet they recognized that a sizable number of officers were able to decline participation and suffer little more than social censure by the hard-core who did participate. With seeds of dissension sown by the administration and a largely compliant inmate population, Bridgewater officers had "nothing else to do there but just look at the next guy," "gossip," and "get on each other's nerves."

At prisons like Walpole where officers and inmates are in open and sustained conflict, officers consider group solidarity essential not only to the accomplishment of shared goals, but also to their very survival as individuals. They feel strongly the necessity to aid and support one another. As a group, they are willing and able to bring considerable pressure on members to conform. But norms of solidarity at prisons where cohesion is not necessary to survival often conflict with the desire of officers to do "easy time" if they can. At the Bridgewater Treatment Center, for example, inmates scarcely ever dared raise a hand against an officer. Officers there were bored, not scared. The officer subculture was but a shadow of what could be found at Walpole. An officer at the Treatment Center contrasted his institution with Walpole.

> With the guys at Walpole, it's a do or die situation . . . If they don't stick together they're dead. Let's face it, down here you don't have to stick together. You're going to exist and get fat at the same time.

What cements norms of solidarity at prisons like Walpole is the fear that, without them, officers in the midst of the fray not only will not get fat, but also might not survive.

# 6

# Prison Violence

In Chapter 4 violence was considered as a form of power in the hands of officers and inmates. Violence at Walpole and other Massachusetts state prisons, however, far exceeded the bounds of such an analytically dispassionate perspective. It was Walpole's violence more than anything else that seared the lives of the officers and inmates who worked and lived there. In this chapter, violence by inmates against both inmates and officers and violence by officers against inmates are considered from the *officers'* perspective. As in previous chapters, the focus is on Walpole, but because of the reportedly high levels of violence at Bridgewater State Hospital and the contrasting circumstances there, particular attention is paid to that institution as well.

## Inmate Violence against Inmates

Walpole in the 1970s was characterized not merely by violence but also by sadism. Inmates did not just die at Walpole. They were mutilated, castrated, blinded, burned, stabbed dozens of times or more. Then they died. The violence of Walpole was not the explosive, impersonal violence associated with the Attica confrontation in 1971. Rather, year after bloody year, it was the sort of vengeful savagery that characterized the mayhem at New Mexico Prison in 1980.

New officers expressed bewilderment at the sadism of inmate attacks on fellow inmates—the need, as one put it, for "overkill." "Strangle a guy, castrate him, stab him fifty times while he's alive, stab him where it's not going to kill him, just for the sake [of it]. And then, after he's dead, stab him fifty more times." Only those officers who had fought in Vietnam found parallels in their own experience or imagination. "It's unbelievable some of the stuff they do. I can't comprehend it. I mean, after the guy is dead—. But then I've seen it in Vietnam, too, where a guy would be dead and then they'd have to have a good time playing with the body."

A few officers, mainly those who had themselves come from the streets, saw the necessity for an inmate on finding himself in the Walpole jungle to arm himself and demonstrate a willingness to meet violence with violence in order to survive. "I'd be just as bad as they are . . . You have to adapt to the situation you're in. Somebody is going to come after you and you've got to handle it. And if it means hitting somebody, then you hit them. If it means whacking them with a chair, you whack them with a chair." But many more officers witnessed the violence and sadism and concluded that inmates were a breed apart, that they "aren't really like people, most of them are animals." Underscoring these attitudes was what appeared to be acceptance, almost indifference, on the part of inmates toward the violence around them. Even inmates who were victims of the violence ideally affected a nonchalance to others if they were not too badly hurt.

> They blew my mind. Whew! I don't know how to explain. I was amazed, just bewildered, like it happened nonchalantly. A lot of times we didn't even know it. The guy would . . . say he wanted to see the doctor, so you'd put his name down on the list and when it's his turn to go you'd bring him out and he'd have blood on his shirt and you'd say, "What happened?" "Oh, I got stabbed." It was like nothing. It was just like, "I got stabbed."

Inmate self-abuse—suicide, self-castration, mutilation—at times took on some of the same bizarre characteristics as violence inflicted on other inmates. The capacity to inflict abuse on oneself was nowhere more evident than in the inmates' quest for drugs:

> I've seen guys slice their veins open with razor blades and try to stuff dope in it because they don't have works . . . Or shoot up with a Bic pen. Get a Bic pen and melt it down so the plastic will be hard and then put on some kind of needle and shoot up with it. Or cutting your throat. These guys would get wire mesh . . . covering their jugular veins because they've cut their throat so much.

Another officer recalled an inmate who "put his hand in [one of the big metal doors] and shoved it on his hand, crushed his hand so he could get more dope. Did it on purpose . . . To *himself*. Shattered his hand . . . He got his dope."

Most officers, at least initially, were sickened by the carnage. Some made sincere, often courageous efforts to lessen the toll, stopping fights, watching out for new young inmates they thought might be raped, doing what they could to aid victims. Once, while interviewing an officer up in the gallery overlooking the cell blocks at Walpole, I watched an inmate destroy the contents of his own cell with a club and threaten anyone who approached. A young officer courageously stood before the open cell and talked the inmate into relinquishing the weapon and going quietly from the block. The officer was backed by half a dozen other officers and clearly could have used force had he chosen not to take the personal risks that he did. (This incident, which was not unusual, illustrated other problems at Walpole. This same inmate had gone berserk before. As the officer I was interviewing at the time bitterly pointed out, the inmate would once again be placed in an isolation cell rather than receiving the psychiatric treatment this officer felt he desperately needed. The block officer, meanwhile, had not and never would receive training for tasks that would challenge the most skilled psychologist. Nor would the officer receive any reward for his efforts.)

Many officers expressed frustration in the interviews over their inability to protect inmates in their charge, even a sense of guilt over deaths or serious injuries they had been unable to prevent. There were officers who felt a personal stake in ensuring the safety of at least some of the inmates. "I can think of some [inmates] up there that if they happen to get hurt or if they were being pushed around [or] something it would affect me greatly. I would do almost anything I could to stop it or make sure that it didn't happen again."

But the level of violence at Walpole, the apparent indifference of inmates to what happened to their fellows, and the officers' inability to stop it inevitably led most officers to adopt at least a facade of indifference, "to try," as one officer put it, "not to let the inmates know that it actually did affect me." An officer who on several occasions had risked personal injury to subdue inmates nonviolently but now viewed those attempts as worthless, reflected on the inmates' brutality to each other and the officers' impotence in dealing with it.

How can you stop it? What they do, they'll take a room way up on the third tier, the farthest one away that you can't see into from where you are. You're protecting yourself. You had to be near the grill and you had to be under the covering of the tiers so nobody would drop anything on your head. You can't see what's going on in their rooms. And you're too concerned about yourself to get the hell out and to walk around and check what they're doing in their rooms. If they're going to do it, they're going to do it . . . The only thing you can do is to lock them up twenty-four hours a day to stop stuff like that. And you can't do that. So you can't stop it. There's no possible way to stop it . . . A lot of [officers] jump in between knife fights between inmates . . . just to stop it. And why should they, really? Why shouldn't they just step out?

Walpole officers daily saw inmates beating, raping, stabbing, and killing one another. If only a minority of inmates were perpetrators of these acts, the remainder let them happen without even an outward expression of dismay or revulsion. It was a short step for the officer to take from thinking that he need not risk himself to stop it to a point where "he'd just sit back, put his feet up on his desk, and too bad . . . Because they figure the guy did something out on the street that he shouldn't have done and he's in prison and that's part of being in prison." Even when violence took the form of self-abuse—overdosing, mutilation, attempted suicide, setting fire to one's own cell—some officers sanctioned indifference. "They'd tell you to leave 'em. If he's going to set a fire, let him."

By the officers' own accounts, some officers did more than turn a blind or disinterested eye to events. A well-placed word about an inmate's past as a child molester or his present as an informer might gain that inmate a severe beating, even death, at the hands of his fellows. Old animosities or racial antagonisms could be inflamed, inmates placed in jeopardy, or elementary precautions not taken to protect their lives. Officers accused their superiors in particular of such transgressions. A Walpole officer asked:

Why do you put ten Muslims on one tier and why do you put ten Irishmen on the tier below that hate each other and are always thinking about ways of stabbing each other? Why do you do something like that? But they do it. Half the time I think it's a game. When —— and —— came back here from Bridgewater they put them in "X" Block. Well, the guy that ratted them out

at Bridgewater ended up in Walpole. They put him in "X" Block. He was killed that night. They stabbed him about eighty times. They weren't convicted. But who else did it?
    *And you think that that's not just incompetence but—*
    I don't think it's incompetence.

Concord officers may have been the worst offenders, especially in inflaming racial tensions among inmates. In 1978, for example, three white Concord officers were fired when they "donned Ku Klux Klan–type hoods, fashioned a wooden cross and then taunted some inmates" (*Herald*, 10 June 1978). A former Concord officer charged,

> They'd actually stimulate [the racial problem] sometimes . . . If something was found in [a cell], they'd say, 'Well, so-and-so, he's black, gave us this information, or so-and-so that's white'— even though it's probably not even true, just so the blacks and whites were always fighting . . . Because it kept the inmates at each other's necks rather than at our necks.

Inmates' supporters accused officers of being directly responsible for much of the violence inmates inflicted on inmates, but by and large prisoners found reasons enough for creating their own mayhem without direct aid from officers. A former Concord officer who became a bitter critic of prisons and prison officers nevertheless concluded that officers were not responsible for most inmate violence. He blamed it instead on "too many people too close together."

> If you ask me, "Do guards perpetrate a lot of [inmate versus inmate violence]?" I don't believe so. I believe they do and they have, but I think it's very minor. I think guards set up inmates. They have in the past. But as far as the personal problems that go on between inmates, I don't think a lot of it's even seen, so it can't be stopped. Especially the rapes, a lot of knifings, the burning out of somebody's room. I don't know how you stop that stuff except give people space.

Most inmates responded to their world of wanton violence with a pose of indifference. Overwhelmed by the level and sadism of the violence and bewildered by its almost casual acceptance within the institution, most officers responded in kind.

## Inmate Violence against Officers

*Frequency.* While officers may have felt or affected indifference about inmate violence when *inmates* were the victims, they felt passionately about inmate violence when *officers* were victims. Incidence of inmate violence against officers is hard to quantify. As previously noted, two staff members were killed and two others seriously wounded by inmates at Norfolk during the 1970s. A Department of Correction study reported 85 assaults on Walpole staff between 1 July and 31 December 1976 (the period during which the longitudinal subjects in this study began their prison service), but the nature and severity of assaults were not indicated (Massachusetts Department of Correction, 1977). During a particularly volatile period in 1979, Walpole officers staged a walkout charging that over a three-month period "39 correction officers were stabbed, blinded, beaten severely and scalded" by inmates (*Boston Globe*, 30 March 1979).

Inmates and their defenders alleged that most of these "assaults" were fabricated by officers looking forward to a few weeks on sick leave or hoping to cover up their own violent actions. Assaults by inmates that did take place were, they charged, usually provoked by officers. Thus, the Executive Director of the Massachusetts Correctional Legal Service considered that

> What is remarkable about assaults on guards by prisoners is not that they occur, but that they occur so infrequently. In fact, serious incidents of this type seem to occur only when an individual prisoner is under extreme stress (as in the case of men on Block Ten of Walpole, who are locked up 24 hours a day, seven days a week) or goes "berserk" as a result of imprisonment . . . In fact, the certainty of retaliation against a prisoner who attacks a guard is so great that it is very unusual for a prisoner to commit such an assault without great provocation. (Martin, 1978, p. 68)

Other than the fact that almost anyone living in Walpole during the 1970s could be said to have been "under extreme stress," I think he seriously underestimated the problem.

More important in shaping officer attitudes than the actual number of assaults (whatever that number may have been) were officer *perceptions* of the threat against them. Every Walpole officer interviewed could cite dozens of cases where officers had been injured or had narrowly escaped serious injury at the hands of inmates. Some of the officers interviewed had themselves been attacked. All reported they had been threatened repeatedly. The possibility of serious injury, even death, at the hands of inmates was very real to them. They considered it a matter of luck that no Walpole officer had been killed, only a matter of time before it happened. "Everybody in these institutions is afraid. I don't care who they are. That's a fact." "It's just the idea that within one second they could kill me. I can't see how anybody hasn't gotten killed . . . It's suicide. It really is."

With nearly the entire inmate population "packing" (carrying a weapon, usually a "shiv,"a homemade knife), a Walpole officer felt at risk any time he was in contact with inmates. If not stabbed, he could have boiling water thrown at him (inmates were allowed hot plates, or when denied them could rig makeshift ones), have his head caved in with a large can of food or a heavy mop handle, or be injured by a variety of makeshift weapons devised from an inmate's own belongings or the meager materials around him.

Assaults by inmates against officers were far less frequent and usually less serious at Norfolk and Concord. While Norfolk was the only Massachusetts prison in which staff were killed by inmates in the 1970s, officers reported that assaults against them were usually minor and normally occurred less than once a month. Concord's young inmate population was more volatile than Norfolk's, and officers reported more threats against them, but the actual rate of assaults did not appear to be any greater at Concord. A Concord officer contrasted his institution with Walpole:

> There's not that much time for the hate to build up really that much. There is hate there. I'm not saying it's less than Walpole's. But it's a different kind of hate . . . You can have an argument with one of these guys one day, and the next day, with many of them, it's another day. So things build and fall, build and fall. Coupled with being a quick place to get in and out of . . . So it's not a long-standing thing that will last for years, a particular grudge between an inmate and an officer.

Bridgewater State Hospital housed an inmate population both violent and insane. Although those most prone to violence were usually heavily medicated, one officer estimated that at least three times a week an inmate attacked an officer in some fashion. The medical director at Bridgewater reported that he "frequently saw officers who had sustained painful and disfiguring fractures of the jaw, nose or cheek, who had had teeth knocked out, or fingers broken by being bent backward; one officer had to have a testicle removed after it was irreparably damaged by a kick" (James F. Gilligan, personal communication, February 1987). Despite their frequency and occasional severity, inmate attacks against officers at Bridgewater were nearly always performed without a weapon and without moral or physical support from other inmates.

*Spontaneous, unprovoked violence against officers.* The violence many officers feared the most was that which was spontaneous on the part of inmates and unprovoked by officers. In a sense such acts of violence were the great equalizers among officers. Any officer in contact with inmates, regardless of his relationship with them, was seen as vulnerable to these random and unpredictable attacks. This is the type of violence that, as a Concord officer pointed out, "could happen any time, any day, any minute. In this business you just don't know."

Officers considered drugs to be the chief culprits in such acts of violence. Legal and illegal drugs of all kinds were available everywhere in Walpole and the other Massachusetts prisons. Whether an inmate was on downers, uppers, or hooch, those officers (and inmates) who were in his way were the ones who got hurt. "I don't know if you've ever seen anybody really screwed up on downs, but it's like being drunk, crazy, not caring about what you do." And not caring to whom you did it. A Walpole officer on good terms with a particular inmate recalled,

> When he got drunk he . . . [would say], "I'm going to cut off everybody's head and I'm going to hit you over the head and we're going to fight," and everything like that. So when they got drunk or on the drugs or something like that there was no distinguishing [an officer I like] or a guy I dislike or something like that. They were like blind to everything. So you were afraid a lot of times.

Officers bitterly blamed the prison's doctors, and by extension the administration, for many of the most volatile situations leading to violence. Inmates could get high on drugs doctors prescribed for them by hoarding the drugs or by forcing weaker inmates to hand over their own dosage. Much more dangerous, they could be made desperate by the precipitate withdrawal of those same drugs:

The worst cases were guys that had Talwin. Now they had it four times a day, right? The doctor wouldn't even tell him he was taking him off it and he'd go flat, cold turkey. Those guys, they're addicted to it. One time you miss it at breakfast and already they're going crazy. But you miss it at lunch and they're worse. And you miss it the next time and, oh Jesus, they're going absolutely berserk by this time . . . We were the ones they'd take their aggressions out on. The doctors wouldn't go down there.

Officers at Bridgewater State Hospital were by far the most vulnerable to spontaneous, unprovoked attacks. "These guys are unbelievable . . . They're so erratic that they can explode any minute." A Bridgewater officer recalled an inmate who hit him without warning:

A lot of inmates up there are hearing voices, different things. Like I got whacked by one inmate one day and two days later I walked up to him and said, "Why did you do that?" He said, "An Indian told me to." "What?!" "An Indian told me to." Stupid things like that. I feel bad for people like that; they can't control themselves.

Officers working with people prone to act without calculation were in constant risk of sustaining serious injury. As this officer pointed out, "the Walpole inmate would be a little bit cuter. He'd know how far he could push you and then he'd maybe lay back, where these guys, they just go off the deep end. They didn't even care what the consequences were." Immune to consequences, immediate or long-term, such inmates posed a formidable threat.

I'll never forget the first time I went on a beef—locking someone up. It was incredible. It took nine of us just to put him in the cell he was so flipped out . . . It's incredible how strong they are once they go berserk . . . I couldn't believe that a person could turn into an animal like that so fast and be totally violent—I mean, ready to kill you. I just couldn't imagine somebody doing that.

*Calculated, unprovoked violence.* Officers also risked injury from calculated, albeit unprovoked, acts of violence. Here, too, the victim was anyone in uniform, no matter how well regarded he was by inmates. Officers believed that some inmates "would kill their mothers to get out of there," not to mention those who would kill purely for the sake of killing. An officer observed of one notorious inmate at Walpole, "He gets a kick out of putting guards out . . . He's just like a machine that's there to function and destroy things in its path." Other inmates seemed to "take hates to people for their looks . . . [and] they'll go after him." Even those officers who felt relatively immune from attack by virtue of their good relations with inmates realized that "there was quite a few out there that would have killed me with no second thoughts about it." This random vulnerability applied particularly to riot situations and escapes. "If the shit hits the fan, you are wearing the uniform. No matter who you are they're going to get you . . . You could be the nicest guy in the world. But it's them, and it's you."

*Spontaneous, provoked violence.* By no means, though, were all inmate attacks on officers unprovoked. Whether through ineptness, miscalculation, or sheer perversity, officers often triggered spontaneous onslaughts against themselves. There are many ways to aggravate a man in prison, and many ways to force him into a situation where for reasons of "image" he feels he must fight. "You don't ever put a man in a situation where he's going to lose face to the other convicts, the other inmates. You just don't do that. You're asking for trouble." Observed another Walpole officer, "In this kind of environment when you give somebody an ultimatum, put them in the corner, they are going to lash back. They have to. On the street they can go the other way. In here they can't. They have to go forward . . . And I have seen so many instances of that it's ridiculous." A Norfolk officer recalled an incident involving a "little" inmate who avoided trouble whenever possible.

He had taken a chair from downstairs and this [officer] went upstairs and saw the chair and went right at him and just kicked the chair around and snatched it all around and . . . made the inmate feel like he was a hunk of trash . . . They feel like they are low enough as it is without having to be put down more . . . And that incident caused a big eruption. They had four or five uniform officers up there to drag him down. I mean, that was ridiculous. The guy wasn't nowhere near that big. But he was so turned off and so turned on—wound up, whatever—about the whole thing that he really became violent.

Perhaps the most common location for spontaneous, provoked conflicts at Walpole was in an inmate's cell block at the time of his removal to segregation. Some inmates would put up a fight when moved regardless of how they were handled. Others would fight either because they had been provoked or because they thought they would get a beating anyway.

> The biggest threat to the other officers' getting hurt is me going down to the cell and saying, "Oh, the maggot's all ready to go," or "Do we have to take your kid with you?" (They used to have . . . sexual partners if the guy was a fag.) I mean, you look at the guy and know the guy's going to come out with his shiv or whatever it is and I can get hurt because this [officer] is acting nonprofessional or stupid, out and out dumb.

Merely the presence of a known officer provocateur was often enough to unleash the violence.

> He'd have his clothes all packed, all ready to go. He'd see [Officer ——]. The eyes popped out of his head. He'd grab something. He says, "I know I'm going to take it so I'm going to take it fighting. I'm going to take it like a man." They have their masculinity or their image or whatever it is to protect . . . They figure they're going to get bumped over the head so they are going to go fighting and screaming and kicking and everything else.

*Calculated, provoked violence.* Potentially more lethal for the officer than these more or less spontaneous conflicts were those acts of violence by inmates that were both provoked *and* carefully calculated. The random violence of drugged or desperate inmates created a constant atmosphere of fear at Walpole, but the calculated act of retaliation, or the threat of it, played the greater part in defining limits for the officers' own behavior. And it was used by inmates for just that purpose. The officer who wrote too many tickets, beat too many heads, aggravated too many inmates knew that, in the language of Walpole, "payback is a motherfucker." "It might not be tomorrow. It might not be in a year. It might be in two years. But 'payback is a motherfucker.' . . . So sooner or later, you will get paid back. You will get yours." In conflicts where the officers had apparently won—the inmates locked in their cells, their leaders in solitary—it was that chant that let the officers know it was only a battle, not the war, they had won.

## Officer Violence against Inmates

Inmates, of course, were not the only ones implicated in the violence of the Massachusetts prison system. Charges of officer brutality were a constant feature of the Walpole scene during the 1970s. They were made by inmates, their families and friends, the prison chaplain, outside observers, and state legislators, and they were repeated in newspaper columns and in court. These charges were regularly denied by officials of the prison and the Department of Correction, in editorials of various newspapers, and in court. Official investigations into officer brutality consistently exonerated the officers. In 1978 three state legislators claimed to have nine hundred complaints of brutality at Walpole, precipitating investigations by both the Massachusetts Attorney General's Office and the United States Attorney's Office. But the state investigation found only three instances of use of force by officers that "merited disciplinary action, but not criminal prosecution" (*Boston Globe*, 20 September 1978), and the federal investigation found no abuses at all. Of the federal investigation, the *Globe* (20 December 1978) reported under the headline, "Guards at Walpole cleared of brutality":

> Guards at Walpole State Prison have not used excessive force in carrying out their responsibilities of maintaining order, a Federal Bureau of Investigation probe has determined.
>
> US Attorney Edward F. Harrington announced today that allegations of guards' brutality are unfounded and that a study of recent serious incidents at the prison "failed to establish the willful and wrongful use of unreasonable force on the part of the guards at the institution in carrying out their official duties . . ."
>
> In announcing that there would be no prosecution, Harrington said that the investigation showed that guards are forced to react firmly to inmate violence and failure to do so "would result in total chaos at the prison."

Of the numerous civil suits filed against Walpole officers for brutality in the 1970s, only one was successful.

Yet according to most Walpole officers interviewed as a part of this study, physical force beyond the need for restraint or self-defense was used on a regular basis throughout the 1970s as a means of maintaining control and deterring assaults on officers. Furthermore, the force that was used was characterized by many of the officers as far in excess of what was required for restraint or self-defense. In the interviews, officers occasionally discussed specific incidents of officer brutality that had been reported in Massachusetts news media or had been made public in legislative hearings. With only one exception, the officers' accounts corroborated the allegations that had been made by inmates and their supporters. (This was not a consequence of informed probing by me. I did not inquire about specific instances of officer brutality in the interviews. These were cases that the officers discussed spontaneously. I did not, in any case, read the press files until 1980, that is, after the bulk of the interviews had been completed.) Furthermore, although allegations of brutality were rarely aired against officers at Massachusetts prisons other than Walpole, officers themselves reported systematic use of violence against inmates at the Bridgewater State Hospital and there were indications that some violence was used at Concord.

*Frequency, nature, and severity of officer violence.* If the incidence of inmate violence against officers is hard to measure, the incidence of officer violence against inmates is very much more so. Some Walpole inmates asserted that "vicious, sadistic beatings" by officers were the norm at the prison (Cambridge, Massachusetts, *Real Paper*, 14 October 1978). Other members of the Walpole community, like the prison's superintendent, maintained that problems within the institution were solved "peacefully. There is no tension. There is no violence" (quoted in *Herald*, 28 August 1979).

A few Walpole officers claimed in the interviews never to have participated in, witnessed, nor heard of a beating in their time at the prison. Yet the majority said that they had either participated in or witnessed beatings and that their occurrence was common knowledge within the institution. Because independent accounts of the same incidents corroborated each other, and because there was almost certainly a greater incentive for officers to assert falsely that there were no beatings than to assert falsely that there were, I feel confident in concluding that officers who claimed there were no beatings at Walpole were wrong. (Whether they had or had not remained oblivious to the beatings is another matter.)

Part of the problem in determining incidence of assault lies in its definition. One officer described often heated debate on the topic among officers. "I'd say, 'What do you mean that you're telling me that you've never seen a beating? . . . What about this guy?' He'd say, 'Well he deserved that. I've never seen a beating that wasn't *deserved.*' " One of the interviewees expressed this sentiment at the time of the 1978 federal and state investigations of Walpole.

> All these things they are talking about, the big inquiry up there about . . . brutality and everything, that's a bunch of crap. It really is.
> *Why?*
> Because there's no such thing as a guard deliberately beating up an inmate at Walpole. I mean, I was only there for eighteen months and I *never* saw it happen. I saw a lot of guys get beat up. But not for the reason of just to beat him up—for the reason that he did something bad enough for them to beat him up. That's the only reason why. That's a bunch of crap when they say that on TV or the newspaper, or the inmates are saying that.

Also complicating assessment of the incidence of assaults by officers against inmates is the necessity to distinguish between force legitimately used to restrain a violent or berserk inmate and force that goes well beyond that needed to restrain. One officer whose accounts seemed invariably accurate estimated that in his nearly four years at Walpole he knew of only ten or twelve beatings that "were close to being criminal . . . when the guy really didn't deserve it and there was no justification behind it whatsoever, that even they couldn't justify or anybody else couldn't justify." In addition to these major incidents, this officer went on to say that he had

> seen some guys maybe a little roughed up, but it would have been hard to say you overdid it or didn't overdo it . . . There were a lot of instances that were, as far as they say were justified—I say it wasn't justified—but they were only minor. It wasn't a real vicious beating. The guy got pushed or shoved or kind of coaxed into something, but it was nothing really big, big or major.

I would not like to estimate the frequency of assaults by officers at Walpole in the 1970s on the basis of the interviews alone. The officers varied in their estimates partly because of differences in their personal experiences and variations in the length and period of their employment. In addition, the same incidents were sometimes repeated—albeit from slightly different perspectives—in interview after interview. This repetition may produce exaggerated estimates of the incidence of assaults, although probably not exaggerated estimates of the importance of such assaults. I think it is safe to say that officer assaults on inmates in the 1970s at Walpole were not nightly, and probably not weekly, occurrences. But nor were they unusual or isolated events.

At times the conflict took on a certain casualness. "You're feeding the guy and the guy take[s] a hot cup of coffee and throw[s] it out there on you and I've seen the whole pot going back in on him. And just go about your business. I've seen that happen because that's just giving him a taste of his own medicine. That's just letting him know."

Far more important than such casual exchanges between an officer and an inmate were beatings inflicted by groups of officers against a single inmate. According to one Walpole officer, "Some of those guys got beatings you wouldn't believe." Officers rarely went one on one with an inmate at Walpole (the "slam" system was designed in part to prevent this). Nor did officers usually attempt to move against an inmate unless the rest of the block had been locked. When an inmate was moved from a max block to segregation, for example, a group of officers were dealing with a single inmate. If there was to have been violence, the situation would have been "five or six guys beating up on the one single guy." An officer recalled the first beating in which he was involved.

> There was a black guy who threw some urine in [the supervisor's] face. That might be reason to bring him to the blue room, but that's not a reason to beat him. Here there were nine [officers] beating the shit out of one guy. Then they'd back off and they'd taunt him and say, "Had enough, had enough?" And the guy would stand there and start swinging. These [inmates] in here are crazy. I don't know whether they are just dumb or are trying to prove themselves or what. That particular guy didn't deserve what he got. But there are guys who deserve what they get.

Such situations were potentially dangerous for the inmate not only because of his numerical disadvantage, but also because of the group psychology involved. "Once one guy threw the first blow and they like all get their courage up and say, 'Okay, it's accepted. Let's do a number on him.'" According to another officer it was a "mass hysteria, mob rule type of thing where the officers would all get together and start beating up on this one guy." These assaults were usually in spontaneous response to some provocation by the inmate. Once the violence had begun, officers at times seemed out of control.

We were moving a guy and he was really mouthing off, and he caused almost a major confrontation between us and the rest of the block. We... started moving him and he "accidently" bounced off a couple of walls here and there. But some of the guys really started overdoing it ... One of the guys was beating him with [a club]. And I, I held back. I didn't do anything because I believe this guy should have gotten a good beating, but to a point. Not to where, hell, it's really everybody in the world getting their licks in just to get something out of their system.

Sometimes attacks seemed random and irrational. Recalled an officer who normally worked the 7–3 shift,

I worked overtime one day. There was an inmate who I had [worked with], a real quiet guy. There was trouble on the 3-to-11 and they were trying to get the guys back in their rooms. I went up on the tier and they were giving this inmate I knew a real beating. I told them to leave the guy alone. His goddamn door was shut. He *couldn't* go back in! I'll never forget it. He was scared to death. His eyes were like saucers.

Some beatings clearly had the potential for causing serious injury, especially when weapons were used: clubs, handcuffs, keys.

There were five or six [officers] beating up on this one [inmate]. They had handcuffs and the chains in the middle, and you fold them over and the two points where the chains hook up to the handcuffs, they were beating the guy's head, punching him in the head with it, and the keys, the big keys.

Recalled another officer of the first beating he had seen, "They kicked him in the gut until he shit his pants ... He was all bruised and black and blue—totally."

Despite the reported severity of some beatings and the mob psychology involved, the interviewees believed that no inmates had been killed by officers. (According to several interviewees, however, in at least one instance officers contributed substantially to psychological pressures on an inmate that led directly to that inmate committing suicide.) If no inmates died as a result of the beatings they received, that was due at least as much to luck as it was to prudence on the part of the officers involved.

*Do you think it is possible that they could ever get so carried away that they would really hurt someone?*

Oh, sure, without a doubt, without a doubt. There are so many parts of your body that—head injuries or whatever—that could totally ruin a guy for life or cripple him or kill him.

*Did you ever have the sense that the inmates could have been killed in that kind of [situation]?*
Oh, yeah. They could've been . . . How many times could I hit a guy in the face before I kill him? . . . I would hope that it didn't happen. I guess that's all you could say is that you hope it wouldn't happen.

*Do you think it's possible that the situation could get out of hand sometime, that an inmate could actually be killed or seriously injured in that kind of situation?*
There's no question.
*Why hasn't that happened?*
Luck.

None of the officers I interviewed as part of this research felt that fellow officers would intentionally kill an inmate. (An officer I interviewed in a different prison system, however, confided that he had once set out to murder an inmate. He relented in his plan only after making the inmate thoroughly sick. And, as reported in Chapter 5, a Walpole officer related an incident where another officer "flipped out . . . and told a man to get down on his knees and beg for his life.") Those officers who voiced the fear that a beating might prove fatal felt that if it did occur it would be something that would happen in the heat of the moment. "If an inmate were killed, I think it would still be in that state of hysteria." "I don't think it comes to your mind that you might kill someone when you're hitting him. And if their intent is to give him a beating, their intent is not to kill him." They generally agreed that they did not "know of any officer that is that bad that would have beat up . . . an inmate to intentionally kill him. If he does it, he is only doing it to get even and he never expected it to go that far."

Public charges of staff brutality in mental institutions seemed nearly as common in the 1970s as charges of officer brutality in prisons. Perhaps it should come as no surprise, then, that levels of officer violence may have been highest in Massachusetts at the facility that was both prison and mental institution—Bridgewater State Hospital for the Criminally Insane. The actual number of incidents of officer violence may have been greater at Walpole (which had a larger inmate population), but the ratio of officer violence to inmate violence (including inmate violence against officers and inmates) may have been highcr at Bridgewater.

These conclusions, however, are tentative. Far fewer Bridgewater officers were interviewed for this study than Walpole officers, and most of these officers usually worked in parts of Bridgewater other than the State Hospital. Furthermore, violence normally took place only in certain sections of the State Hospital. Officers deemed unsympathetic to the use of force were not assigned to those areas. A former Bridgewater officer who was permanently assigned to the State Hospital recalled, "I knew that there was a lot of violence thcre but I didn't see any of it . . . because 1 was never allowed to work where it was." Thus, officers' assertions that violence occurred were based in some cases on hearsay information. Nevertheless, those interviewed were in agreement: officer violence against inmates at Bridgewater State Hospital in the 1970s was widespread and often vicious. Reported an officer who participated in the violence,

> At Bridgewater there's a lot of beatings going on. Oh, it's incredible . . . I've seen people get beat up there so bad that they're almost dead. I've seen guards go home at night where . . . they're worried that night, are [these inmates] going to make it through the night or not?

As noted in the section on inmate violence against officers, Bridgewater inmates were prone toward spontaneous, unprovoked attacks against officers. The officers, in turn, were apparently prone to harsh retaliation. "Bridgewater State Hospital is the last stronghold of corrections where the law of the land is if . . . you hit me once, we're going to hit you three times." Or, as another officer put it, "it's a cardinal sin at Bridgewater for an inmate to hit an officer. If he hits an officer, whew! good night, because you are going to get creamed almost until you're ready to die. That's tradition up there."

Some inmates seemed to invite aggression against themselves. An officer recalled,

> At Bridgewater when you lock somebody up he's going to get it and he's going to get it good. Wet towels around the neck, around the hands, the whole bit. We locked this one guy up one time down in the maxes, and this guy loved to fight and everybody knew it. And he was a loudmouth. He came in, he was in good shape, and once a week he'd flip out—he'd want to fight . . . Black people seem to swell up a little bit more than white

people for some reason, and his face would be just puffed up, blood all over him, and he'd be sitting there shaking, laying on the ground with no clothes on with ten officers there, "Come on, let's do it again. I love it. Come on. Beat me again." He'd start swearing, "You pigs, you screws," and start all over again.

The severity of some of the beatings that occurred was in part explicable by the perception that inmates like him were almost oblivious to pain (whether this was because of the type of medication they were on or their psychosis officers did not know). The officer just quoted spoke in more general terms later in the interview of this phenomenon in relation to Walpole, and its effect on him and his colleagues.

You get to the point where the officers have been—say three officers—struggling with an inmate and your arms get weary from hitting him and it's not even bothering him. You're really laying into the guy and it just doesn't do anything to him. He's still calling for more. That's incredible to see. It's violent. It's very violent. They just don't care. Walpole's like—you got a harder inmate and that, but I don't know . . . When it comes down to the nitty gritty, most of them, when they get hurt, they'll back off . . . But at Bridgewater, they just don't care. They get that strength—all pumped up. They're just flowing . . . And you find yourself as an officer up there getting the same way.

Not only did Bridgewater inmates frequently provoke—occasionally even invite—assault by their own behavior, but they also offered little or no deterrent to assault. In fact, officers reported getting hurt as much by other officers joining in the fray as by the inmates they were assaulting.

The officers go at him like a pack of wolves going after prey. Most of the time when you get hurt, you don't get hurt from the inmate, you get hurt from the other officer kicking you or something. I've been kicked by other officers up there. I've been in a room where I've punched another officer. You usually get hit by the officers because there's so many of them and everybody's trying to clean house.

Another officer recalled an attempted escape by an inmate:

[All] of a sudden, one kid runs for the fence on me . . . So I said, "We got one going for the fence!" and I went after him. So they hit [the] emergency alarm and about ten officers come charging like a herd of animals from a building, right? I mean, you need that in a way in case somebody really was getting hurt, but the way it happened! I grabbed him from the fence. I put him down. All of a sudden—I put him down—I get trampled. Boom! I fall on the ground. They hurt me more than—The guards, they hit the guy, they kept whacking, punching. I'm on the bottom. I ended up getting a black eye from somebody's foot . . . I was covered with mud . . . All these guys are covered with blood, the inmate's blood . . . He was really busted up.

Furthermore, officers who assaulted inmates had little or no reason to fear calculated "payback" in the future. A Bridgewater officer contrasted his institution with Walpole:

At Bridgewater, you tell a guy to go in his room. If he doesn't go to his room, you throw him in his room. At Walpole, you *ask* a guy and, if the guy doesn't go to his room, you don't throw him in his room, you get somebody else to throw him in his room— somebody higher than you. You start throwing people around in their room [at Walpole], you're going to get something in your back.

An inmate beaten or thrown into his cell at Bridgewater, on the other hand, was very likely to forget the circumstances the next day or, if he recalled them, to assume the blame himself:

One time [I] saw this officer whip this guy to the ground, just pounding the heck out of him. But the [inmate] was trying to kick him between the legs . . . He just got the hell beaten out of him. And then he was put in . . . seclusion and three days later he came out, came back on the ward, and was as nice as can be, "Do you want me to do this, do that?" . . . He was just sorry he did it.

An inmate at Bridgewater State Hospital was also unlikely to file a lawsuit or complain to a newspaper or state legislator about beatings. To some extent, the therapeutic staff at Bridgewater acted in the inmates' stead. In an effort to crack down on the violence, the administration decreed that "a psychiatrist has to come over within two or three hours after the person has been locked up to interview him to make sure there's no marks on him because we've been accused of really beating on the patients." But ways existed to circumvent even this problem. As the officer just quoted pointed out, psychiatric staff for the most part worked a forty-hour week and were not present in the evenings and on weekends when most beatings occurred.

> It would seem that quite a bit of the time it would happen on the weekends. That would be the time that the officers, if they didn't like a particular inmate, that would be the best time to do it because the doctors don't come in until Monday and nobody sees them for two days. So if you puff them up a bit, maybe . . . his puffiness will come down.

And, as prisoners the world over know, there are many ways of inflicting violence on a person without leaving a mark.

Absent any real restraints some officers apparently became very violent indeed. An officer recalled an incident when

> nine or ten officers and the supervisor is there hitting him. Boom! Boom! Boom! You put him in a room, right, and you are holding him down and he's wiping the blood off him. And while the supervisor walks out of the room, there's four or five guys punching him. That is ridiculous to me. You're standing there saying to yourself, "Come on, enough is enough. When you beat a guy, you can't even see his face and there's blood all over you and all over everything, give the guy a break." But no. We had other guys that were headhunters . . . Whenever there was a beef—they wouldn't open the door and go in first, but whoever went in first and got him down, then they'd come in and grab him by the hair and just boom! boom! boom! to the face. That's all they wanted to do was just mess up a guy's face. It's ridiculous to do something, to beat—to even want to be labeled like that. But some guys like that.

Under the circumstances, inmates at Bridgewater appeared to be at even greater risk of serious injury or death at the hands of officers than were Walpole inmates.

Concord and Norfolk were quite different stories from Walpole and Bridgewater. At Concord, the junior officers I interviewed reported stories of violence past and present but said they had never witnessed such events themselves.

> I've never seen any physical force used on an inmate . . . I've never seen an inmate hit an officer . . . I've heard officers tell me stories, I've heard inmates tell me stories, and for some reason I've never run into it . . . I've only heard one or two stories

where the officers have brutally gone overboard in using force
. . . and I've never witnessed it. And I'm very surprised myself at
that . . . There's not as much violence as I thought there would
be really.

The violence that did take place was believed to be perpetrated by a
small clique of officers who trusted one another to keep things
quiet.

It doesn't get out past a certain wall. It doesn't go beyond that.
Do I hear rumors of someone getting beat up here, someone
getting stomped over here? Yes. Twice a week you might hear
something like that happened. But the majority of just plain old
smacking somebody to slow them up or being excessively physical, that never gets out. You don't hear none of that.

At Norfolk, officers reported hearing stories of abuse in years past
but believed that it rarely happened in the late 1970s. They ascribed
the absence of violence in part to the "laid back" character of the
officers and inmates and in part to the open access of inmates and
officers to each other. "You have 700 [inmates at Norfolk] . . . and
you can't beat on one inmate and not expect 699 . . . to retaliate or
to feel that they have an access to you."

A measure of the low level of officer violence at these two institutions was that some officers there complained bitterly about the
*absence* of beatings. A Norfolk officer contrasted his institution
with Walpole. "If an officer in this place got beat up by an inmate,
the officers wouldn't do anything about it. But in Walpole, if an
officer got beat up, they'd get him and they'd whale him. And I think
that should be done." A Concord officer agreed, "A lot of the time
they don't even—they just take them to the can. And I don't think
that's right. I think they should give them a {whacking} and see how
they like it."

*Which officers are involved.* At Walpole and Bridgewater State
Hospital, officers who actually instigated violence were relatively
few in number. These officers looked for trouble, instigated it, rev-
eled in it. "They're the type like Hogan's Heroes—kick heads and
ask questions later." As at other prisons where violence occurs in
violation of official policy, at Walpole and Bridgewater it took place
most often on the 3–11 shift, when administrators, psychiatric staff
and other "outsiders" were gone and the institution was inhabited

almost exclusively by inmates and officers. A Bridgewater officer explained,

> On the day shift there's more doctors and more staff around so they kind of clean up the way they want us to. So when we come in [on the 3–11 shift] there's hardly anybody there doctor-wise, so we can take care of the business. Whereas on the day shift they kind of lay back a little bit, on the night shift there's no problem.

At both institutions, officers who instigated violence were sufficient in number and stature on the 3–11 shift to attract followers and sustain a pattern of violence within their respective institutions.

On the 3–11 shift at Walpole, these officers were known as the supervisor's "boys." They were seen as acting at their superiors' behest and thus bore a mark of legitimacy in fellow officers' eyes. Where such officer "hard asses" led, other officers inevitably followed, giving an impression at least on the 3–11 of majority support. The 7–3 and 11–7 shifts steered a somewhat different course from the 3–11, partly due to differences in circumstances (understaffing on the night shift and chaotic conditions on the day shift, with the inmates free in the blocks and out in the corridors) and partly to differences in style and temperament of the officers and their supervisors. (These differences and reasons for them are explored further in Chapter 8.) As noted in Chapter 4, the 7–3 shift was more likely to try to persuade or induce compliance than was its evening counterpart. According to an officer on the 7–3 shift,

> [The] 3-to-11 [shift] has the reputation of handling situations in a way that they won't bargain with you as much as some other shifts will . . . The 3-to-11 may come up and say,
> "You, you're going to 10 Block. We know you got a knife or you got a [ticket]. You're going to 10."
> "Hey, what the hell did I do?"
> "Open the door!"
> They open the door, right.
> "Let's go, step out of the room."
> The guy might say, "Wait a minute, wait a minute, wait!"
> "Get out of the room."
> "Wait a minute, let me get my pants on will you?"
> Bap! Bap! Bump! And the guy {gets down} all bruised, all banged up. They're a little more macho, shall we say.

With officer hard asses at the helm and sufficient men behind them, the 3–11 at Walpole was known as a "heavy-handed crew."

Yet, as will be discussed below, even on the 3–11 most officers appeared to have serious reservations about the violence. ("It was," as one officer put it, "all how you looked in their eyes.") Observed an officer critic of the violence, "The number of bad officers is really, really small . . . But the effect they have on so many others, it throws the balance [off]." In assessing officer participation in the violence, I share this officer's perspective: "I don't want to give a bad, a wrong impression about . . . beatings, or [that] everybody beats them every night, because I don't think it's true. We have a lot of good officers in the system. There's a lot of screw-ups, too. But there's a lot of good officers."

## Why Officers Engage in Violence

The question of *whether* officers were perpetrating violence at Walpole and other Massachusetts state prisons was the subject of impassioned public debate during the period of this study. The answer to that question, by the officers' own testimony, was "yes," although perhaps less at Walpole than they were sometimes publicly accused and perhaps more at Bridgewater. Largely obscured by the debate over *whether* officers were engaging in violence was reasoned consideration of *why* they might be doing so.

Justifications and explanations that officers themselves gave for their use of violence focused variously on (1) the inmate recipient of the violence, (2) relationships among officers, and (3) the individual officer who engaged in violence.

*The inmate recipient of violence.* The most common justification for violence centered on its use in controlling inmates. Physical force and coercion as forms of power were discussed in Chapter 4. I shall not repeat that discussion here other than to reiterate that many, perhaps most, Walpole officers felt themselves unable to maintain even minimal control without at least some reference to violent sanctions.

An even more fundamental concern for officers than maintaining control over the institution was ensuring their own physical safety. Officers who work in a prison system as chaotic and violent as that in Massachusetts are afraid. One of the primary justifications officers offered for their use of violence against inmates was that they believed it deterred inmate violence against themselves. They used physical force to restrain aggressors and defend themselves from immediate assault. More important, they systematically used violent reprisals in an attempt to prevent future assaults and to punish past ones.

Restraint and self-defense are two occasions for the use of physical force that, when that force is judiciously applied, are officially sanctioned. At Walpole, the need for officers to restrain or defend themselves against violent or unruly inmates occurred frequently. Even so, definitions of "self-defense" were very broad at Walpole. They were anticipatory in two senses. First, amidst Walpole's random, unrelenting violence, the need to defend oneself often became translated into the need to "t.k.o. this guy before he t.k.o.'s me." To an officer who argued,

> "Well, before I'd do anything to him, he'd have to do something to me" . . . they'd say, "You are a *sucker* waiting for that point . . ." And then they'd give you point after point. "Well, what about Officer Jones? He was like you. He thought he was a good guy. They ripped his eyes out." Or, "He's the guy that got hit over the head in the last riot and he's still like a watermelon."

Second, at Walpole most officers and inmates believed that in order to survive they had to establish and maintain a reputation for willingness to meet aggression with aggression. Demonstrations of such readiness were commonly considered matters of self-defense by both sides. Asserted an officer of occasional clashes with inmates in his block, "There's guys that could cave my derby in on their worst day and my best day. But I figure that if it had to be done it would have to be done. You've got to expect it. If I backed down, I'd better never show my face in there again. I'd quit."

Once an officer was assaulted, reprisals were deemed by many to be not only appropriate but essential. An inmate who assaulted an officer "should be beaten until he can't stand up anymore. And if he does stand up, beat him some more. Beat him until it gets through his head what will happen and then he'll think twice about what he is doing."

Morris and Morris (1963, p. 258) observed of officers at Pentonville prison, "Although most officers realize that the greatest threat comes, typically, from the unpredictable psychopathic inmate, the vast majority are utterly convinced that it is only the threat of a flogging which prevents assaults on the staff from rising to an intolerable level." Massachusetts officers for the most part shared that perception. "When an officer is struck, you have to come back, you *have* to . . . That's the only thing that stands between us and the inmates taking a pop at every officer they come across." Recollections of the past served to substantiate such perceptions. A Walpole officer recalled, "It used to be that if an inmate hit an officer they would go up and get the guy and beat him up. And when he woke up and found himself in segregation for forty-five days with only one meal a day, no correspondence and only the Bible to read he thought twice about doing it again." But no more. Official sanctions were deemed hopelessly ineffective in stemming the tide of assaults against officers in the 1970s. Furthermore, an administration that professed to oppose officer violence took few steps to protect officers from attack. Officers felt justified in taking matters into their own hands. "When an officer gets hurt, that inmate should be really taken care of, a real good punishment—and he goes out of it with nothing. Right away the administration [says], 'Don't touch that inmate! Don't do nothing to that inmate.' But if you gave him a good lesson, I don't think they'd do it again."

The virulence of some of the "lessons" meted out by officers was a measure not of their sense of omnipotence but of their sense of vulnerability.

> You need to do it. When an inmate stabs an officer or throws acid or maybe urine, what have they got to fear? They have natural life already [have been sentenced to prison for the term of their natural life]. What have they got to lose? A guy comes up to you in the cell block and he says, "I want to make a phone call." And then he gets eight guys and they sit down on your desk and he says, "Now I want to make a phone call." And you tell him, "You can do what you like, but you are going to pay the price . . ." If they kill an officer, what are they [the Department of Correction] going to do? If there is always that little element of fear, knowing they're going to get the shit knocked out of them and it will take a long, long time to come back.

Even some officers who rejected violence for themselves, and declined to work on the 3–11 shift for that reason, felt violence meted out by that shift played an essential role in protecting all officers. "We need 3-to-11 at Walpole. We need that element. It's got to be there . . . The cons should not want to fool with the 3-to-11 or fool with any of the guards up there or anybody under the implied idea that the 3-to-11 is going to come and collect the bill."

At Bridgewater State Hospital, the importance of *immediate* retaliation for inmate assaults seemed all the more apparent in efforts to deter future assaults. There the officers were dealing with inmates who "are really psychotic and just really crazy and you're not dealing with someone that can reason." Inmate behavior was very erratic. A man could be quiet and cooperative one moment and a "raving maniac" the next. To postpone punishment for hours or days until a hearing could be held was seen by some officers as irrevocably severing the link between sanction and offense. A beating applied immediately, however, was seen as effective. An officer reasoned,

> You're not dealing with the regular inmate. You're dealing with crazy people. And they do know—most of them know—what a good beating is. Maybe they don't know too much about anything else, but they do know right from wrong in that aspect. They don't like to get hurt. Most people don't, mentally ill or not.

Officers did not like to get hurt either. Many, though far from all, felt justified in hurting inmates in order to avoid the possibility of being hurt themselves.*

Officers, of course, had other motives for violence that focused on the inmate recipient. Many sought not only to deter future assaults, but also to seek revenge for past offenses committed within (and occasionally without) the institution.

Even if the beating inflicted today fails to deter an attack tomorrow, at the very least it settles the score from yesterday. It was the officers' version of "payback." As a Walpole officer put it, "If you hurt [an officer] seriously enough, then you goddamn well better

---

* Although some officers may have seen the inmates' mental illness as a justification for physical punishment, other officers took the opposite stance. An administrator familiar with Bridgewater at the time of this study considered that "one of the more surprising aspects of the officers' attitudes toward the patients at Bridgewater was the sharp distinction they made between those they saw as 'mad' and those they considered 'bad.' When a patient whom they identified as mentally ill was violent, the officers amazed me by how much punishment they could take without retaliating; I am not sure I could have remained as benevolent, paternal and understanding as many of them were even after being 'sucker-punched' (hit suddenly and without provocation or warning), or having had to subdue someone who had 'gone berserk'—as long as they saw him as 'sick.' But let an inmate whom the officers saw as merely a sociopath or a 'Walpole con' hit anyone, and it was, for some of the officers, 'open season ' " (James F. Gilligan, personal communication, February 1987).

believe I'm coming back and hurt you if I can." This was not to the officers a question of brutality but of just deserts. An inmate who assaulted an officer *deserved* a measure of his own medicine. "Say this guy assaults me, he punches me right in the face. They'll grab him out and pull him out in the corridor and beat the shit out of him. But he deserves it. *That* way he deserves it." Some officers at institutions where violence was less common than at Walpole also felt retaliation for assaults against officers was just and appropriate. A Norfolk officer expressed a desire shared by others that if "somebody laid me in the hospital, I'd like to see the officers go in and kind of educate the gentleman . . . I'd want revenge taken in my name."

Officers at all the institutions were bitter about the unwillingness of the Department of Correction to seek justice on their behalf. Even though inmates involved in offenses against officers were likely to suffer in the future when they were considered for furloughs, special programs, or parole, that provided little solace to officers in the short run when penalties were mild or nonexistent. An officer at the Treatment Center assailed the efficacy of such distant sanctions, "What good is that for me today? . . . Five or six years from now that's fine. But . . . I live in that population day-to-day."

In the absence of satisfactory official punishments, officers sought their own form of "justice." A Bridgewater officer reasoned about offenses committed by inmates within the institution, "You did a crime, you're going to pay for it. That's the way it is in this country . . . [And] the officers up there were the judges." They were the judges, the juries, and the plaintiffs, too. Not surprisingly, theirs was not a dispassionate vengeance. The provocation was too often personal and great. A Walpole officer spoke passionately,

> It's not easy just to stand there and take it with an inmate pointing a razor blade at you and saying that he's going to get you or he is going to get your family when [he gets] out . . . You take it when what you'd like to do is swing at him and bury his head under concrete. But you had to just stand there and take it. You hear it day after day after day . . . You are waiting for the chance that he is going to take the first swing.

The ferocity of some officer assaults on inmates in response to what in the particular instance might have seemed minor provocation could at times be accounted for by an accumulation of grievances with officers waiting for "an excuse now to go in there and give him a hard time." As was true with inmate revenge, "payback" by the officers might be long in coming but severe when it did. One officer claimed to have been waiting years for the opportunity to "get" an inmate who had betrayed him, even foregoing opportunities to transfer to better positions within the Department of Correction.

Such carefully calculated acts of revenge were apparently far less numerous and less important at Walpole than spontaneous retaliations triggered by inmates' attempts to harm fellow officers. Asked how he would justify officer behavior in the aftermath of a hostage incident "to somebody who cried officer brutality," a Walpole interviewee replied,

> I don't know if I could defend it . . . I think I would just try to tell them this is somebody that is important to us. We are all important to each other . . . We're comrades in arms . . . The feeling to me would be if you had something unreplaceable stolen, a family heirloom or something, and some young punk with no regard for you whatsoever came in and took it away from you and then treated it disrespectfully or broke it or misused it or in some fashion like that. And you had an opportunity to catch him and get it back. But when you got the item back you found, "Well, look what he did to it!" That sudden—maybe it would only last a few seconds—but the feeling you had right then, how much you wanted to whack him in the mouth for what he had done. Take that exact feeling and that state of tension and leave it like that. It doesn't decrease . . . from the time the hostage was taken or the incident happened until the end results happen. Because you get this—*I* get it . . . —the urge that if I ever get my hands on this fucking guy that's got my [buddy] . . . If I had the guy right {down there} I probably would have choked him. Because he violated my number one, my basic principle, "Don't touch the officers, don't hurt them, don't take them hostage."

Although this officer's record at Walpole was one of relative nonviolence, he recognized the potential within himself to kill an inmate under such circumstances.

> If I saw one of my men down and being physically assaulted, seriously assaulted, I think it's within my power to kill a man for that. I think I could do it. I'm thinking about it now, I'm

starting to get upset. It's completely against everything that I believe in: "You don't touch an officer. If you do, I'm going to kill you. It's as simple as that. I will hurt you."

(With these same emotions, interviewees expressed understanding for those officers who participated in bloody reprisals against inmates in the aftermath of the 1972 Attica prison uprising in which officers had been held hostage and had died. But they also universally criticized New York State officials for having permitted officers to take part in retaking the institution.)

Inmates were not innocent victims in officers' eyes. They were men who had done in the past—and in all probability were willing to do again in the future—at least as much harm to other people as officers did to them. Especially at Walpole, officers reasoned that what they did to inmates was not cruel "because that's what they deserve. What *they're* doing is cruel, too. What they're doing to officers is cruel. What they're doing to *other inmates* is cruel."

What inmates had done to their victims outside the prison was also often very cruel. Officers at Walpole and Bridgewater State Hospital—the two state prisons where the most violence occurred—did not usually point to crimes that inmates in their charge had committed in order to justify violence against them. No one denied that incarceration at Walpole was substantial punishment, and there were too many problems within the institution to pay much attention to what had happened outside in years past. At Bridgewater State Hospital, many of the inmates had committed appalling crimes, but officers tended to accept the diagnosis of "criminally insane" and focused on deeds committed in their presence.

In comparison to Walpole and Bridgewater State Hospital, incarceration was relatively easy for inmates at Norfolk and the Treatment Center for Sexually Dangerous Persons. Many officers at these two institutions did not believe that the inmates there were paying sufficiently for the crimes they had committed. A Norfolk officer expressed feelings shared by many of his co-workers. "I'm not gung-ho about being a prison guard, saying, 'Oh, wow! I'm a prison guard.' But I don't feel like I'm also doing what people who have been hurt by these people are expecting me to do."

These sentiments were magnified at the Treatment Center, where the crimes committed were considered among the worst and the officers were most constrained in what they could do to inmates. In the prison world, sex offenders rank lowest and often suffer most at the hands of fellow inmates and officers. They constitute one of the few classes of offenders singled out for systematic retaliation by officers (along with inmates convicted of violence against children and those who have killed law enforcement officers). Many of the inmates at the Treatment Center for Sexually Dangerous Persons (SDPs) had committed "atrocious" crimes against adults and children. Nevertheless, the regimen at the Treatment Center was fairly benign, befitting the residents' status as "patients," not inmates. Furthermore, unlike their "criminally insane" neighbors at the State Hospital, many of the SDPs were of sound enough mind to challenge officers' actions against them through administrative and legal channels, thus deterring most direct officer violence.

For the most part, officers at the Treatment Center did not accept the notion that the people they were guarding were "sick" or deserved the status of "patient." "The way I look at it, we're dealing with the scum of the earth, right here. This isn't your typical bank robber or murderer . . . These guys, whew! little kids, molesting little kids. I just can't see that." "I mean you're not talking about a crime where a guy ran into a store with a gun and held somebody up for $50, $100 and ran down the street and went to Walpole and did eight years. You are talking about a guy who went out and diddled some kid or raped a woman, I mean *viciously*. And these guys get out on the street in one year. How would you feel?"

Treatment Center inmates did not present serious behavioral problems within the institution (other than by their open homosexuality, which enraged many officers, especially as it was seemingly condoned by the administration). Many inmates were almost fawning in their compliance with officers' directives. But more than officers at any other Massachusetts institution, officers at the Treatment Center focused on the inmates' crimes and their victims outside, rather than on their behavior within the institution.

> A guy [comes] here . . . with forty-two counts of rape against him . . . and [he's] the sweetest little sweetheart you ever saw in your life . . . That's hard. You don't know the victims' families, but you know what they're more or less going through. And here's this guy, the state's spending fifteen to eighteen thousand a year on him to feed him, clothe him, to give him "educational benefits." Unbelievable!

Such violence and lesser acts of vengeance that officers at the Treatment Center committed against inmates stemmed principally from their rage over the disproportion between crime and punishment. Said one who used some violence when he was first an officer there, "My mistake when I first came here was, when an [inmate] come down, I'd look at his record. That was the biggest mistake I ever made because you develop such a hatred for these guys." The death penalty was the least these officers felt many inmates deserved for what they had done, but instead they lived unrepentant in relative comfort.

> There's a good majority of these [inmates] who deserve the death penalty and it should still exist. These women and these kids have to live out there the rest of their lives with what these guys did to them. And these guys, it seems like they did what they did, but it doesn't bother them. It's over with now. "I did my time. I'm in jail, I've been here for five years now, I deserve to be back on the street now." It doesn't matter that he cut her breasts off or this guy bit this kid's penis off, or he stabbed this girl forty times but she's still all right, or he fractured her skull and put 190 stitches in her face or knocked her teeth out. That's not important. What's important is "I'm back on the street. I'm getting out of here. I'm on a program." . . .
>
> More and more these guys are not feeling any guilt. They should just hang, hang, hang. "I killed somebody. I cut her head off. I ripped her breasts off. I ripped her open." Big deal. They're still sitting in here, still living. And all they're worried about is their goddamned rights and their radio, and they want a color TV, and black and white ain't good enough, and "I want a stereo and I want to get out of here in five years." What they did was fine . . .
>
> I have to cater to this asshole . . . who committed the crime. Who's the goddamned inmate in here, them or me? So why don't they hang some of these bastards? . . . Sometimes I wish that one of these real animals would slug me so I could slug them back. I think I would get a lot of satisfaction out of it—the satisfaction it would give me that I could sink my fist into their face.

This officer fantasized about machine gunning half the inmate population to death, another officer of gassing them, a third officer of flying "over this place with a little bomb. Get all the officers out and it wouldn't faze me in the least. I'd feel I was doing humanity a big favor getting rid of these guys."

These were fantasies born of frustration. But clearly some Treatment Center officers would have played the role of society's avenger had they not been held in check by what they saw as an unholy alliance among the inmates, the courts, and the Department of Mental Health. Psychotherapists are trained to approach their patients analytically and to consider the crimes they commit dispassionately no matter how grotesque. (The officers I interviewed held less flattering theories about why therapists, especially female ones, were willing to work closely with sex offenders.) But the officers were not similarly trained or emotionally constrained. They saw no reason to aid the Department of Mental Health in its efforts to "cure" their charges. "Help these son of a bitches? What they've done out in society that brought them here? . . . No way! For what? To have them 'rehabilitated' and go out and diddle *my* kids just to come back here again?" Although the Treatment Center was in many ways the easiest and safest prison in which to work, the officers' unresolved rage often took a heavy psychological toll. As the officer just quoted assessed his situation, "For the money you can't beat what I'm doing. But as far as my head goes, it's a drag."

*Relationships among officers.* The need to control the unruly, to deter aggression, to punish offenses committed inside the prison and without: these were justifications for the use of violence by officers that focused on the inmate recipients of that violence. They concerned transgressions inmates had actually committed or their relationships with those officers who inflicted punishment on them. However, other explanations for the use of violence by officers largely ignored the inmate recipients of it and focused instead on relationships *among officers.* Especially important was an officer's desire to be accepted, respected, and promoted.

Regardless of their own views on violence, Walpole officers were under considerable pressure not only to acquiesce in it, but to participate in it as well. Norm 5 of the officer code, "Always support an officer in a dispute with an inmate," and the more specific injunction, Norm 6, "Always support officer sanctions against inmates," were mainstays in the systematic use of violent reprisals against inmates. As previously noted, most officers who participated in the violence were followers, not instigators. Many of them had serious reservations about their involvement. But few saw options not to participate. Walpole was, as one officer put it, a place where "you do what the majority does."

A young officer on the 3–11 shift who at first found his involvement in the violence "hard" explained,

I fell into it kind of. I got the feeling from the place and I realized that this was the way it was. I never really went looking for it, but if I was on the moving crew and these people were doing the lugging [moving an inmate against his will, not bringing in contraband] and it was their job to rough the guy up, then he'd be roughed up. But I wouldn't go out of my way to get him. It was just like, "Okay, you guys are moving him and if something happens to him on the way, whoops! it's okay."

The pressures to conform were more than those of the ordinary peer group; they were reinforced by genuine fears for survival in a situation in which individuality might well be rewarded with death. An officer thoughtfully assessed the problem:

I think the biggest problem in a place like Walpole is that a lot of guys aren't leaders and they are really, really followers to the degree that they may be doing something—like when someone hit somebody and they kind of like follow not really wanting to follow—and you kind of don't blame them . . . If you're adding up the figures, "Well, how many officers hit somebody?" and I say, "Well, Jesus, that number is pretty high." But it's not really a true picture of what really happened even though all these guys hit this guy, this is what happened and this is what did it. And it wouldn't never happen—them guys would never thought about doing this . . . because inside that's really not them. But they say, "I have to assume this role in order to make it as a correctional officer. I *have* to do this." . . . Because that environment is like no other environment. They probably wouldn't do the same thing out in the street, or in the house. But you go there, deep down inside there's a tension or something that eats away at you constantly. And you say, "Well, okay, there's only one way to live here. There's only one way to survive." And you do what you have to do to survive.

At Bridgewater State Hospital, survival was not the central issue. Officers opposed to the violence there may have found themselves shunted off to parts of the institution where violence was less common, but they apparently were not imperiled by their nonparticipation. On the other hand, in contrast to Walpole recruits, rookies at the State Hospital faced a long, uphill battle to be accepted by their fellow officers (see Chapter 8). Their understandable desire to be readily integrated into the officer corps accounted for the initial participation of some in the violence. An officer ambivalent about the violence recalled his own initiation into it:

> When you first start there you don't know anybody, so what you had to do is do what the other people do. So when you work a certain ward, and with certain people, I'd act the way they acted. If they wanted to be hard, I'd be hard. If I worked another ward and they were easy, I'd sit back and just be easy. That's the way I kind of did, just to fit in with everybody up there. Which was wrong. I should have been able just to do what I wanted to do. But if I worked with these people, I [would have] had these people talking behind my back. So instead of doing that, I just kept my mouth shut.

While most officers at Walpole and Bridgewater State Hospital, especially new ones, felt pressure to go along with the violence, some officers saw their own participation in it as an opportunity for gaining prestige among fellow officers. "An officer thinks, 'If I do this I'm going to be thought of highly.' " These officers instigated violence. Theirs was the prestige of being able to "come out of the room a hero in front of the rest of the officers. 'Oh, I just knocked the shit out of this inmate!' "

At Walpole, where key supervisors and administrators were seen as supportive of (or at least acquiescent in) much of the violence, prestige was not the hard-ass officer's only reward. He might be "trying to impress the people who are in control who make up the roster so he can get good jobs" and avoid lousy ones. One irony of Walpole was that an officer who was "in on all that stuff, beating everybody in sight" could not be assigned to work the blocks (the most difficult and among the least prestigious positions in the prison) because his presence alone in the block might "cause a riot" or at least provide inmates with an opportunity to retaliate against him. For this reason, these officers were seen as being able to secure relatively easy posts (for example, the control center) and yet maintain their reputation through periodic involvement in the blocks lugging inmates and responding to crises. What is more, they were seen as able to use their reputations as springboards to eventual promotion.

*The officer himself.* Justifications and explanations for violence have centered so far on an officer's relationship with inmates or fellow officers. The popular image of the "brutal screw," however, focuses not on an officer's relationship with others but rather on the officer himself—his personal predilection for violence and need for aggression. There were clearly elements of that, too, among the officers studied, although reasons why officers felt a need to act out aggressions were perhaps not as straightfoward as officers' critics (including some fellow officers) might have believed.

According to those interviewed, there were officers who apparently enjoyed the violence. Walpole officers reported, "Some of the guys thrive on it." "[They] get into it, they really get into it, and they get high on it. Something goes down, somebody gets killed, they get high on it and like it." "There were some guys working at Walpole that enjoyed it, they looked forward to making a move. And they instigated it—a lot of the trouble." It was exciting, dramatic, a break in the routine. Said one officer of his work at Walpole, "I really enjoyed it. . . . I like having action." Responded another when asked if he found "the brutality of the institution depressing," "No, because to be honest with you I looked forward to some incidents and stuff to happen . . . Sometimes really it peps up my day, cause at least *something* happens during the course of the day." Similarly, at Bridgewater State Hospital, officers pointed to "a few that just loved to just whack people around." "Some guys like that. That's all they look for. They call that the 'goon squad' up there . . . The heavy hitters . . . I don't know what makes them guys do that, but they love it." Officers at Concord and Norfolk also pointed to men who seemed to thrive when tensions were highest and the possibilities of violence greatest.

Despite the public deference accorded those officers who initiated violence, fellow officers were frequently scathing in their private assessments of them. Beneath the machismo, they discerned fear. "I think a lot of them are scared deep down inside and that's how they—'I've got to prove that I'm not scared.' And they are constantly proving themselves, constantly proving themselves." Behind the excesses, they saw "frustrated cops." "They like this kind of authority. They like to wear the badge." "They get into this macho type of thing. They're feeding their own egos and they think that other people look up to them." One Walpole interviewee perceptively compared such officers to the men they were hired to control.

They are just like an inmate . . . It's just that they have found their relief through other avenues. "I've got this desire to be powerful. Now I can either be powerful by going out and saying to someone, 'Give me money,' with a gun and he gives me money, or I can . . . get a job as a correction officer and do the same thing and say, 'You sit down here!' " Basically it's the same thing. You're filling the same needs that you have but through different avenues.

Bridgewater officers also compared their more violent colleagues to the inmates they guarded—in this case the criminally insane. "Some of them belong in here, I think, the way they freak out. They're like crazy, too." A colleague agreed, "Some officers up there are really banana heads. They look for trouble . . . Sometimes an officer has a fight with his wife, and he'll go in there and, 'Oh, you maggot, shut up,' and . . . they take it out on them . . . They would just do 'hard time,' always yelling, screaming."

Some rookies who went to Concord were struck by the fascination for guns among their older colleagues. One officer who liked most of the men with whom he worked nevertheless recalled, "Even when I was first starting, I noticed there was a bloodthirsty attitude for some officers. They would collect guns. They would get into fights, barroom fights . . . There's a type of individual that will start an argument with an inmate and would like nothing better than to beat someone up." Another Concord officer was more sweeping in his critique: "Gun toting, macho, insecure within themselves . . . A lot of them . . . were really into authority, or being an authoritarian and needing someone to put their thumb on because it made them feel better."

One of the officers I interviewed conformed closely to the image of the "gun toting, macho, insecure" officer. Assigned to one of the peripheral institutions, he set out to make a "bad guy" image for himself. He was an officer who claimed to hate inmates, especially blacks ("I just don't like their attitude, their walk, their talk, just everything about them"), and hoped inmates reciprocated in kind ("I know they hate me and I like them to hate me"). In his view, "men are supposed to be domineering." He derived "a lot of satisfaction out of locking a guy up" and sought confrontations, preferably violent ones, although they were out of keeping with the tenor of the institution where he worked. He acknowledged being a heavy drinker and having an uncontrollable temper. In an effort to emulate an admired officer at a different institution, he cultivated a "mean reputation" and a suspicion that he was "crazy." Of his mentor he observed,

Nobody gives this guy any bullshit. He just doesn't have that many hassles to put up with, because he'd formed a reputation. You've got to start someplace. He built his reputation. And now . . . none of the inmates give him any trouble because they know. So I figure I'll do the same thing. That way it may be tough at first, but after [that], these guys'll never bother me and I'll have it easy.

He was determined to maintain a reputation within the institution for the ability to dominate, just as he did outside.

I'm still full of piss and vinegar. I'm not going to bend . . . I'll never bend to these people, because if I bend to these people, I'm going to think they beat me and there's no way I'm going to voluntarily let somebody beat me. I don't do it on the street. I don't see why I should do it in here.

He traced the roots of his aggression and desire to dominate to childhood experiences.

*You said that one of the things you admire about ——— is that people don't give him any shit. Why is that something you admire about him?*
You're in school. You see this one kid that everybody picked on. Did you want to be that kid? All right, that's it in a nutshell.
*But then there's also the other extreme. There's the kid who gets picked on and there's the kid that everyone's leery of. And then there's everybody else in between.*
No, no. There's the other kid—not the kid that does the picking, but the kid that saves himself and his friends and he's just got an atmosphere of just total confidence about himself. And nobody's going to mess around with this guy. Not that they fear the guy, but just that they respect the guy . . . To be truthful with you, when I was being brought up through school, in the younger grades, I was the kid they picked on . . . I was a real skinny {bastard} when I was a kid. I was skinny, bucked teeth, glasses. Everybody picked on me . . . Then all of a sudden I started working out . . . And I just started getting stronger, started getting a lot of confidence. Finally, [when] some of these people started picking on me, I reacted different. I got a lot of respect out of it. To this day, people don't pick on me anymore. And it's not a toughness thing. It's just that I like to be the guy that nobody bothers.

In the prison he became the officer no inmate ever bothered, although he admitted being scared in a prison where most officers had little reason to be.

His aggression toward inmates served other purposes besides satisfying personal needs for domination and control. He also justified his violence in terms of his relationship with his fellow officers, whose respect he sought to gain by the very tactics that allowed him to dominate inmates.

> The night I banged the [inmate's] head in the wall, the night I walked in the room and smacked him . . . they all started respecting [me]. And now [I] fit right in with them. They know that if . . . something goes down in here or on the street, I can take care of myself. If something happens to a buddy, I'll help my buddy out.

As an officer he felt able to achieve both dominance and approval (though his perceptions of approval were not always verified by interviews with his colleagues). A price he acknowledged paying was burying what he also saw as an important part of himself. "Inside I'm a sensitive person I guess is what you could say. But a lot of people don't know that because I keep my sensitive emotions inside of me. I don't let them out."

A few of the other officers I interviewed apparently shared his need for forceful domination, his emotional instability, his insecurity: qualities that at least in his case seemed to precede and transcend the prison experience. But these officers were atypical among those I studied. Origins of the officer subculture and its aggressive stance toward inmates are explored in the following two chapters. Suffice it here to say that most aggression by officers, especially Walpole officers, appeared to come not from men who brought aggression *to* the job, but from those for whom aggression was a product *of* the job. These were men who "had learned to hate," their hatred provoked by inmate treachery and brutality. "Leeches . . . cannibals . . . On the outside they preyed on other people. In here they can only prey on each other, their own kind"—and on the officers. A Walpole officer who had entered the prison optimistic about his relations with inmates bitterly assessed those relations two years later.

> I don't give a damn about the inmates. You can't please them.
> If you do a guy a favor or you give a guy a break, you expect that

sometime maybe in the future they will give you a break. But they just turn around and grab a little more, or next thing you know they are threatening to kill you . . . [You get] no human response from inmates.

Recalled this officer,

When a buddy of mine got stabbed that I really cared for—a good friend of mine, that's when I couldn't stand {anybody there} anymore . . . I realized that I'd probably been fooling myself for two years . . . that they were people or something . . . There's certain cons I hated—if I hated anybody in the world it's them.

Depression—anger and hatred turned inward—appeared widespread among the officers that I interviewed, especially at Walpole. As will be discussed in Chapter 9, the resulting aggression was often inflicted first on an officer's family and friends. Later, if not sooner, that aggression was turned against those who had provoked it. The violence that resulted did not really stem from a desire to exact due punishment for wrongs actually committed, as when retribution was the motive for violence. Instead, it represented the venting of officers' pent-up rage against inmates as a group. In the context of the daily tension and anxiety under which officers worked, almost any inmate was seen as an appropriate outlet for that rage. Explained one officer,

I think a lot of times if the inmate was to get a beating, let's say it could be just from the tension of whatever happened at that particular time. They might not have set out to beat him, but he might have said something on the way that they didn't like and they might have {flipped} out and next thing you know you take out your aggravation on some inmate that maybe didn't have anything to do with the circumstances.

*Denial of the need to justify violence against inmates.* Some officers I interviewed had thought carefully about officer violence. They offered justifications and explanations for it of their own accord. When explanations were not forthcoming, I pressed for them in the interviews. By implication, violence was something that required justification and explanation. But that was not a perspective all officers shared. In part what distinguished Walpole as an institution in my eyes was the apparent acceptance by individuals on both sides—keepers and kept—that violence, at least in some forms, needs no justification: it is natural, a way of life, even a game if played within certain rules. "It's like the environment of the {place}, getting beat," commented one Walpole officer. Observed another,

> It's a completely different culture [in there] . . . Officers *and* inmates think differently in that type setting . . . That's the way it's been evolved over the years. That's the way corrections is . . . Human nature takes its course and finds its own way to deal with things, the best possible way.

This officer went on to give examples of ways in which violence was accepted within the prison culture:

> Something was done in a block [by inmates] and we did a shakedown. So we went through the whole block. And all the inmates were yelling "payback's a motherfucker, payback's a motherfucker!" Because we went in there, we turned the place upside down, shook down all the rooms, and they didn't want to be disturbed like that. But when an officer was stabbed one night and we went in there and turned the place upside down afterwards, [the inmates] didn't say a word. Because they know this is their payback. Like they were saying, "You disturb us and 'payback is a motherfucker' " to us, but "we disturbed you so this is a payback." And they knew it. That's the type of game that you play. These guys expected that and in that way it's a different culture.

Nor was the acceptance of violence always one-sided. Occasionally when an officer was the victim of assault other officers recognized a certain legitimacy to events. When one officer deemed a "regular ticketron" by his colleagues for his excessive use of D-Reports was stabbed, the other officers were neither surprised nor particularly exercised over it. Violence and retribution were understood and accepted by both sides. " 'You do it to us, you're going to get it back.' That's the way it is."

Officers who shared this perspective on violence viewed it as so routine a means of resolving differences that they often failed to consider other courses of action. One officer when confronted by inmates for having beaten another inmate told them he had done so because that inmate had called the officer's mother a "punk." On hearing the officer's side, the other inmates had "understood completely." When pressed by me to justify his actions then and elsewhere, this officer simply repeated what to him seemed obvious,

"You would do it. Anyone would." Said another officer of an inmate who had taunted an officer and gotten a beating, "This is expected by this guy. He goes and mouths off and that happens. And he knows this is coming. He's going to take it, too, which they normally do. That's part of the game."

To some extent the conflict did take on the dimensions of a game with elements of humor, a respect for rules, and a sense of proportion and fair play. An inmate who spent years in Block 10 reminisced about the pitched battles that occurred. "I admit it. I threw shit at the guards. It got to be a game. They tried to dehumanize me and that's the one way they ended up succeeding. I threw the only thing that was around to throw" (*Boston Globe*, 7 March 1980). An officer there during roughly the same period recalled that the combination of urine, feces, and feathers from the inmates' pillows made passage down the tiers extremely difficult with "fifteen pounds of feathers and everything else stuck to your shoes." Officers weighted down made easy targets for new onslaughts. What happened, then, when inmates wanted officers to come down to deliver meals or mail? A "truce" was called. The officer dispensing the desired articles was permitted to make a path before him with a broom, after which

> they'd fill it all in right behind you, figuring the next guy coming down, he wasn't going to get no path . . . We used to call these truces, made it out like a big game, which it was, a lot of it was a game . . . "You play fair by these rules and I'll play by these rules and everybody'd be happy. You got to do what you've got to do, and I've got to do what I've got to do." . . . It was like fair and square. And we fought and everything, but it was like a lot of fun, like we were kids.

But, of course, the conflict was not always "a lot of fun," at least not for everyone, and that was in large part because the rules of the game—especially what was considered "fair" violence—varied widely among officers and inmates. Some officers, such as the one just quoted, limited their definition of "fair" violence to restraint and self-defense. Others extended their definition to include measured defense of one's own reputation. And then there were those who simply saw violence as a natural and routine part of human relationships. Officers in this last group were not unconcerned about concepts of fairness. In fact, some became exercised over distinctions between different forms of violence that might be lost on those more categorically opposed to violence. For example, to beat up an inmate one-on-one might have been justified in their eyes, but to gang-beat him or beat him while he was handcuffed might not, even if the inmate received no worse a beating from a group of officers than he did from a single assailant, while restrained or free. What was the worst thing one recruit could do in his own eyes as an officer?

Beat somebody up with handcuffs on him.
*Why would that be the worst thing?*
Because he doesn't have a chance to fight you back . . . That really disgusts me. One-on-one is fine, but give the guy a break, give him a chance.

An experienced officer objected along the same lines, "if the guy punches a guard in the mouth, all right, bring him out here and let the guy that he's punched at him. If they want to duke it out that way, let them duke it out. But don't let five or six guys jump on him and beat the crap out of him."

A concern for "fair violence" is, of course, a concern of individuals who do not see violence per se as problematic. Such a perspective if leavened with a soldier's sense of dispassionate duty might have engendered a regime of harsh but disciplined control. But at Walpole hate was as "natural" as violence. It was their combination that sparked many of the brutal excesses on both sides.

## Officers' Arguments against the Use of Violence

The justifications officers put forward for their use of violence were in many ways compelling. Violence against inmates did offer some control and protection, especially at Walpole, where officers had little of either. It also provided a means of avenging wrongs actually committed against officers and of releasing some of the enormous stress and anger that were by-products of their association with inmates. Yet, many officers themselves were unpersuaded by arguments favoring violence. They argued against it on a number of grounds, practical and moral.

Perhaps not surprisingly, officers most categorically opposed to violence worked in those institutions where there was least call or occasion to use it. A Norfolk officer observed that a generation ago, the "first thing you did when you got here was you made a name for yourself by knocking a couple of guys around. But you can't do that now . . . You don't get any respect by using force . . . Now you have to outsmart them." Officers like him rejected violence as unnecessary ("that's not the way to handle people") and inappropriate ("I can't see overextending your authority to the point where you are going to beat people up . . . That doesn't make you any better than [the inmate] . . . Where the hell is the sense?"). Although they had an easier clientele to work with than did their counterparts at Walpole, Norfolk officers pointed to numerous instances where they were able to deal nonviolently with the very same inmates with whom Walpole officers had had aggressive relationships.

One Norfolk officer felt that even at his institution officers were too inclined to threaten force or sanction because they mistook aggression for violence. The officer, who was white, elaborated this point with particular reference to white officers' relations with black inmates.

> I find it among the inmates and among the guards, not so much violence but just a force that's used: eyes . . . tone of voice. Inmates do it, they use a threat . . . It's used at Norfolk more than physical violence is used. Like they go in their room and slam the door, like kids, but it's done, I swear.
>
> And guards use it . . . A lot of guards are panicked into doing something they wouldn't normally do by not understanding this aggressive pattern which is *not* violence . . . If you go in the streets, you can see a lot of it. If you stand back you can see a ritual. If you get closer, you don't see it, you just see a bunch of hoods. But it's really a ritual. It's their way of being somebody . . .
>
> The black guys at home have like a ritual dance, strut, whatever you call it. It's their thing. And if you can do it with them, you're all right. There's no physical attack. But if you blow it, or if you don't understand what's going on and, by not understanding, you don't communicate to them—you say, "What's this shit about, man? This is silly. What are you trying to do?"—you tell him that you're backing out, that he's won, that he's on top. And that to him gives him a feeling of might that really isn't good to have because it really isn't true. But he feels it is and it could cause *him* trouble by having him overstep certain bounds and it could cause *you* trouble by having hurt your head . . .
>
> I just think a lot of guards should be taught more about aggression, how it really is . . . how it's not all necessarily accompanied by force.

If these arguments were not sufficient to dissuade officers from engaging in violence, there were less subtle deterrents at Norfolk. As an officer there pointed out,

If you hit an inmate, nine times out of ten, you're going to get sued . . . Most of the time nothing comes of it, but it's a hassle . . . And out of the 720 [inmates] that are in there right now, there's not more than five or six I'd like to take on one-on-one because they have all day long to work out—weights, boxing and this and that. Probably I wouldn't be the one hitting them, I'd be the one getting hit.

Their situation, of course, was not analogous to that at Walpole. "There's a lot more freedom to roam in here . . . [At] Walpole you close the doors and you've got thirty of them contained in one block. But in here something goes down, you're dealing with everyone that's in this place." Norfolk officers worked in a reasonably congenial institution. They often took a hard line themselves toward officers who rocked the boat.

Objections to violence ran along much the same lines among Concord officers. There, peace sometimes seemed more fragile than at Norfolk.

Any [officer here] will tell you they don't want to work next to another officer who may end up getting them—me—killed . . . I don't want to work with anyone who's going to start trouble with somebody else and I'm going to have to end up coming in or end up being part of the trouble . . . We have enough trouble as it is. If you're creating the trouble, you should be out.

Bridgewater officers were not deterred from committing acts of violence because of fear of reprisal by inmates, but the younger officers I interviewed there were appalled at the extent of the violence, most of which they claimed was unnecessary and unjustified.

It was at Walpole, of course, where arguments in favor of violence seemed most compelling. That was the institution where the officers had least control and were most regularly victimized. I think it is important to appreciate that, as one officer pointed out, many officers "honestly believe . . . that they are doing the right thing. If an inmate hits an officer, then that inmate should be taken care of, that's the only way you can teach them. So it's a belief. They don't honestly think it's wrong. They're really accepting that that's the way it is in an institution."

This view was reinforced by society's perceived acquiescence in the violence. "Society's saying, 'That's okay. I don't care if you beat his head in. The guy deserved it. He stuck up somebody. And to think that he could put a gun—the fear and the emotional stress that he put on that other person. Someone who could do that has got to be sick. Put him away, throw him in a hole, cage him.' " Officers observed that most people outside prisons, including most civic and political leaders, did not care what went on inside as long as problems were handled within the institutions. "They put [the prison system] in a corner and throw a rug over it and it is out of their sight for a while. So they can live with it." "There is no real concern. That's why they build the walls. People don't want to see in here. They don't really want to know what is going on. So it's accepted. As long as it's quiet, they'll let them run it any way they want to." It is not surprising that many officers concluded that "we got the right to treat them any way we want and no one else in society cares." *

Yet even at Walpole most officers had reservations about the violence, and a few categorically opposed it. Some saw it as counterproductive.

> Where is it rational for an officer to challenge an inmate or even go to the point of physically assaulting him? . . . I'm quite sure that when an inmate gets his head broke he remembers. He sits in that cell twenty-four hours a day and just thinks, "I can't wait to get out so I can get even with this bastard." And you go home, you do whatever you do; you're not thinking about this guy. And then, all of a sudden one day—three, four, five, six months, a year later—you go into a block and say, "Jeez, I know that guy. Why do I know him? Hey, hey, oh, that's right! That's why he's coming at me with the mop pail. He wants to kill me because I beat him up a year ago!"

Officers like him recognized that when fear begets violence, that violence begets more violence, which in turn begets more fear.

Other officers opposed violence on humanitarian grounds. Some of these officers were merely appalled at the severity of the beatings

* For such acquiescence, Arendt (1977, p. 126) found German society culpable for the atrocities of the Nazi regime. She wrote of Eichmann, "He did not need to 'close his ears to the voice of conscience,' as the judgment has it, not because he had none, but because his conscience spoke with a 'respectable voice,' with the voice of respectable society around him."

("nobody deserves *that*"). Some saw their own participation as wrong, but were less definite about others. "The worst thing I could do in my own eyes as an officer is to beat an inmate into submission. [*Why?*] Because it's not the right thing to do! Especially when he hasn't got a chance in the world. It's just so inhumane, to me, to take part in it." (This officer recognized that he did not absolve himself from blame by his nonparticipation in the violence. He continued, "I suppose walking the other way when somebody else is doing it is just as bad, but I've got to keep my job . . . Now if an inmate came at me, naturally, I would defend myself. But to have a bunch of other officers hold him and me go at him, I just can't picture myself doing that.")

Finally, a few Walpole officers viewed officer violence as wrong from both a societal and a personal perspective. "[Other officers] are really accepting that that's the way it is in an institution. And to me it isn't. That's wrong." Such officers were able to see beyond society's perceived acquiescence in the violence, to realize how vulnerable the officers were both morally and legally.

> An officer thinks, "If I do this, I'm going to be thought of highly." . . . [Other officers will] say, "You're all right, John." But when they finally say to somebody, "You're going to be the example. This isn't happening. Society . . . isn't going to accept it, and you are going to be the first one who is going to pay for it." And then he's going to say, "Well, where are my friends?" And you're alone, and there's no one there . . . They are going to feel that the system is letting them down because [it's] not protecting them. But the system's not made to protect someone like that and they don't realize this, they don't understand this.

The system may not have been made to protect them, but during the 1970s officers in Massachusetts were not called to account for their violence, and society did not demand a cessation of the brutality. The effect of the violence on those within the prisons and without will be discussed in later chapters.

# 7

# Officer Recruits and
# Their Values

Where do the central values and characteristics of the officer sub-culture come from? Are they principally products of the prison environment itself or are they to a large extent "imported" into the institution by those recruited to the officer role?

These questions parallel ones that have generated considerable debate among penologists regarding origins of the inmate subculture. Donald Clemmer (1940) sparked the debate in his seminal work, *The Prison Community*. He used the term *prisonization* in regard to inmates "to indicate the taking on in greater or lesser degree of the folkways, mores, customs, and general culture of the penitentiary" (p. 299). "Universal factors of prisonization" (p. 300) were considered for a time to apply to all prisons and prisoners—products, as Sykes (1958) was later to suggest, of universal "pains of imprisonment." Subsequent studies have provided evidence for the opposing proposition that central features of the inmate culture are "imported" into the institution. Authors of these studies have argued that the inmate subculture derives its salient characteristics from the "street" world to which most inmates belong before entering the prison, and not from the nature of imprisonment itself. (See Hawkins, 1976, chap. 3, for an overview of this debate.)

The question of whether the *officer* subculture is imported or is a consequence of prison work has been largely ignored, despite its important implications. If the officer subculture principally reflects the types of individuals recruited into it, then the nature of prisons can be substantially influenced by changes in recruitment. If, on the other hand, the officer subculture is principally a product of prison work itself, largely unaffected by the kinds of individuals recruited into it, then the focus of efforts to change the role and behavior of officers must be on the structure and conditions of prisons themselves.

Clearly the popular image of prisons and guards favors the importation model. In her best-seller, *Kind and Usual Punishment*, Jessica Mitford (1973, p. 10) championed this view:

> A reading of recent congressional hearings on prison conditions reveals, *not unexpectedly*, that beyond those men and women who become guards because they have no alternative, this occupation appeals to those who like to wield power over the powerless and to persons of sadistic bent. (Emphasis added.)

Mitford inferred that "the guard mentality . . . is not only a natural outcome of the job but a prerequisite for it" (p. 10). As former commissioner John Boone observed of his erstwhile employees, "[What kind of person becomes a] prison guard? Somebody that's going to have the heart and the guts to keep their brothers! To control and contain them!" (*Boston Globe*, 26 January 1975). From this perspective, the values of officers *prior to* their employment in prisons correspond with the worst features of the officer subculture. Once such men become members of the subculture, their private values serve to reinforce and perpetuate the values of the subculture.

Although social scientists who have studied prisons have not directly addressed the origins of the officer subculture, they, too, appear to lean toward the importation model. In those rare instances where officers are discussed in sociological literature on prisons, it is frequently their characters that are in question. Thus, the most common policy recommendation appears to be the recruitment of *better* prison officers, implying that there is something seriously wrong with those currently employed.

My personal experiences as an officer inclined me toward the opposite view. I had assumed the position of prison officer with attitudes sympathetic to inmates and skeptical of officers. Within a very short time at the prison my sympathies and loyalties lay with officers and my skepticism was directed toward inmates. Other new officers appeared to be as influenced by their prison experiences as I, and to undergo similar transitions in their attitudes and allegiances.

The longitudinal study of officers reported here led to different conclusions. Neither "importation" nor "prisonization" by itself accounted for what happened to officer recruits and the "society of captors" that they joined. The officer subculture and the process of acculturation appeared to be products of a complex inter-action of importation, socialization, deportation, and cultural evolution. In this chapter I shall consider the contribution made to the subculture by the importation of values.

If the officer subculture is "imported" into the prison, then the values of new officers should be closely in line with the values of the subculture as it already exists. I shall devote this chapter, then, to an examination of demographic characteristics, recruitment patterns, motivations, and attitudes of the forty Massachusetts recruits who were part of this study.

## Recruitment

Massachusetts in the 1970s had a depressed economy with high unemployment. At the same time, the Massachusetts prison system had a high turnover rate among officers and a chronic need for new officers. Yet the Massachusetts Department of Correction was hard pressed to fill each new training class with recruits. The waiting lists of applicants to police and fire departments were years long, while corrections with its similar salary and benefits was in reality a "walk-in" job. Screening and selection were largely limited to investigation of possible criminal records of applicants. So haphaz-ard was the system that the correction officer exam was not even given for six years. The prison officer recruit was largely self-selected.

Who were these Massachusetts recruits? How were they recruited to the job? What motivated them to become prison officers? In what ways did their attitudes coincide with the officer subculture as portrayed in Chapters 4–6, and in what ways did they differ?

*Demographic characteristics.* Most of the forty Massachusetts recruits who were part of this study were young, white men who had no formal education beyond high school and a history of blue-collar employment. The average age of the recruits was 24 years, the range being 19 to 31 years. For almost two-thirds of the recruits schooling had stopped at high school; only 15 percent had a college degree. Three-quarters had been exclusively employed in blue-collar jobs since entering the work force. Four (10 percent) were members of a racial minority group. Demographic data for all recruits and for recruits sent to Walpole are presented in Table 1.

*Recruitment patterns.* Three-quarters of the recruits were prompted to apply by relatives or friends who were already em-

*Table 1.*  Demographic characteristics: Massachusetts prison officer recruits and Walpole recruits

|                              | All recruits (N=40) | Walpole recruits (N=13) |
| ---------------------------- | ------------------- | ----------------------- |
| Age                          |                     |                         |
|   Mean             | 23.9                | 24.4                    |
|   Median           | 23                  | 23                      |
|   Range            | 19–31               | 19–31                   |
| Marital status[a]            |                     |                         |
|   Married          | 20 (50%)            | 6 (46%)                 |
|   Not married      | 19 (48%)            | 7 (54%)                 |
| Education                    |                     |                         |
|   College graduate | 6 (15%)             | 1 ( 8%)                 |
|   Some college     | 9 (23%)             | 3 (23%)                 |
|   High school      | 25 (63%)            | 9 (69%)                 |
| Race                         |                     |                         |
|   White            | 36 (90%)            | 10 (77%)                |
|   Black            | 3 ( 8%)             | 2 (15%)                 |
|   Native American  | 1 ( 3%)             | 1 ( 8%)                 |
| Military service[a]          |                     |                         |
|   Yes              | 12 (31%)            | 5 (38%)                 |
|   No               | 27 (68%)            | 8 (62%)                 |
| Previous employment[b]       |                     |                         |
|   No previous full-time job | 4 (11%)    | 1 ( 8%)                 |
|   Prior blue-collar employment | 28 (74%) | 9 (70%)                |
|   Prior white-collar employment | 5 (15%) | 3 (23%)                |

[a] Data missing for one recruit.

[b] Data missing for three recruits.

ployed by the Department of Correction, usually as prison officers. Recruitment in these cases was often casual in nature. One recruit reported,

> A friend of mine works at Walpole. He's been there three years now. Called me up one day and he said he knew I was looking for a job that I could make decent money. He said, "They're hiring for correction officer, are you interested?" I said, "Ah, I don't think so." So then I started thinking about it and I said to myself, "Jesus, it doesn't sound too bad." He started telling me about the money he made and the security in there. So I said, "Well, I don't know." He said, "Well, why don't you fill out an

application and give it a shot. If you don't like it, you can always quit." So I said to myself, "Gee, that's all right with me. I'll try it." So here I am.

A recruit's acquaintance with individuals already employed in prisons appeared to play two important roles in his becoming an officer. First, such individuals were a source of information. Corrections is not a high-profile career, one that readily comes to mind to the average job seeker. According to a Louis Harris survey, only 1 percent of high school students ever consider becoming a guard (reported in Jacobs and Grear, 1980, p. 275). Important information about the job—availability, application procedures, salary, and so forth—were thus more accessible to those with an inside contact. Second, and probably more important, contact with individuals already employed as prison officers served to "normalize" the job in the eyes of the prospective applicant. Even if employment as a prison officer does come to mind, most individuals would be deterred from applying by the stigma attached to the guard role in American society. Personal contact with officers helped to counter prevalent stereotypes about officers and made the job seem less foreboding. After all, this friend or relative seemed not to conform to the steel-booted stereotype of the brutish guard, and he had survived the job with body intact and a few good stories to tell. The role played by relatives and friends already employed in prisons in encouraging the recruits to apply should not be confused with any sort of organized effort by the Massachusetts Department of Correction. Indeed, the failure of the department to generate candidates was perhaps the most striking feature of officer recruitment.

The remainder of the recruits found their way to corrections via diverse routes. Four were law enforcement majors in college who were encouraged to apply for a job in prisons by college placement officers or teachers. Two were steered toward corrections by contacts on the police force. Another two had had independent contacts with prisons—in one case via a church group, in another through incarceration of a close relative. Finally, several, such as the officer quoted below, simply wandered into the job.

I was basically out of a job for maybe eight months or so and I needed to do something. I went into a bar, right, and this guy was in there. They were talking about the correctional institute . . . And I said, "Are you people guards?" And they said, "Yeah." And I started questioning them about it and how much money they made and everything like that. One of the guys was doing some hiring for the training academy and I said, "Hey, why not? I'll try it. I'll give it a try." And that's how—before I went into that bar I had no idea that I would have been interested in corrections.

## Motivation

How a recruit came to learn about the job still does not tell us much about why he actually applied for it and, when offered it, accepted it. Friends, college teachers, and officers in bars must suggest employment as a prison officer to many individuals who reject the prospect out of hand. As one officer dryly observed, "Who the hell wants to be a prison guard?" What, then, were the principal motivations of the recruits in this study for becoming prison officers?

Mitford, as previously quoted, suggests that "beyond those men and women who become guards because they have no alternative, this occupation appeals to those who like to wield power over the powerless and to persons of sadistic bent" (1973, p. 10). But in Massachusetts we need not look far "beyond those . . . who . . . have no alternative" to find the predominant recruitment pattern for officers. In fact, Mitford's rule of thumb might be reversed: beyond those interested in law enforcement or social work careers, this occupation appealed to the unemployed and to individuals from communities in which *any* state job was considered upwardly mobile.

*Economic motivation.* Slightly more than half (53 percent) of the forty recruits in this study cited economic considerations as their only or primary reason for becoming prison officers. Of these, most had been or were about to be laid off from their most recent job. Virtually all of the remainder of this group were working in blue-collar jobs without security or long-term benefits. Many had applied for a range of civil service jobs accessible to men with only a high school education, principally fire fighters, police officers, postal workers, and prison officers. Lacking the political connections or minority status deemed necessary to obtain highly sought-after positions in the post office or fire and police departments, invariably their first and only offer had been from the Department of Correction. An officer from southeast Massachusetts explained, "Where I come from . . . it's the factories. You either work in a factory and don't make a heck of a lot of money or you get a break and go to an

institution or get a break and become a police officer or something."
A young recruit who rejected college for the factories and then the
factories for the prison reasoned,

> Why should I go and spend my mother's money . . . to go to
> college and then if I ain't going to make it, and I ain't the
> smartest student in the world either . . . I says, "Well what am
> I going to do?" So I says, "I'm going to make myself money and
> get ahead." So I went to the factory and I started working and I
> started putting money in the bank. And I did it for a year with
> all greenhorns . . . they all spoke Portuguese. A real sweatshop.
> Sweat every day and get black and clean up all the muck. I'd do
> real filthy jobs. And then I'd get out of there and I'd say, "Some
> day I'm going to get a job where I'm going to be clean, and I ain't
> going to have to be punching the clock . . . and really get so
> filthy and tired" . . . And that's why I come into a job like this.
> This is like a big thing for me. I was making sixty dollars,
> seventy dollars a week. This is more money. And I feel, if
> they're going to give me this much money, why shouldn't I do
> my best at it?

Mitford appeals to our common sense regarding the moral inade-
quacy of those who go to work in prisons. "For after all," she in-
quires, "if we were to ask a small boy, 'What do you want to be when
you grow up?' and he were to answer, 'A prison guard,' should we
not find that a trifle worrying—cause, perhaps, to take him off to a
child guidance clinic for observation and therapy?" (1973, p. 8). The
answer, of course, is "no," not if he were from a lower-class, immi-
grant community in southeast Massachusetts, and not just because
parents there are unlikely to take their children to a therapist no
matter what they said they wanted to be. The fact of the matter is
that the recruits were typically drawn from towns and cities with
high unemployment rates—communities in which a state job, *any*
state job, was considered an extraordinary opportunity not only for
the individual but for his immediate and often extended family as
well. Taking such a position was regarded as upwardly mobile not
for its *power* but for its financial security and benefits. (So proud, in
fact, were the families of these recruits for becoming prison officers
that some officers found it extremely difficult later to quit the job
even when they were desperate to do so, a matter to be discussed in
Chapter 9.)

> I'm in there for a job for my family . . . I've worked in construction and [been] laid off three Christmases in a row and that's hard. But now we're seeing checks come in and . . . we'll be able to start a future. And that's the whole thing with us, is some future, getting things going right . . . We want to have children . . . And a correction officer, it's got the security, and it's got advancement, and it's got a career.

Another recruit with a young family who had held a succession of blue-collar jobs echoed these sentiments.

> I just want a good job really. I don't know how that sounds, but that's what I really am looking for, a good job that I can get things that I want. And I'm married. I want a pretty good pay check every week and that's about it.
>
> *But when you say it's a good job, what about the job do you think makes it a good job?*
>
> The pay and everything, compared to—. . . There's no other jobs around, really. So I'm going to have to say the pay and the security and that's all I can think of.

Even when a recruit was not married, family and security considerations often played a major role. A recruit who was all of twenty years old explained,

> The biggest thing was I was looking for a job that had a future to it and I figured that this job definitely does have a future to it . . . And it was a job that paid well, whereas I checked out a lot of places around and they're offering poor hours and poor benefits and poor salary. And I can't see myself working in a factory all my life for three, three-fifty an hour . . . See, my father worked for a place for twenty-two years . . . and it closed down and he lost all his seniority. See? So security is playing a big part in my family right now . . . If there was jobs all over the place right now offering two hundred dollars a week to do this and to do that and there was a future in it or something I might say maybe this isn't for me. But somewhere in your life I really feel that you have to decide. You do, you have to.

One-third of the recruits could cite *no* reason other than economic need for taking the job.

*Social work motivation.* Eleven of the recruits (28 percent) reported that they applied to be prison officers primarily out of a desire to help inmates. Theirs are what I have termed "social work" motivations. Some of these recruits spoke of the satisfaction they would feel from helping a single individual:

*What will you like best about the job?*

Knowing that if I can go into . . . one of the institutes and help even just one person out, that will make me feel good and that's what I want.

To some extent such sentiments may have been but a thin veneer over a more fundamental drive to be employed. One seasoned Walpole officer wryly observed:

I didn't want to be a correctional officer. There was no way I could see working in a prison . . . But yet you do it because you feel you need to for your family . . . [Department officials] say, "Why do you want to be a correctional officer?" And everybody, because of the modern correctional philosophies, they say, "I like to help people." But that's a bunch of bullshit. They are doing it because it pays two hundred bucks a week and it's a difficult job to get but not that difficult for a good-paying job with state security, if you are looking for security—financial security and job security.

What this officer had felt himself and observed of other officers may have been true to an extent, yet I think it is hard to deny the sincerity and depth of motivation of some of the recruits, especially those who saw their helping roles in more comprehensive terms. One such recruit said,

It takes a certain type of person to be a good correction officer, the helping correction officer and not the screw . . . I feel I'm a genuine, caring person. And as long as I have this attitude that I give a damn about this person, that attitude will come across in responses from inmates, knowing that I'm not there just to write them up and keep them in their cells, but to give them the break they need to get back on the street.

A surprising number of recruits reported that they themselves had had scrapes with the law as youths or had friends or family who had been in trouble, even gone to prison. These experiences often provided the motive to reach out to those currently incarcerated. One recruit had given up a job in a trade with good pay to become an officer. A close relative of his had spent years in different institutions before his death. This relative was someone who the recruit felt "could have been cured and never was."

> I like the feeling of helping someone. I've never done college or nothing, so I really don't have the education to do it. But I feel as though I am capable of helping someone to a certain degree. And I feel as though I can help these people . . .
>
> *And [in your previous job] you don't think you're able to do that?*
>
> Not on a personal basis. My job, I wasn't in contact with people personally. I just did my job and that was it. This way here I'm in contact with different types of people and their attitudes . . .
>
> *How do you think you could go about helping somebody in an institution, say someone like [your relative]?*
>
> Just being like a friend to them, I think. Understanding his problem, where I could understand his problem because I've lived with it and I just feel as though maybe me talking to the person about their problem might be able to help them to a certain extent.

The possibility of helping people was a dimension lacking in this recruit's previous job, a disaffection shared by others. A recruit who had had repeated scrapes with the law himself as a youth and had held several blue-collar jobs before joining the Massachusetts Department of Correction reflected,

> I think basically all the other kinds of jobs I did, I never really got into a job where I could do some good for people. And I really don't know if I can in this job, but I think maybe the opportunity is there where maybe I can do some good for somebody, rather than having a finished product being material. Knowing that I actually did a human being some good.

Four of the eleven recruits who gave social work motivations as their principal reason for becoming officers were, or were about to be, college graduates. The prison job was typically their first full-time job and was seen as a way station to other careers in counseling, criminal justice administration, law, and related fields. These college-educated recruits tended to see themselves more as critics and reformers of the system than as members of it.

*Law enforcement motivation.* Eight (20 percent) of the recruits gave as their principal motivation for taking the job their desire to be law enforcement officers per se. This group is worth examining in greater detail for they would seem to be the recruits most likely to be attracted to the position of prison officer by its power and authority.

One of the stereotypes of the prison officer is that of the "frustrated cop"—individuals whose real ambition to be a policeman has been thwarted. For them, corrections is second best. If they can't bust criminals on the streets, they can at least do it in the joint. As mentioned, a number of recruits in this study had also applied for police officer positions. Some of these were individuals who gave economic or social work motivations for taking the prison job; they had generally applied to police departments in the same spirit in which they had applied to postal, fire, and correction departments. But the "law enforcement" recruits appeared more intent on the police jobs, and most had in fact applied or considered applying to police departments (two had considered military careers). When their police applications were unsuccessful, some turned to corrections as a "foothold in the door of law enforcement," with the hope of eventually making the shift to police. As one Massachusetts officer (not a member of the longitudinal study) admitted, "I'm a correction officer because I wanted to be a cop and I couldn't make it. And I'll be honest, I took the state police exam, I took it twice, and I never, never made it. So I says, well this is the field I want to get into. So I'm a correction officer." What was it that attracted recruits to the role of law enforcement officer, be it prison officer or police officer?

In explaining their attraction to the role of officer, the law enforcement recruits focused primarily on external considerations: family tradition and a desire to achieve status in the community. Five of the eight were sons or nephews of police or prison officers. (Of the thirty-two recruits who claimed economic or social work motivations, only six mentioned that they were sons or nephews of officers.) Several had a family tradition of uncles, fathers, and brothers in the criminal justice system. They had "grown up" with the law and saw themselves maintaining a continuity as naturally as sons enter a family business. Others were attracted by the status of being an officer. In fact, it was in large part the greater glamour and prestige of the police force that made it seem preferable to prison work. The officer's relationship with the *offender* was surprisingly absent in most of these interviews, but there were exceptions.

Two officers were attracted by what might be called the fantasy role of the officer vis-à-vis the offender. Both traced their ambitions to be a law enforcement officer to childhood fantasies that had been in large part created and sustained by television.

> You know when you're a little kid, all the kids want to be either a fireman or a policeman? I wanted to be a policeman, and this is on the same idea, law enforcement. So I think that's really all it was.
> *Why do you want to be a correctional officer now instead of a policeman?*
> Probably because my [relative] is. I'm just following him.
> *What is it about law enforcement that you find very interesting?*
> Cops and robbers. Like the type of thing like you see on TV. Just a little childhood fantasy I guess . . . Still a kid [*laughter*].

> *How did you get interested in law enforcement back when you were a kid?*
> I had a lot of idols from TV, law enforcement people.
> *[Like the] lone ranger?*
> Yeah. That was one of them. I used to always look at the Texas Rangers. I can remember . . . all the big law enforcement men from out west.

Cops versus robbers, Texas Rangers versus outlaws: the orientation of these two recruits takes on an almost stylized character. In both cases, though, these fantasy images were related to conceptions of authority and, eventually, to the way in which these recruits would deal with real life inmates.

Finally, two of the recruits saw themselves as society's avengers. They couched their motivations in terms of their personal hostility to criminals. As one of the two put it:

> It really burns me that people . . . commit crimes day after day and beat up people and do things and get away with it. I'd like to see it changed. Being a police officer maybe you can do your job just so much better to see these guys put away. I used to have to go around backing up my brother who's a lot younger than me. And they're punks. That's all they are. They just gang up and try to beat him up and I wouldn't stand for that, cop or no cop. Just lay it on the line. "Touch my brother and you're going to mess with me and you're going to have a lot of problems." I think that a good cop can get a good charge on some-

body. They can put them away where they belong. I've seen corrections that you're part of it, too. And that I like.

It was these two recruits out of the forty interviewed who came closest to the stereotype of the punishment-oriented recruit at least in terms of expressed motivation.

Motivation for taking a prison position does not tell the whole story regarding a recruit's orientation to prisons and prisoners. An individual who is motivated to become a prison officer solely by economic concerns may still hold inmates in contempt and see his role inside the prison in punitive terms. Alternatively, an individual who is attracted to the job for the prestige of being a uniformed officer may yet have sympathetic attitudes to inmates. To what extent, then, did the attitudes of the recruits seem compatible with the values of the officer subculture, especially as exemplified at Walpole? More specifically, to what extent did their attitudes reflect hostility or lack of sympathy to inmates?

## Attitudes

The recruits ranged from those who personally and politically identified with inmates and categorically rejected the officer subculture to those who held the opposite views and allegiances. Thus one recruit asserted, "It's an 'us' against 'them' type of code of ethics we're working against. I'm not comfortable with that because I've been 'them' too long . . . I find being 'us' now is not the best thing in the world. I think 'them' is the better type of people." These views would have been anathema to another recruit who identified with "us," the officers, and observed of inmates, "These guys are animals. They're really animals in there . . . [The officers] are on the right side of the fence . . . The good people look up to the law because law is good, law is right, law is what is right." While these two recruits may have represented extremes along the continuum of attitudes and allegiances of all the recruits, they were not alone in their views.

Those whose attitudes were mainly positive toward inmates tended to view criminality as the result of poor environment or bad parenting or as symptomatic of an unjust society. They viewed inmates as not unlike themselves or, at the very least, emphasized their common humanity. Many either had preexisting friendships with inmates or expected, as officers, to develop such friendships.

They were capable of taking the inmates' perspective on problems within the institution and, if not always adopting that perspective as their own, they at least advocated good (or better) treatment of inmates. Finally, they often expressed a desire to help inmates or at least were supportive of treatment strategies within the institutional framework.

Recruits who were less sympathetic toward inmates tended to see criminality as the fault of the individual, something that marked him as fundamentally different from other people, especially law enforcement officers. In keeping with this perspective, these recruits usually rejected the idea that an officer could be friends with an inmate. They felt deeply the harm inflicted by criminals on society, especially victims of violent crime, and were inclined to think that inmates, even at Walpole, were insufficiently punished. Some nevertheless expressed a desire to help selected inmates (particularly young first offenders) and most were supportive of at least some treatment or educational programs in prisons, although they suspected that the majority of inmates abused such privileges.

The interviews were not sufficiently standardized to permit reliable categorization of recruits along this continuum of attitudes to inmates, but careful reading of the interviews suggests that a far higher number of recruits conformed to the first profile—that of the recruit sympathetic to inmates—than to the second. Twenty-two of the recruits appeared to hold views that were predominantly positive or sympathetic to inmates while only seven held views that seemed on the whole negative or unsympathetic. The remaining eleven recruits expressed ambivalent attitudes.

Recruits' attitudes toward officers also varied considerably, although the recruits were much less definite in their ideas about officers than they were in their opinions about inmates. One out of every four expressed serious reservations about at least a sizable portion of their future colleagues. One recruit sketched a fairly stereotyped picture of the cold, brutal "screw":

> I would say that the typical screw is one that is basically a cold-hearted person who has no feeling for the inmate, thinks [of] every inmate as being like this—a table—having no feelings. "They're animals, they're not people." And I'm sure that most of them get mistreated. It seems to be a real vicious cycle . . . in the correctional system and the typical screw seems to perpetuate this type of cycle . . . Hopefully, hopefully I'll be different.

Such attitudes were far from universal, however. Most recruits seemed unsure of the nature of the officer corps and were hopeful of good relations with fellow officers, yet wanted to maintain some autonomy in their own behavior. A considerable number of recruits were clearly looking forward to their future association with officers and anticipated that officers would form a close-knit, supportive association of which they would be a part both within the institution and without.

Although the interviews with the recruits were not standardized and most questions were open-ended, all of the recruits were asked before the interviews to fill out a questionnaire regarding attitudes toward inmates and treatment strategies. In addition, during the interviews every recruit was asked, "What would be the worst thing you could do in your own eyes as an officer?" Responses to these questions shed some additional light on attitudes about becoming a prison officer.

The questionnaire presented a series of hypothetical dilemmas confronting officers in their relations with inmates and fellow officers. Respondents were asked to indicate not only how they felt about the way in which a hypothetical officer handled each situation, but also to predict how most other officers would feel. (The text of the questionnaire and a detailed analysis of responses may be found in Kauffman, 1985, pp. 399–409.)

On most of the questions, recruits approved of the hypothetical officer behaving in a way that was sympathetic to inmates or treatment strategies. Thus,

100 percent approved of an officer defending a treatment staff member to the officer's colleagues even though the treatment staff member had been critical of "the way some of the correctional officers had been handling one of the inmates."

95 percent approved of an officer volunteering for assignment in a treatment program in order "to help inmates."

95 percent felt that an officer who broke up a fight between inmates should investigate and do nothing if the fight was not serious, rather than give the inmates an automatic "write-up."

93 percent approved of an officer informally defending an inmate to his fellow officers.

84 percent approved of an officer formally defending an inmate
at a disciplinary board hearing against charges levied by a
fellow officer.

In their responses to all five of these questions the recruits indicated
considerable sympathy for the inmates' position and for treatment
strategies in a prison. The responses to three other questions suggested less sympathy:

79 percent approved of an officer refusing to discuss controversial new rules with inmates.

63 percent approved of an experienced officer applying for a job
in the gun towers—a position remote from the inmates and
symbolic of the conflict between officers and inmates.

45 percent approved of an officer *not* intervening when fellow
officers were roughing up an inmate.

Recruits who approved of refusing to discuss controversial new rules
with inmates may have been demonstrating their loyalties to their
new employers more than anything else. Those who approved of an
officer applying for a gun tower position seem to have been posi-
tively disposed toward an officer applying for any job that he desired.
(The recruits as a group registered much stronger approval of an
officer taking a position in a treatment program—95 percent—than
they did of an officer taking a position in the gun towers—63 percent. Furthermore, only 8 percent of the recruits said they "strongly
approved" of an officer applying for a gun tower position while 69
percent "strongly approved" of an officer applying for a treatment
position.)

The question on which the recruits' responses seemed least pos-
itively disposed toward inmates' interests was the one that inquired
whether an officer should intervene when fellow officers were
roughing up an inmate who had caused a disturbance. The question
did not ask whether the respondent approved of an inmate being
roughed up by officers, but only whether another officer should
actively interfere with the way in which his fellow officers were
handling the situation. Such intervention would represent a much
more serious breach of officer solidarity than, say, defending an
inmate informally and privately to fellow officers. Nevertheless,
responses to this question suggest limits on sympathies for
inmates—or willingness to act on those sympathies—on the part of
at least a sizable minority of recruits.

Significantly, the recruits as a group apparently perceived that their future co-workers were far less sympathetic toward inmates and treatment than they were themselves. For example, while 93 percent of the recruits approved of defending an inmate informally to other officers and 84 percent approved of defending an inmate at a disciplinary board hearing, their perceptions were that only 47 percent and 30 percent, respectively, of all officers would similarly approve. The pattern was consistent on all but one question. (On the question regarding whether an officer should discuss rules with inmates, 21 percent of the recruits approved of an officer refusing to discuss the rules; their perception was that approximately 23 percent of all officers would give the same response.) *These data suggest that most recruits entered prison work without the expectation that their attitudes would coincide with those of the officer corps as a whole.* At least at this stage, the recruits did not apparently feel the need to tailor their own views to those of other officers.

Most responses by the forty recruits to the question, "What would be the worst thing you could do in your own eyes as an officer?" could be classified into one of the following five categories: (1) to misuse inmates, (2) to let oneself be misused by inmates, (3) to become like the other officers, (4) to antagonize other officers, and (5) to violate major rules of the institution.

Twelve (30 percent) of the recruits felt that the worst thing they could do would be in some way to harm an inmate: to punish him unfairly, push him around, show him lack of respect, or, at the most extreme, to injure or kill him. Theirs was a concern for misusing powers they were soon to acquire as officers over the lives of inmates, whether it be the power of the man in the gun tower or simply that of an authority figure whose actions and demeanor could undermine feelings of self-worth of those under their control.

> What's the worst thing I could do? Mentally damage an inmate . . . Just harass him to the point where he flips out or he comes to [have] such a chip on his shoulder when he gets out that two days later he's going to be back . . . That would just [be] the one thing I want to avoid because I think it's so easy for a correction officer to mentally change an inmate . . . I think you're supposed to build up a person and not tear him down.

Half as many recruits (15 percent) feared the opposite: misuse *they* might receive at the hands of inmates, such as being hurt physically by them, losing control to them, allowing inmates to get something on them, being placed in a position where, rather than being superior, the officer is cast in the subordinate role.

Four recruits (10 percent) felt the worst thing they could do would be to become like the other officers, to "become one of 'them'—or one of 'us,' I mean—. . . a full-hearted one of 'us.' " "Go out there and just lose my identity, become a real pig." "Become the mechanical robot type of correctional officer." "Conform to something I don't want to be." Theirs was not just a sympathy with inmate interests but an outright rejection of the officer corps. Their opposite number, in a sense, were two recruits (5 percent) who feared nonacceptance by fellow officers—being denied the opportunity to "become one of us."

Finally, ten of the recruits (25 percent) responded that the worst thing they could do would be to violate a major institutional rule such as "lugging" drugs or permitting an escape. In almost every case, the underlying concern was with doing something so serious that their jobs would be jeopardized. This concern for job security is consistent with the economic motivation that led most of the recruits to seek the job in the first place.*

In sum, the recruits as a group seemed far more concerned about endangering the interests of inmates or becoming stereotyped officers than they were about being abused by inmates or not being accepted by fellow officers. But within this context of a preponderant sympathy toward inmate interests, there was considerable diversity in orientations and points of view among individual members of the group.

## Assignment

Clearly the values of the recruits *as a group* were not closely in line with those of the officer subculture as characterized in Chapter 5.

---

* Four of the six miscellaneous responses were: not do the job, lie to someone (anyone), bring problems into the prison, and be "buddies" with an inmate. In addition, two recruits responded that the worst thing they could do would be to participate in gang-beating an inmate or in beating an inmate who was handcuffed. I did not classify the last two responses as ones indicating fear of misusing inmates. Both of these recruits condemned the types of beatings they mentioned on the grounds that unequal odds would render the beatings "unfair" rather than because beating an inmate was in itself a bad thing. The vigor of their statements was directed more at officers who did such things than at concern for the inmate victims. In the context of the interviews with these two men as recruits and later as officers, I would interpret their statements as being consistent with fairly hostile attitudes toward inmates. (See Chapter 6 for a discussion of officers concerned about "fair violence.")

Theirs was not an unquestioning loyalty to the officer corps. Few offered automatic support to fellow officers in conflict with inmates nor, for that matter, to their fellow officers in conflict with the administration, the public, or the recruit's own personal beliefs. If anything, they seemed more inclined to portray themselves as partisans of the inmates than as partisans of the officers.

But while the values of the average recruit may have varied markedly from those of the officer subculture at an institution like Walpole, the values of *some* of the recruits did not. Furthermore, the institutions themselves varied in character. Violent, punitive Walpole represented an institutional extreme, as did the rigors of the officer "code" observed there. Other institutions were more relaxed and free of sustained hostility between officers and inmates.

The recruits were not randomly assigned. If they had been carefully matched with the different institutions according to their personal philosophies and styles, then an argument might still exist for the importation of subcultural norms. Furthermore, differences in institutions could also then in large part be accounted for by differences in the recruits sent to them.

The recruits in this study were hired and sent to the training academy without knowing to which institution they would be assigned. During their weeks at the academy they were assessed by the staff, who waited until the final days of the course to make their decisions about who would go to which prison. Their decisions were heavily constrained by institutional staffing needs, geography (recruits living within commuting distance of a major institution where vacancies existed were not expected to move), and to some extent by the preferences of the recruits (who could effectively veto an assignment by resigning at the end of the course—a not insubstantial threat for a training academy staff under pressure to produce bodies).

The training staff were well aware of Walpole's reputation. They hoped to effect a gradual change in that institution by the slow infusion of a new type of Walpole officer trained and assigned by themselves. But they were also cognizant of the harsh realities of prison life at Walpole and sought to prevent gross mismatches between institutions and recruits. Thus the most militant advocates of inmate rights were not sent to Walpole, nor were the physically weakest or those whose appearance or behavior might have been construed as effeminate. (The militant, weak, and effeminate did not fare well wherever they were sent, but perhaps they fared better than they would have if they had gone to Walpole.)

Of the thirteen recruits assigned to Walpole only one had expressed a strong desire to be sent elsewhere. The other twelve had rejected Concord as too far, Norfolk as too dangerous, and Bridgewater as either too distant or its inmate population too distasteful. As a group, those sent to Walpole were slightly older, less well educated, and more racially diverse than the twenty-seven recruits who went to the other prisons, but the differences were not substantial. The Walpole recruits were also somewhat more likely to have cited economic or law enforcement motivations for taking the job. Social work motivations predominated for only one of them. Furthermore, I classified four of the thirteen recruits sent to Walpole as among the seven recruits having the least sympathetic attitudes toward inmates. On the other hand, I classified seven of the thirteen who went to Walpole as among the twenty-two recruits having predominantly sympathetic attitudes toward inmates. Though these seven may not have been as outspoken in their sympathies to inmates as some of the recruits sent elsewhere, their positive attitudes were for the most part clearly expressed in the interviews and seemed deeply felt. Thus, though the average recruit sent to Walpole tended to be somewhat more "conservative" than the average recruit sent elsewhere, the disparity between the attitudes of *most* of the Walpole recruits and the Walpole subculture remained great. (The disparity between the values of the most "radical" recruits and the institutions to which they were sent was even greater, especially at Concord.) It seems fair to conclude that assignment by training staff brought the attitudes of the recruits more closely in line with variations in the officer subcultures at different institutions than random assignment would have allowed, but that substantial disparities remained.

# 8

# Conflict and Change

Most prison officer recruits who were part of this study began their careers holding values that were different from, and in some cases opposed to, those held by their more experienced colleagues. How were these incongruities between the values of the officer subculture and those of its newest members handled? Did individual officers change to adopt the values of the subculture (socialization)? Or, failing that, were nonconformists, regardless of how numerous, excluded from the subculture (expulsion)? Or were the incongruities somehow tolerated and, under the influence of the diversification of membership, was the subculture itself made to change (evolution)?

## Socialization

Socialization implies a good deal more than mere accumulation of knowledge by new group members about group norms and attendant sanctions. Socialization at its most complete involves taking on values of the group as one's own (internalization) and, in the process, developing a sense of belonging to the group (identification). By implication, the values and perceptions of new group members are not initially identical to those of the group. The greater the divergence, the greater is the need for socialization or resocialization of new members.

Orville Brim (1968, p.559) noted that socialization in adulthood is usually concerned with overt behavior rather than with values in large part because values are much more difficult to instill in adults than in children. Brim cited two principal solutions used by society to deal with incongruities in values between adults and organizations.

> One is anticipatory, with attention being given to the selection of candidates for an adult organization, in order to screen out those who do not have appropriate motives and values for the anticipated roles. This helps to assure that those who enter the organization will not present difficult problems to the socialization program.

As discussed in the preceding chapter, the Massachusetts prison system was not notably successful in recruiting new members whose values at the outset closely matched those of the existing officer corps. In any case, "anticipatory" socialization may be of little relevance at an institution like Walpole, where the values of the officer subculture diverge substantially from those of the communities from which new members are drawn. Brim continued:

> A second solution is that society may accept conforming behavior alone as evidence of satisfactory socialization and may forgo any concern with value systems. This entails risk, for if the social system undergoes stress, then the conformity, since it is superficial anyway, may break down rapidly.

Of course, a characteristic of prisons like Walpole is constant stress. The drastic consequences of breakdown in conformity had been demonstrated often enough to make uniformity of *values*, not just behavior, seem essential to group survival. Thus, Walpole and other prisons like it may represent one of those rare contemporary arenas of adult socialization in which the inculcation of *values* takes precedence over adherence to behavioral norms. This emphasis is reflected in the discussion of socialization of officers at the four prisons studied.

*Socialization at Walpole.* To understand socialization at Walpole in the mid-1970s we should first look back to a less chaotic time. Walpole was a fairly stable institution in the 1950s and 1960s. The prison was run by a steady core of experienced officers; officer turnover rates were manageable. The prevailing pattern was socialization through silence. A new recruit, unless perhaps the son or nephew of an established officer, was studiously ignored. He had to glean what he could about expected behavior from watching experienced officers or frequently by seeking assistance from inmates.

The recruit was only gradually admitted to membership in the officer society and only as he proved himself worthy.

A Walpole officer of southern European descent described his initiation at Charlestown prison (Walpole's predecessor) in the 1940s:

> The old officers wouldn't tell you nothing at first. They resented us. Up in Boston everything was Irish. They had all Irish at Charlestown, so when these guys came in from New Bedford, they said, "Well here come the fishermen." So they resented us. It didn't bother me in the least. Once you proved yourself, then you were one of the boys.

Not long after he became an officer he successfully subdued a violent inmate. "The older officers saw that and that's what got me into the club."

Things had not changed appreciably two decades later. An officer hired in the late 1960s described his initiation on the 3–11 shift at Walpole:

> When I first started it was very, very difficult because in order to be accepted you had to be like everyone else . . . Everyone put [you] through a ritual, a big ritual like a voodoo dance or something like that where no one talked to you . . . After a couple of days, no one had really said anything to me other than saying, "This is how we take the count on this shift and this is how we do that." Nothing personal, all business, until like about the end of the first week, and I was saying "Holy mackerel, this is traumatic. No one's really talking to me." You had to be accepted first.

The turmoil of the early 1970s put an abrupt end to socialization through silence. While effective, the silent treatment as a socialization method took time, and during the years of crisis time was something Walpole officers did not have. Desperate for replacements for those of their colleagues who resigned each week of the crisis, they greeted anyone wearing the uniform with open arms. In an abrupt reversal, new officers were accepted unless they proved unworthy.

Walpole was not again in the 1970s to regain the order of the old regime, but by 1976 sufficient stability had been restored for a new socialization process to emerge, in many ways as inhospitable as the old. For most Walpole recruits it consisted of four phases: (1) the training academy, (2) on-the-job training (OJT), (3) the 7–3 shift, and (4) the 3–11 shift.

*Training academy.* A formal training program for officers had been inaugurated by the Department of Correction in the 1950s. In the mid-1970s, the course (which lasted approximately four weeks) was attended by all officer recruits prior to their assignment to any of the state's penal facilities. The academy was directed at that time by men committed to modern correctional philosophies, and it was staffed by former prison officers who had proved themselves capable in the day-to-day realities of prison work and yet were open to modernization of the system.

The first three days of the course were dramatic. On their arrival at the academy, the recruits were taken without prior notification to an old, renovated jail in Connecticut where they were locked in individual cells and treated as inmates by experienced Connecticut prison officers. Although no "real" inmates were present and the trainees knew that they would soon be released (how soon they were not quite sure), the experience was a powerful one for someone who had never "done time." The sense of vulnerability, the feeling of solidarity with one's fellow "inmates," the resentment toward guards who refuse seemingly minor and reasonable requests such as an extra match, the anger at being given a D-Report for a trivial offense, the positive role of raucous behavior (which at least reminds the individual in his isolation that others are nearby), the seeming morality of deceit that benefits the "inmate" and his fellows at the expense of the system: these lessons were powerfully taught. It was an experience that inevitably created sympathy with inmates, for it quite literally forced the new officer to stand in the other fellow's shoes. (I knew these feelings well, as my own training as a Connecticut officer in 1972 had begun in this fashion.)

The remainder of the training course provided an introduction to the Massachusetts judicial and correctional systems (including visits to all of the major prisons), taught rudimentary skills (use of firearms, cell and body searching techniques), and attempted to instill positive attitudes toward "modern" correctional approaches with emphasis on "interpersonal communication."

Armed with their minimal skills and a desire to fulfill the heady goals set for them at the academy, the rookie officers reported to their designated institutions for on-the-job training.

*OJT.* On-the-job training at Walpole was significant for the lost opportunity it represented. For their first one or two weeks at the prison, the new officers received a thorough physical orientation to the institution and "just went around and saw what was going on." Usually, although not always, the first week or two also included some time in a block with an experienced officer who would "show them the ropes." But that was the extent of their "training."

The officer in charge of training at Walpole apparently put as much effort into disabusing the new officers of attitudes acquired at the academy as he did teaching them about their new assignments. As he complained in a memorandum to the superintendent of Walpole regarding one class of trainees,

> They had an 'cmpathy attitude' towards the inmates that would certainly have created problems between the older experienced officers and themselves in innumerable ways—possibly leading to having to censure or dismiss from the service one or more of these new officers, if this empathy was not put into proper perspective, in a relatively short period of time.   (Memo dated November 18, 1976)

*The 7–3 shift.* Without further ado, the rookies were assigned cell blocks on the 7–3 shift. "They gave us about a week's training, a *week*! . . . Of course they told us we wouldn't get any blocks right away. I think we made it maybe another three or four days after that, then we started getting blocks." Those rookies who were assigned to a minimum-security cell block had another, presumably more experienced, officer working with them; those assigned to Block 10 worked with a number of other officers. But those who were placed in one of the maximum-security blocks were on their own. "It's like throwing fresh meat to the animals," observed one officer. Recalled another,

> I worked a block I think when I was there a week. A *block*! I didn't know what to do. I didn't know anybody. But they threw me in there . . . You'd go to feed a block and you'd have forty-five cons and you'd have enough meals for fifty and you'd end up twenty short. Guys would take three meals. You didn't know. You were brand new. But the administration doesn't care . . . And to find a guard that had been there for a while, you couldn't find him. There's more hiding places in that place than you can imagine—up in the gallery and down in the canteen and outside somewhere. They're hiding everywhere.

Even Block 10 with its high complement of officers was a terrifying experience for the rookie. "Ten Block is where you threw the rookies . . . They'd put as many rookies down there as they possibly could to fill up space. And they were so scared they could hardly walk."

Cell blocks are the most important and sensitive posts in a prison. The significance of assigning rookie officers to the blocks on their own without adequate preparation cannot, in my opinion, be over-emphasized. It had profound impact on the institution and on the new officers themselves. They were abandoned by the administration, isolated from their fellow officers, and left virtually at the mercy of inmates in their block. These initial weeks and months had a traumatic and lasting impact.

The rookie officers had entered Walpole confident of the administration's support. They had spent weeks at the training academy learning the principles of modern corrections and had been led to believe that the Department of Correction was prepared to practice those principles in concert with them *and* that the administration would provide them with such support as was necessary. The first few weeks in the institution provided overwhelming evidence to the contrary. Not only were brand-new officers immediately thrust into the most difficult and dangerous positions in the institution, but they were also given virtually no support in carrying out the task at hand. Officers reported that the day-shift supervisors took such little personal interest in them as rookies that the supervisors rarely knew the names of the new officers under them. Anonymous and unprepared, the rookies were sent immediately to the front lines where many became early casualties of the Walpole war. "A lot of these guys are just taken and thrown in there saying, 'Okay, this guy's going to be here for a while. If he doesn't work out, bingo! he's gone.' And they just put them through the academy like that."

More devastating for the Walpole rookie than his abandonment by the administration was the lack of support he received from his fellow officers. Two groups of officers predominated on the 7–3: rookies awaiting eventual transfer to the 3–11, and officers who had served their years on the 3–11 and had enough seniority to bid for positions on the 7–3 that involved scant contact with inmates. The latter group generally showed marked indifference to the plight of the former.

*How did you feel about them putting you, a brand-new officer, in [a max block] right from the beginning? Did you think that was a pretty crummy deal?*

Yeah. You're kind of lost. And one thing that I found out, that there were few officers around that were willing to help a new guy. You'd come in and here you are in a place like this, and you have to make decisions, and there's no one here to say, "Okay, what's normal procedure, and how do you handle this." Because you don't want to go overboard, yet you don't want to be lax about it. You'd like to know how they generally handle those things. So the whole time for me I had trouble knowing who I could talk to to find out how things are done. A lot of the officers weren't good officers and you didn't know whether to trust that person. So it was really hard in the beginning to find out and to judge who was a good officer . . .

*Was it hard to figure that out because you're so isolated in your own cell block?*

That was a problem. If you were working with a guy, the whole time you could watch him. But it was hard. And a lot of times you were there by yourself and had to handle things. And you couldn't constantly get on the phone. And the senior's running up and down the corridors, got things to do, and everybody in different blocks are asking him things. And you've got to try and grab him in between. Meanwhile, you've got five or six inmates yelling at you and trying to get something out of you . . .

*Do the officers seem to care much about the rookies?*

No. I'm the type that just goes along and most people get to know me as I go. There's some guys that are really outgoing . . . and they don't have any problems. But . . . that was difficult for me because it takes you a little bit longer for everyone to get to know you . . .

*Did [officers give] you a really hard time or [test] you? . . .*

Yeah. I ran into that a lot—not really even testing that much, but just not giving me the time of day. I would walk into a situation where you were with another officer and you'd come up and say, "How's it going," to the other guy, but he'd turn and start talking to an inmate before he would you . . . He just wouldn't give you the time of day, much more concerned with the inmate or talking to him. And then [he'd] just hand you the keys and say, "Okay, I'll see you later." And you'd have to say, "Hey wait a minute. What's the count, and what's going on, and give me a little feedback." And "Oh, the count's [*mumble, mumble*]." And then he wanted to get out of there . . .

*Is it really . . . them just not caring?*

To me it was more like just not caring. Because when someone comes along and everybody sits back, more or less sizes that
person up . . . I mean, just the basic hospitality, or whatever you
want to call it, they could give to you, like, just tell the basic
things. You're not asking for any big information or any ins and
outs of things. Just tell me what I'm supposed to do and I'll do
it . . . It got to be a thing where a lot of people were all for
themselves . . . "I'm going to go hide in here while this guy does
that chore" or whatever.

The actions of a rookie, of course, did not pass unnoticed. Some
officers observed and judged in a manner reminiscent of the old
silent treatment:

They just sit back and watch how you handle yourself. They'll
watch you in pressure situations and see if you're getting flus-
tered and nervous and excited and worried. And they can kind
of judge from there. But it takes a few incidents just to get your
name around . . . having people watch you dealing with inmates
before . . . something comes out saying, "Okay, he's okay."
People start accepting you.

Still others took note of a rookie's presence only to make him the
vehicle for their own amusement.

I had only been in the place for maybe two days when the
supervisor comes up to me and says, "Walk down [with] this
guy and pass out medication with him. Don't say nothing and
don't do nothing. Just walk down with him and take a peek in
room —— and look at this guy. Don't sit there and gawk at him,
but just look at him." I walked down there and a guy threw a
bucket of piss at me . . . Everything was going smooth until that
happened. Then I went right down and felt really depressed.

Incidents like that not only provided comic relief for some officers,
they also underscored the rookies' low status among officers and
served to alienate them from the inmates.

Thus the rookie was received by his fellow officers on the 7–3
shift with indifference seasoned with mild harassment and an occasional helping hand. It was a reception only slightly less hostile
than the "silent treatment" of the past. It served to impress the
rookie with his vulnerability, his lack of negotiating power regarding his own role within the prison community, and the necessity to
do things their way.

If the indifference of the administration and fellow officers served to isolate and alienate the new officer, there was still another group to which he might have turned—the inmates. One might expect that inmates would grasp such an opportunity to co-opt the rookie, to entice him to forge a different alliance, one sympathetic to the inmates' own plight. But to expect such an outcome would be to overestimate the rationality of forces at work at Walpole. Inmates used the inexperience and isolation of their new block officer to shorter-term advantage: to con the ignorant rookie into permitting, or failing to prevent, forbidden activities, from stealing food to murder, and to engage in the sport of mocking and intimidating their keeper. "It's constant testing over little things. One after another after another guy would come up to you and constantly test you. It was like unbelievable. When they had nothing to do, bingo! 'Okay, let's go play head games with the officer.' "

Even if only a small proportion of the inmates actually engaged in hostile and manipulative behavior, it was they who dominated the new officer's experience. Those inmates who were neither hostile nor manipulative were prevented by their own inmate code of conduct from positive interaction with the officer. And even if an inmate were to have made friendly overtures, the officer would have been likely to interpret it as simply part of another "con." Ironically, the officer most likely to bear the full brunt of the inmates' harassment was precisely that officer who was most easygoing and, at the outset, most sympathetic to the inmates. An officer who entered the institution with attitudes very sympathetic to inmates and ended up indifferent to their fate reflected on his first several months.

> I got so depressed and I hated the place, I couldn't stand coming in here.
> *What was it about it that depressed you about being here?*
> Just the environment, the whole environment, harassment [by] the inmates . . . Being a new officer, they're going to harass you, they're going to harass the hell out of you. They are going to test you and test you and test you. And being basically a nice guy, I was very subject to it, and I was open to it. I still get it, but I just sort of say, "Yeah, I know what you are doing, but it doesn't bother me any more."

Officers often compounded the problem by their own reactions to it.

> [Of] course, naturally I was a little uptight myself getting a block for the first time, so I might have said something to the

wrong person [in] that block. They put rats in my desk and everything! . . . First of all they wouldn't let me in the block—they knew I was new—and they had about ten inmates standing around the grill. They wouldn't let me in. So I didn't know whether they got mad at me because I pushed my way into the block—I put the key into the door and I just pushed my way in. And then there was somebody sitting in my chair so I asked him to get off the chair, and he did, but the next guy was sitting on the desk right in my way. So I told him, "Well, listen, you'd better get out of my way." And he wouldn't get out of my way. So I told him, "If you don't get out of my way I'm going to [*inaudible*]." Well, that was probably where I made my mistake. So he got off the desk. And then the whole block dispersed and they didn't bother me for the rest of the day . . . And they kind of stayed away and watched me. And after they watched me for that one day, I think they got right on my case. I couldn't believe it!

Putting rats in desks, holding doors closed, taking an officer's chair are petty harassments, the sort one might expect of unruly schoolchildren with a substitute teacher. But beneath it all was the reality of violence and the pervasiveness of fear at the prison. An officer described his reaction to his first few months:

It is kind of scary, especially when you hear a slam and you run to the slam and you don't know what you are going to expect. Fear of the unknown. And you hear all these other stories of all these other officers who are retired because somebody hit them over the head with a mop bucket or they were stabbed. Sure, it is scary!

For some, it took only the first cup of boiling water thrown in their face or their first sight of a sadistically mutilated corpse to harden their attitudes. Said one officer attacked twice in his first weeks, "I changed fast. Within two weeks my whole attitude had changed. What we were taught out at the academy went out the window. It was a bunch of horseshit." Even those not so radically changed often adopted a facade of toughness, which in turn reinforced the inmates' negative perceptions of officers, new or old, and helped perpetuate the cycle of hostilities. The outcome, in any event, was that whatever sympathetic attitudes an officer had held toward inmates on entering the institution were quickly, and permanently, extinguished.

Walpole recruits were even denied the "fellowship of suffering" that characterizes other groups who experience socialization through ordeal, such as military conscripts, medical interns, or fraternity initiates (Moore, 1969, pp. 878–879). The cell block officers were too isolated, the number of rookies at any one time too few, the hours too long to facilitate a banding together of fellow initiates on or off the job. Nor was such a fellowship encouraged at Walpole, as is done in other settings to promote esprit de corps. The rookie officers at Walpole suffered largely alone. If theirs was a fellowship at all, it was a fellowship of despair.

Their months on the 7–3 shift left few of the rookies unscathed and many deeply depressed.

> They come in [with] the same attitude all the time. But you can see some changes in the new guys. You really can. I think when they come in they are really nervous, as *I* was, and everybody else was, whether they admit it or not, was scared . . . They will come in and they will try to listen and be kind of funny and everything and then a few weeks later you see them and they have a frown on their face and they look so depressed. And I can only empathize with that, because I went through the same thing. The same thing.

Whatever ideals the recruits had held on entering the institution, whatever hopes they had had for playing a positive social role were long gone. Their once lofty goals had been reduced to a desperate desire to make it through each day—and onto the 3–11.

*The 3–11 shift.* Most of the rookie officers were transferred to the 3–11 shift after several months on the 7–3. Transfer to the 3–11 came as a major relief. The switch in shifts heralded immediate changes in the rookie's relations with his supervisors, his fellow officers, and the inmates.

The 3–11 was dominated by a single shift supervisor. He had risen rapidly through the ranks during the turmoil of the early 1970s despite the fact that he consistently bucked the administration. "He was the only guy that was going up and still fighting the administration . . . And everyone looked up to him because he was so powerful because he could do this and he never licked anybody's boots and he was still getting up on his own." Those who worked with him described him as "ramrod tough," "hated" yet "respected" by the inmates, a "General Patton," but "very, very fair" and devoted to his officers. As is crucial at an institution like Walpole, during times of crisis he "had enough common sense to seem to make the right decision all the time."

> Some man! He was one of the best. I'd take him before I'd take any of them out there because, number one, all the guys out there respected him, officers and inmates alike . . . A problem can arise, he can come in and talk to [the inmates], smoking his cigar and he can really bring things back under control. It's just the way he carries himself.

> Great supervisor . . . This is one guy that can maintain a level head in stressful situations. When you're working for a guy like that you feel a lot safer than if you're working for somebody that is going to get nervous and blow up and not be able to think in a stressful situation. When this guy is on, it's fantastic.

It is probably not too extreme to say that the 3–11 was run in his image. As he exemplified central values of the officer subculture, including the acceptability of violent sanctions, so did his shift and, eventually, the new men on it.

> He had us running things his way, but I liked it that way. He [made] you {aware of} what he wanted and what you were going to do . . . He had everything the way he wanted it and it was going to stay that way. When he needed a man in the block, he told you to work in the block, "You go work there." And you don't complain. And, see, it wasn't like that on the first shift.

The force of his personality was felt immediately by rookies assigned to the 3–11.

> [He] took us aside and . . . he put us here and there. He introduced us to people. He told the 3-to-11 shift to "make these guys feel as comfortable as possible and give them all your knowledge you can." And he took time to get to know you. He knew my name off the bat . . . And like he sat down and went through our files and said, "Oh, you've been here. Good, good." And he asked us personal questions like he was interested. And he *was*. It was real.
> *Sounds like the basics of good management.*
> Definitely. That's all it was. He knew his job, and he was doing it sincerely, too.

He paid close attention to each officer's progress, offering both criticism *and* praise—the latter a very rare commodity at Walpole. And he systematically weeded out those who failed to meet his standards. He instilled a pride in his officers that they had desperately lacked in the preceding months. "He made the job seem like it was a worth-while job." And he put an instant end to the rookies' isolation.

These *were* merely the basics of good management, but they were basics so sorely lacking in the rest of the institution that it gave this supervisor enormous stature in the eyes of his officers. What is more, it earned him their devotion.

Wilbert Moore (1969) contends that strong, positive affect in relations between socializer and socializee is necessary for the internalization of norms. He observed that "it is the expectations of significant others that induce normative compliance and, normally, an actual sharing of attitudes and beliefs. This sharing, whether or not fully articulated, then constitutes an occupational identity, which is collective as well as individual. The individual *belongs*" (p. 878, emphasis in original). No other figure loomed so large in the lives and affections of the officers. Members of the 3–11 shift developed strong bonds with one another, but this supervisor was central to the bonding process. To rookie officers in particular, he was *the* "significant other" and the embodiment of their occupational identity.

His example was followed by officers on the 3–11 in their treatment of rookies. Gone was the indifference of the 7–3. "They said, 'We're glad to have you,' congratulating me like it's great being on this shift, and telling me all about it. They sat down and they took the time to tell you what you had to do . . . And I think the officers, the supervisors, deputy, on that shift had a lot to do with that. I think they were the best." Officer unity was emphasized. Every officer was primed to safeguard his fellow officers.

> Everybody's communicating with each other [on the 3–11], everybody's together with everything and it's just the way the operation is run. And you feel a lot safer working with something that's organized than something that's not organized. You [are] going to go [on the 7–3] and take somebody out of a block and don't even know how? What procedures you're going to use? All you know is you're going down there? With the 3-to-11 shift, they know exactly what's going to happen when they go down there.

With the officers united and disciplined, the balance of power between block officer and inmates was dramatically altered. The inmates could no longer press their advantage over the lone rookie in their block.

> See, the 3-to-11 shift had their system together. They have everybody organized. They don't do anything without the other officers there. If an incident come down, they walk outside, slam that door, everybody locks their door, and everybody gets together and goes down and they deal with it. I don't care if it's just two guys getting ready to fight. But they see that they're in unity and that whatever goes down, all the officers [are] going to be there together. So [the inmates] respect them in that way. If they've got to feed, they feed prompt, right on time. If you come down and get your food, you get it. If you don't, you don't. Everything is tick-tock around the clock and this is the way that the 3-to-11 shift carry themselves. And the inmates just fall into *their* system instead of the officers falling into the inmates' system.

The price the rookie paid for deliverance from the 7–3 was adoption of, or at least accommodation to, the philosophy and tactics of the 3–11. As discussed in earlier chapters, control on the 3–11 was exercised not merely by the *show* of force but by the *use* of force as well, sanctioned and guided by their superiors. So traumatic were their first months alone and vulnerable on the 7–3 shift that it was a price most rookies were willing to pay. Abandoned by the administration, scorned and threatened by the inmates, they had been offered no other alliance. With rare exception, they saw no alternative means of coping with what otherwise seemed an untenable situation. There are few individuals who, forced into the same circumstances, would not have accepted the bargain.

The typical Walpole recruit had entered the training academy sympathetic to inmates. At the academy he had been taught to take the inmates' perspective and had been imbued with the spirit of "modern" corrections. He had been assigned to Walpole—often his institution of choice—where he had received cursory orientation before being flung alone into the most hazardous and difficult job in the institution. There he had suffered deeply from his isolation from his fellow officers and had learned to distrust the administration and hate the inmates. His transfer to the 3–11 had offered him survival, acceptance, and pride. The price he paid was surrender of old values, behavior, and identification and adoption of those of the officer subculture as characterized by the 3–11 shift. His socialization was complete.

The story, of course, does not end there. Some officers seemed at peace with the idea that "when you're working in a place like that you do what the majority do." But many of the officers grieved deeply over the changes that they saw occurring in themselves. As detailed in the next chapter, it was a destructive accommodation for them. Despite the rookies' adaptation to the 3–11, there were few "true believers" among them. Furthermore, for all that it offered officers, the 3–11 was characterized by almost constant confrontation and crisis. Under the continuing stress, most officers rapidly burned out. The vast majority quit the institution within the first four years. Of those who did not, most withdrew as soon as they had sufficient seniority into low-inmate-contact positions on the 7–3 or 11–7 shifts. There they became part of the shadow corps of officers whose indifference had done so much to enhance their own agony as rookies. Now they too would ignore the plight of new officers as the socialization process repeated itself.

But not all officers left the 3–11. Those few officers who had actually thrived on that shift remained there, active and eventually in charge. Some had entered the prison with values compatible with those of the officer subculture; others had come to adopt them. In either case, it is they who became the bearers of the culture, the agents of socialization for new generations of rookies.

It is tempting to look for villains or conspirators in the Walpole socialization process, but none existed. The socialization of the Walpole officer—from the recruit sympathetic to inmates and opposed to officer violence to the seasoned officer hardened to the fate of his charges and accepting the need for force, often brutally applied—was not a product of scheming administrators, supervisors, or even hard-ass officers. Recruits were not first abandoned on the 7–3 to harden them toward the inmates, embitter them toward the administration, and render them susceptible to the claims of the 3–11. This rite of passage was a result not of planning but of incompetence and the failure of successive administrations to counter the continuing legacy of chaos, violence, and rapid turnover of staff that rendered the rookie anonymous and all those around him callous to his fate. That one supervisor on one shift was able to use this chaos and indifference as the backdrop for forging unity among officers and, through that unity, rigid, if brutal, control over the inmates was far more a testament to his leadership skills than to any Machiavellian influence within the institution. If his regime was harsh, at times unlawful, it was also based on genuine devotion to the welfare of his officers. Such concern, if only for a select few, was as rare as fresh air in Walpole.

I have focused thus far on the career pattern of the typical Walpole officer. Not all officers, of course, were socialized to the same extent. Some escaped the brunt of socialization as described above because of important differences in their experiences at the prison. Perhaps the most striking example of variation in institutional experience was one recruit in the longitudinal sample who entered Walpole with among the least sympathetic attitudes toward inmates. He was one of only two recruits who, when interviewed at the training academy, advocated use of violence by officers. ("I may go over and take the handcuffs off and beat him up because, let's face it, if a guy stabs an officer you might have to teach him a lesson . . . I don't know whether you'd call it beating him to submission . . . but there are people you can't control verbally, you have to physically control them.") Given his predisposition toward the use of violence, I had expected that this officer would become one of its foremost practitioners in the receptive environment of Walpole. But instead of going to the 3–11 shift, this rookie was one of the few assigned to the 11–7 shift. He stayed there for several years, by which time he had enough seniority to bid onto a low-inmate-contact position on the day shift. Thus he never had the occasion to become involved in officer violence, nor did he ever become well integrated into the officer subculture.

Other officers stayed on the day shift long enough to develop their own styles and strategies of coping, which they were able to maintain for some time after transfer to the 3–11. But even they eventually changed if they stayed on the 3–11 long enough. One officer described his own slow transformation after an extended introductory period on the day shift.

A lot of guys come on and hold onto it for a long time. Say I'm what they call a nice guy off of days. "Oh, you're a nice guy from days? Oh well [*pounds table*], this is how we run it on the 3-to-11." You hold out for a while but you find yourself—it's like a wearing down process. "Listen, if you do that on this shift and that guy escapes or this guy got hurt and that could have been because of you." Everything happens for a particular reason. Say an officer got hurt on the 3-to-11, they say, "See, this is what happens. This guy didn't sign out and that is why we have them sign out." And after a while they can talk you into just about anything. They can say, "That's why we should have the electric chair." And after a time of this, you're programmed. And finally you don't want to bid off the 3-to-11.

*Socialization at Bridgewater.* Socialization through silence prevailed until the 1970s at all four Massachusetts state prisons for men. At Norfolk and Concord, as at Walpole, the upheavals of the early 1970s forced a change in these patterns. To a considerable extent, however, socialization through silence survived at Bridgewater. There,

> no one wanted to teach you anything. The old-timers didn't like the young guys. The young guys couldn't get anything out of the old-timers. You had to pick up everything on your own . . . It's just like, "If you don't have five years in, you're wet behind the ears. Don't even talk to me kid. I don't even want to look at you."

A Bridgewater officer recalled his introduction to the State Hospital. "I walked in [the first] day and they said, 'Go to this ward.' And that was it . . . There was really no training once you got in there." Some older officers took advantage of his presence by having him do all the work. "All they did was play cards all day in a back room where I didn't even see them. I'd be on the floor all by myself. 'Hey, kid, do this; hey, kid, do that.'" Others used him for their own entertainment.

> The first day at the institution I worked one of the maximum units. I sat down and they unlocked the inmates and they all came out. They told me just to sit there and watch. So I sat there. This inmate came running out, completely bare, with his fists clenched, came right over—I'm sitting in the chair—and he just started screaming and putting his fists in front of my face . . . I almost shit in my pants. That was it right there. I didn't know what to expect. They grabbed him . . . he was harmless, but I didn't know that. My hair went up. I thought, what am I getting myself into here? . . . I'll never forget that as long as I live. It was incredible . . . I had [inmates] walk up to me and tell me they were going to kill me. Now, it's all a joke, because the officers that work that particular ward know what they're like, but to me it wasn't a joke.

Unless a Bridgewater officer ingratiated himself with the "in-group," especially by participating in violent reprisals against inmates, or found a mentor among the older officers, "you could be there ten years and not know anything." On the other hand, although seasoned officers (and some administrators) seemed to go out of their way to make life miserable for the rookie, they also made little effort to instill specific values or codes of conduct. If a new officer kept his mouth shut and was unconcerned about integration into the existing officer corps, he could pretty much do and think as he liked without reprisal.

*Socialization at Norfolk.* Turnover among officers at Bridgewater was very low during the 1970s and the trickle of new officers could be accommodated in a slow fashion, but the situation was quite different at Norfolk. There, new officers predominated on the evening shift (4 P.M. to 12 A.M.), where they were largely insulated from their older colleagues.

Norfolk rookies in the mid-1970s typically spent their first months on the 12 P.M. to 8 A.M. shift, where they were treated "worse than the inmates." "New guys took the rookie heat . . . The rookie thing is to take harassment as far as being cut up or told, 'You don't know it yet. You're a rookie, listen to me.' Despite whether you knew the guy was off the wall or what, you had to step back, take second." "Rookie heat" applied by old-timers "bothered the hell" out of some new officers, but most sloughed it off until the next batch of rookies arrived to divert attention. (A more lasting bitterness was felt toward shift supervisors for pettiness, favoritism, and lack of assistance.) After a few months on the 12–8, rookies welcomed the opportunity to transfer to the 4–12 shift or to become house officers.

The 4–12 shift was considered a "good shift. Almost everybody wanted to help you out." It was a "tight" shift precisely because it was populated almost entirely by young officers, a consequence of turnover within the officer corps and the seniority bid system. While new officers liked that shift, most were uncomfortable with the lack of experience among officers on it. An interviewee with less than two years as an officer remarked,

There's been nights where I've been senior man in the yard. Now this is ridiculous . . . We got nobody to go to, follow ahead, no old-timers on the shift. Guys here with four, five, six years experience, they don't stay on the shift, they go to the day shift.

And so you're flying by the seat of your pants and make a mistake, or you try to think before you speak but it just never seems to work out right a lot of times . . . I wish there was more experience . . . Experience of knowing how to handle [the inmates].

This officer articulated why experience is so important—and correspondingly why a seniority bid system is so disastrous—in a prison:

A fourteen-year-old kid could come in here and do the physical part of the job. He can turn the keys, he can know what doors to unlock, he can know the schedule, he can know where he has to be at the time. The only difference comes in the job is when you have to deal with the inmates . . . [It] drives me up a wall— not knowing what to do, how to handle it and what to anticipate when you run into something . . . It gives me great pleasure to sit down or to work with somebody that's got more time and to watch them, to see how they handle it. Because you just don't see it. You're doing it by yourself or with another guy that's got the same amount of time, or a year or two. And it doesn't {amount to} a hill of beans, a year or two—I'm talking ten or twelve years, to see what they do.

A colleague spoke bluntly, "A guy that's been here a year-and-a-half don't know piss. I've been here two, and *I* don't know what's going on. And I talk to guys that have been here five years and *they* don't know what's going on."

House officers (Norfolk's counterparts to cell block officers) were left even more to their own devices because they worked most of the day alone. Prior to the mid-1970s, their isolation from the rest of the officer corps was tempered by the fact that most house officers had served at least five years as uniformed officers before they had acquired sufficient seniority to bid into a house. By the end of the decade, however, house officer positions had lost their appeal. Brand-new officers were being drafted directly into houses, effectively insulating them for their first months or years at the prison from attitudes and expectations of more experienced officers.

The failure of the old corps of officers at Norfolk to socialize their younger colleagues resulted in a situation where evolution of cultural values and norms of behavior was possible, a matter to be discussed at the end of this chapter.

*Socialization at Concord.* Concord had apparently been the toughest master in days past, especially for those rare individuals who landed a post there without being related to another Concord employee or, worse yet, were not from Lowell, Massachusetts (see Chapter 3). During the heyday of the "forty cousins," when the prison was dominated at all levels by staff members who came from the same town and were related to one another, few differences apparently existed between the values of the officer subculture and those who sought membership in it. (Although we may thus speak of the officer subculture as having been largely "imported" from outside the prison, the transmission of cultural values and behaviors no doubt went both ways, with mores and attitudes of the community outside the prison reflecting the realities of prison life for those of its members who worked inside, and vice versa.) In any case, the need for socialization of values, as opposed to the learning of specific skills and behaviors by new members, would under those circumstances have been greatly reduced.

The efforts of the Department of Correction in the mid-1970s to wrest control of the prison from the "forty cousins" led to a drop in morale and a corresponding increase in turnover rates, and eventually to the hiring of substantial numbers of new officers from communities outside Lowell. New officers were subjected during their first months to a fair measure of harassment and ostracism, especially if they were not from Lowell. They were thrust without training or orientation into positions alone in the prison hospital or the protective-custody ward, or were left to languish for months in the gun towers on the midnight shift. An officer who was not from Lowell concluded that the older officers "were there to make it as unpleasant as possible." Even those from Lowell were harassed. "You get your initiation . . . They let you know that they know you're new . . . A lot of them won't talk to you." But men like him benefitted nonetheless from their contacts. "[If] you know a few people in here you get along better and faster with the other guards . . . I'm from Lowell [which] . . . helped a lot. I knew a lot of people, a lot of people, which was good."

As the chaos persisted and the Lowell contingent became increasingly dilute, the old-timers retreated into "their own little clique . . . the 'Forty Cousins Club' " with its intense loyalties and own mores. New members of the club were admitted only grudgingly. Most rookies were momentarily harassed and then forgotten. The old corps saved its wrath for the administration and for those new officers who most flagrantly violated the old ways—a problem to which I now turn.

## Expulsion

When selection and socialization fail to produce sufficient congruity between the values and behaviors of the initiate and the norms central to a culture, that culture may still protect itself through the expedient of expulsion. Businesses may fire the inadequately socialized, schools may expel them, and the military may court-martial them. Imprisonment, itself, may be seen as temporary or permanent expulsion by modern society in response to failures in socialization (or perhaps more accurately, in response to the triumph of counter-socialization), as in earlier times were banishment and transport to alien soil. Capital punishment represents expulsion in its most extreme form.

Few if any societies, large or small, lack the self-protective mechanism of expulsion regardless of how infrequently they may use it against their own members. But rare, too, is the society that uses expulsion as the sole or even principal mechanism for maintaining cultural continuity. The costs of doing so are staggering, for such a society would have to expend enormous resources and energy in socializing new members to produce but few eventual "carriers" of the culture. To succeed with such a strategy, a society would have to have great resources and a supply of potential members substantially greater than demand. (Some such societies come to mind: Green Berets and Trappist monks are perhaps two examples. Even in these cases, however, initiates are not accorded full membership in the society until after certain standards have been met. Once full membership has been accorded—the green beret awarded, the final vows taken—expulsion rarely occurs. In that sense, these organizations may be seen to have a two-staged selection process—one before socialization begins in earnest, the other after—rather than to use expulsion as a principal means of maintaining normative continuity.)

Brim (1968, p. 559) ascribed the reluctance of societies to attempt major changes in adult values to

> the limitations on later-life learning that make it impractical to attempt a thorough resocialization. It may be that the costs are too high and that it simply is not efficient, from society's point

of view, to spend too much time on teaching an old dog new tricks. Perhaps only in the case where the need for a certain kind of manpower is very great and the question of efficiency becomes secondary to the need for personnel can an intensive and costly resocialization effort be made for adults.

In the extreme environment of Walpole, a "certain kind of manpower" was required to maintain cultural continuity. But the values of the subculture diverged sufficiently from those of the community around it and of individuals recruited to membership in it that an intensive resocialization effort was attempted. That effort *was* impractical, inefficient, and tremendously costly in terms of institutional needs and the well-being of the officers involved. And yet, as we have seen, few "true believers" emerged. The subculture maintained continuity of values chiefly through the elimination of the majority of officers, by force or by choice, in fact or in substance.

Formal power to expel an officer from the prison community rests, of course, not with the officers but with the administration. (In Massachusetts during the 1970s it was a formal power very rarely exercised.) What officers may lack in formal authority to expel, however, they more than make up for in the informal exercise of powers. None of the recruits in this study who were assigned to Walpole were forced out by their fellow officers, but three who went to Concord and Norfolk clearly suffered this fate. Each erred in their first weeks in making their sympathies to inmates widely and publicly known. The story of one of these three officers follows.

"My views were very liberal . . . It caused a lot of resentment from other guards." They responded angrily to his pronouncements on the nature of prisons and prisoners. " 'You've been here one week and you're going to tell us how this place is? . . . You're an asshole. You don't know what you're talking about.' " He was "isolated by the real hard-core officers and I never really fit in. I never fit in." At least at first he made no effort to do so.

> They're skeptical of any new officer coming in. You have to prove yourself in a situation like that, and you're not going to get any real respect or acknowledgment even until you're put in a situation, either verbally or physically or even emotionally, that you show that you're one of us. And I was never into being one of them.

The response to his heresies was "complete isolation." He was assigned to the towers on the midnight shift, "the farthest one away,

like out of sight, out of mind." Other rookies spent their first months
in a similar situation, but his banishment appeared to be without
end. "I didn't see inmates at all; I didn't see guards at all . . . I found
myself working in an institution, but yet I wasn't a part of it. And
they wouldn't allow me to be. I didn't want to be, I guess, but they
really made me disappear by putting me in the tower." There was
never any question in his mind that his consignment to the towers
was in lieu of his being fired. "Because it's hard to fire somebody.
'What did [he] do?' 'He was talking to an inmate.' You can't fire
somebody for that. So it's a form of disappearing." There was also no
question in his mind that he was being punished. "I felt rejected. I
felt that I was doing something wrong. Why am I more or less being
punished for doing what I feel is correct? . . . Doing time in the
towers . . . was like being in jail."

Officers brought home his rejection in more direct ways as well.
Many refused to talk to him. Almost none offered assistance. Their
rejection hurt. "Sure you care. You care. Your manhood's questioned; your sincerity is questioned; your naiveness is questioned;
your immaturity is questioned. And those are all negative things."
He had more to worry about than social rejection. He was in constant fear of being "set up, and that's the way of getting [you] fired
. . . I was very leery about where I went, when I went, and how I got
there." He found officers and supervisors "checking on everything
that you do, hoping that something's wrong; really hoping that
something's wrong." Eventually, he came to fear for his physical
safety.

> If an incident went down, there was no one to cover my back.
> That's a very important lesson to learn. You need your back
> covered and my back wasn't covered there at all. And at one
> point I was in fear of being set up by guards. I was put in
> dangerous situations purposely. That really happened to me.
> There was times I went there *scared*, and then I didn't mind
> sitting in the tower.

Some officers personally "threatened to kick my butt in . . . I was
afraid walking into the parking lot. I didn't know what was waiting
for me there. That's why I was scared. I was scared a lot of times in
that place. I'm very serious about that—and the fear came from
guards."

He eventually concluded, "You're either going to have to fit in and
be like these people or you're going to get hurt. Because at that time

I saw no out. I couldn't afford to just quit, although that definitely entered my mind. I had no alternative. So I had to fit in." He began the humiliating process of ingratiating himself with the very officers who had threatened him. "I was on the [night shift] and completely isolated. I wanted to somehow be reintegrated back into a normal day . . . And I figured ways of doing that was to show that I was more like everyone else." When he foiled an inmate escape, he basked in the momentary glory. "I felt that acceptance and it really scared the hell out of me because I didn't know where I was going." He was rescued from his predicament by the sudden offer of a job outside the criminal justice system. But he had few illusions a year later about how he would have compromised himself had he been forced to stay. "A person that's trapped in an environment like that has no recourse . . . I was an outsider messing with an inside-run organization."

The mechanisms of expulsion were much the same at Walpole—ostracism, harassment, assignment to the nether reaches of the institution—coupled with the far greater sanction of abandonment within the prison. Not even the most openly inmate-sympathetic officer was deemed (or deemed himself) able to survive within Walpole without at least some support from fellow officers. The speed and force with which some recruits were expelled from or denied membership in the officer subculture may be seen as compensation for the lack of control that officers had over the selection process. Those forced out may be said to have been "deselected" by the officer corps.

Most officers who quit, however, were not driven to do so by their fellow officers, but rather by circumstances within the prisons themselves. This was especially true at Walpole. To some extent the officer subculture there served to alleviate some of the officers' unhappiness and frustration and thus to counter the forces that made men want to leave. But the demands of the subculture were so great, the values so divergent from those with which most officers had entered the institution, and the negotiability of roles inside so limited that the subculture there almost surely was a major force behind the high turnover rate among officers.

Those officers who formally resigned were not the only ones who abandoned the prison community. It might be said of Walpole that those officers who could, quit, and those who could not, disappeared. The seniority bid system allowed a man with sufficient seniority to obtain a post within the prison that required little or no contact with inmates, the public, or even other officers. Towers and gates must be manned, commissary items ordered, forms filled in at any maximum-security institution. What the seniority bid system at Walpole ensured was that those who filled these positions were as permanently lost to the prison community as if they had joined the majority of their peers in resigning from the prison.

Thus, only the hard core remained at Walpole, active and in charge. The few who were temperamentally and philosophically suited to the harsh realities of the prison became in their turn the central figures of the officer society, the bearers and transmitters of the culture. Their values had not prevailed by virtue of mass *importation*—their views had, in fact, been held by a minority of those entering the institution. Rather, their values had prevailed principally by socialization and the *deportation* of competing values. The majority who could not or, occasionally, would not fit in had long since been forced out, resigned, or retreated to the shadows.

Subcultural values prevailed at Walpole, but the costs were staggering. The majority of recruits who entered the prison left in defeat, their lives disrupted, often severely scarred by the experience. The institution, meanwhile, remained chronically understaffed, seriously hampered by the absence of experienced personnel, with no apparent end in sight to the violence and destruction.

## Evolution

When recruitment and socialization fail to produce conformity and wholesale expulsion is neither desirable nor practical, then a society must somehow accommodate its deviant members. It is through such accommodation of deviant values and behaviors that cultures evolve.

Riots and other crises are common watersheds in a prison's history. One imagines that Attica and New Mexico prisons were very different institutions after their cataclysmic riots, with different values held by members of both the officer and inmate subcultures. Certainly Walpole was a vastly different institution in the late 1970s than it had been a decade before as a result of the intervening years of crisis and strife. Old methods of socialization had broken down and the resignation rate of officers, new and old, was extremely high. As a result, whatever values were held by the bulk of those who hung on through those years were the ones that prevailed. But changes wrought by such events may, in the long run, serve to retard future evolutionary change. A Walpole officer astutely observed the effect that the years of turmoil had on the willingness of officers to entertain any change at all.

> [The officers] are scared of change. Because [Walpole] . . . went from tight to unbelievably loose to unbelievably tight to unbelievably loose. And the officers as well as the inmates can't handle that. They're saying, "Now I'm scared of change." You've been through so much and they say, "Nope, I don't care which way it is, but let's leave it this way. I can't take it no more." It's too frustrating to get the extremes all the time. It's like a Dr. Doolittle "push me, pull me" type of thing. It's really something psychologically that you can't handle.

Walpole in the late 1970s evidenced at least as much cultural rigidity as it had in the 1950s and 1960s.

At Bridgewater, turnover rates among officers in the 1970s were so low that little opportunity existed for the infusion of new values. Nor were there pressures for their dissemination. Concord, at the other extreme, had very high turnover rates in the late 1970s among old and new officers alike, but the prison was in such chaos that it was difficult to determine where, if anywhere, it was headed.

Only at Norfolk did conditions seem favorable to evolutionary change in the 1970s. At Norfolk, unlike Walpole, neither incessant conflict with inmates nor dominance of any senior officer militated in favor of tradition among younger officers. Segregated on their own shift and in the inmate housing units, and thus shielded from the socializing influence of older colleagues, the new generation of officers developed their own styles and strategies for dealing with inmates. "The old style, 'Yes, boss, no, boss,' or 'You caught me, give me my ticket,' it was gone. Now everything was constitutional rights and violation of best interests and things like that." These were changes to which the younger officers often adapted more easily than the old-timers. "Most of these [officers] that have been here fifteen, twenty, twenty-five, thirty years, they've been conditioned, 'This is the way things are. That's the only right way.' . . . Officers [who] have been here five or ten years can see where everything isn't set in a certain category." These differences created divisions among officers ("The older officers all more or less stick together and the younger officers more or less stick together"), and were reflected in the way older and younger officers related to in-

mates and permitted inmates to relate to them. A young house
officer explained,

> I've talked to a lot of [older officers] that worked in a housing
> unit doing the same job I'm doing now—they did it twenty
> years ago. They'll say, "Why do you let that guy talk to you like
> that for?" Well, with the people [inmates] that you have today,
> you have to because if you didn't let them you could cause a
> riot. And I feel that I've got to live in that unit with them.
> Twenty years ago if a guy . . . swore at an officer or something,
> you lock them right up. But it didn't happen that often. It's a
> regular day thing in there now. In fact, if I was to go in there and
> I had a whole day where somebody didn't call me a name, I'd
> think something was wrong!

The younger officers and many of the inmates came from the
same generation with similar language, standards of conduct, and
taste in music and dress. Older officers were forced to accept changes
in style and standards among officers not only because they had
forgone the opportunity to socialize their younger colleagues, but
also because they recognized (if grudgingly) that the changes were
useful in maintaining a stable institution.

> Automatically, being a younger officer, we're considered a lib-
> eral because our hair's long, and we wear bell-bottom pants and
> what not. But I think the older officers also see the need for us
> because the type of inmate you have is changing, too . . . I'd say
> out of the 700 inmates here at Norfolk there's got to be 100 in
> their either late teens or very early twenties. And a guy fifty
> years old just doesn't know how to deal with them. So they see
> the need for the younger officers. [But] I don't think they really
> like it.

Whether the old-timers liked it or not, the old order at Norfolk
was evolving under the influence of a new breed of officers and
inmates. Of the four Massachusetts prisons for men, it was the
only one where conditions in the 1970s favored such gradual
changes.

# 9

# Effects of Prison Employment on Officers

"[When] I started Walpole I had everything," recalled an officer who as a recruit at the Training Academy had spoken with optimism about his new job, his family, and himself. "When I got out of Walpole I had nothing. No family, no morals, nothing. I don't give a shit about anything . . . I like the way I was before. I was easygoing and I liked everybody and everything . . . Those . . . three years screwed up everything—don't feel the same about anything anymore."

Walpole was, according to this former officer, "a major disaster for anyone who goes up there." The lives of the Walpole officers in this study largely confirmed his assessment. Most officers recognized the changes that had taken place in themselves and spoke of those changes with sorrow and bitterness in the interviews. Many of their young marriages were in trouble or destroyed. Some officers were so burnt out that they could not go into supermarkets or take their children to the zoo. Others were so drug dependent that they had to get drunk before going to work on the 7 A.M. shift. Some were so angry and frustrated that they punched holes in the walls of their homes and abused those whom they loved. They suffered severe headaches, hypertension, nightmares. Most of all, they were desperately unhappy and despaired that life could ever seem good again.

*[Did] anything good at all come out of Walpole?*
  Nothing. Absolutely nothing . . . There was nothing good about it. I didn't learn anything except to handle people. It didn't make me more of a man to work there. It didn't make me more of a person. I think it made me less . . . I didn't get any-

thing beneficial out of that place at all. All it did, it took two years of my life out of me that I'll never get back. And it's ruined the rest in a way because I've had that experience. So there's nothing good I can say about that.

In earlier chapters in this book I have painted a grim portrait of Walpole in the 1970s. That this prison would have had a profound and negative effect on those who worked and lived in it must be obvious to all but the most ardent believers in the inherent perversity of officers or inmates. The effect of working in Bridgewater, Concord, and Norfolk was not as devastating for most officers, but few officers at these institutions were happy, and most were depressed. As one of them put it, "It's just an attitude around the place, an attitude that's associated with it once you get to work in here. You just don't feel good about yourself."

Prison work affected all facets of the lives of officers who were the subjects of this study—their personalities, their health, their characters, their families. With rare exceptions, those who could leave did so, bearing the emotional scars of having worked in a prison. Those who had no choice but to stay "mentally anesthetized" themselves to what was happening around them and to what they themselves were doing.

In this chapter and the next, I shift the focus from institutions to individual officers. I do not always identify institutional affiliation of officers quoted (previously I have identified institutional affiliation if the officer quoted was *not* from Walpole). But as with earlier chapters, these chapters were written in the shadow of Walpole. Not only did officers from that prison constitute a majority of those studied, but they also suffered most severely the consequences of working in prison. As in the rest of this book, it is principally their experiences that I chronicle here.

## Emotional Effects

Most prisons seem designed as much to deflate the spirit as to confine the body. With their grey walls, clanging doors, artificial light, and stale air, they are gloomy places quite apart from their mission as prisons. Ever-present rats, roaches, slime, and excrement make institutions like Walpole all the more inhospitable. People do not cheerfully go to work in such places.

Yet the physical environment of the prison is not the most depressing part of an officer's job. He must also contend with the dismal purpose of his employment and with the open hostility of men in his charge. Officers go to work each day not to create goods that others want or to provide services that others esteem. They go there to "maintain that human warehouse." As one officer mused, "What lower thing can you do besides lock up other human beings?" If officers failed to recognize the impoverished nature of their employment on their own, the inmates in their charge seemed to take every opportunity to manifest their hatred and scorn. It is little wonder that, for most officers, "that depression was evident, like really hating to go to work."

Walpole and prisons like it are pervaded with tension and anxiety. They are places where men never completely relax. "You just see that place and everybody's anxiety level rises." Officers reported themselves always on edge, constantly wary, jumpy, suspicious. "Once you're inside those walls you've got to have six eyes." They felt themselves under strain and pressure all the time. One officer likened the anxiety of working at Walpole to months he had spent patrolling the perimeter of a military base in Vietnam. Major incidents only occasionally occurred, but constant watching and waiting took their toll. "It's the mental strain up there," he observed of Walpole. "You might not be afraid and you might not be consciously looking at, watching everything [that's] going on. But your head's always working."

There seemed to be no escape from the confrontation. It began the moment an officer walked on his shift and often continued unabated until he left.

> You get there at quarter to seven . . . you'd lock the doors behind you, start feeding breakfast and then it starts. Seven o'clock in the morning! You're not ready for something like that. You go to a regular job, you're waking up at seven. You don't even get into it for an hour. These guys have been up all night waiting for you. You're not ready for that stuff.

The daily conflict—"fighting with those fools forty hours a week"— wore them down. "Every day an officer is in four or five arguments. No one needs that." As crises repeatedly came and went, officers felt like yo-yos on well-worn strings.

> Something might not feel right to you or a situation might come up—right away, zam! like that—that you didn't expect. And

you're put on the spot and your adrenalin shoots up. And it's tough to go up and down, up and down, up and down constantly over a period of time. It affects people in that way.

Officers at prisons like Walpole are not merely anxious. They are afraid. Jack Abbott, incarcerated for years in prisons as violent as Walpole, wrote of watching the "blackening" of men's hearts after they come into prison. "They enter prison more bewildered than afraid. Every step after that, the fear creeps into them . . . No one is prepared for it. Even the pigs, when they first start to work in prison, are not prepared for it. *Everyone* is afraid" (1982, p. 144, emphasis in original). A few Walpole officers professed in the interviews never to have been afraid, but the rest scoffed at the idea that anyone in Walpole—officer or inmate—could be free of fear. Said one officer of those who claimed not to be afraid, especially new, young, "macho" officers, "I think they are all scared to death. I didn't think at any point that there was anybody [who wasn't] scared, because I saw in situations where their face would turn white, just go absolutely crazy and they'd be running around with their heads cut off." Most officers agreed. "Everybody that's in these institutions is afraid. I don't care who they are, that's a fact . . . These inmates . . . they were scared stiff doing time in there and of course the officer is too. He doesn't know *what's* coming at him." Or who it was coming from. Abbott observed, "Every single prisoner every day must exist with the *imminent* threat of assault at *the very least*—and from any quarter" (p. 133, emphasis in original). So did the officers. "That place has got such a reputation and everybody goes in there, 'I'm in Walpole now. I'm a tough guy.' And, boy, I tell you, you got the skinniest little guys on the street that you wouldn't even think twice about, they're in there and you don't know *what* they're doing."

Fear was not the exclusive province of young, inexperienced officers. Even those deemed most capable by their peers—officers with years of experience—were afraid at least part of the time if they were still in contact with inmates. A seasoned officer recalled,

I've been terrified in there. I've been scared to death. I haven't been scared to death that I wouldn't do what I had to do. But I was scared to death that I might make a mistake and somebody's going to slip in and get a lucky one in on me and I'm going to get hurt, or I'm not going to get there in time and this other guy's going to get hurt . . . Every single guy up there has gone through that.

Another senior officer, highly respected by his peers, described himself as "scared as hell" sometimes even when the institution was running quietly.

> It was like the correction officer made his money, or I made my money, one minute a month . . . You just run a block and everything is smooth. But that one time when you're downstairs when a knife fight breaks out or a guy comes in drunk and you're trying to lock them up and you're alone, you're looking up in the gallery hoping the officer's watching . . . And you've got that feeling of being totally alone with a guy that could waste you if he wanted to.

Officers had had plenty of opportunity to witness close at hand what inmates were capable of doing to their fellow captives. It did not take much imagination to appreciate what those same inmates would be capable of doing to their captors. Officers who had not themselves been victims of serious assault still had frightening stories to tell of things that had happened to them. One recalled an incident when he was on the tier.

> Everybody was acting uneasy. I turn around and here comes [an inmate] flying up the tier. He flies up the tier and he spins around in the air and he comes down and he's got a thing in his hand . . . Goes, "I got you!" I said, "Oh, shit." . . . This man is insane . . . He's crazy . . . He's built very strong. He's a big guy. Talking in slurred language, spitting . . . His eyes were as big as they could be and his pupils were tiny . . . He was gone. He was flipped, completely flipped out! He proceeded in the next hour and a half to tell me how he could kill me in fifteen minutes, in an hour, in two hours; how he could torture me and do this and do that . . . I couldn't believe I was sweating and all of my energy was drained out of me. It was into my ankles by now and I was crazy.

When the officer was finally rescued from the tier he described himself as "a mess . . . I didn't go down that tier for a while." Another officer recalled going up on a tier with several officers when

> all of a sudden [an inmate] came out. His eyes were [large and bulging], his face was like the color of that paper. He was like a

maniac. Came running down like a monkey, right down to the bottom of the floor like a real monkey with a knife in each hand and chased us off the tier.

Even the hardiest officers had their breaking moments, trapped on a tier or held hostage by men who had maimed and killed before. Such experiences were, by the testimony of the officers involved, "deeply scarring" ones. (I recall asking a Walpole administrator how some officers had fared after being taken hostage and eventually released. His eyes misted over as he predicted that those fellows had probably just walked right back in the next day as if nothing had happened. His knowledge of prisons and human nature must have derived more from John Wayne films than from experience at Walpole. Several days after the hostages were released, one of them out on "unlimited disability" described his hours in captivity as the most "traumatic experience" of his life [New Bedford *Standard Times*, 31 July 1979]. His reaction was not atypical.)

Under the circumstances, nearly every Walpole officer was afraid some of the time and some were afraid nearly all of the time.

> I was scared. Every day I was scared to go to work. I really was. I was petrified. At night I had sleepless nights and I had nightmares worrying about what would happen . . . Just walking in there in the morning, you didn't know what to expect, really. You didn't know what was going to happen . . . I was really miserable and I was scared shit.

Officers at the other prisons were also often anxious and afraid. At Bridgewater State Hospital, officers were in constant danger of sudden, unprovoked attack. It was a situation in which, as the former medical director observed, "You have to be 'paranoid' in order to stay in touch with reality" (James F. Gilligan, personal communication, February 1987). A Concord officer regarded as tough and capable by his fellow officers concurred, "Any officer that steps in here, if he's not scared at different points then he shouldn't be here. He's not normal." A colleague of his who quit recalled the "fear that you carry with you all the time . . . I don't mean like shaking or anything. But that frame of mind that you're almost always set for something to go off, and you're ready. And that's a fear. The adrenalin is always like this much from getting ready to boil." Even at normally placid Norfolk, officers were often afraid although they tried not to show it.

You could walk around here and act as if nothing bothers you. But there are times when you are scared in here. A group of inmates will come up to you and you'll sit there and you'll say, "I want to talk to you, and the rest of you get out of here." And now they look at you and they say, "Well, this guy wants us to leave, {so let's} get out of here {pretty quick}." But you may yourself, might be saying, "Jesus Christ, look at all these goddamn inmates around me. They could jump me, do this, do that, do this, do that." You can't *show* that. You have to keep a lot inside of you when you are working in an institution . . . And it can be rough sometimes. A lot of tension. A lot of tension. Your life is in danger when you walk in the door. Don't let anybody tell you that it's not, because it is.

Yet the anxiety that officers at Concord, Norfolk, and the Bridgewater State Hospital experienced was not as debilitating as it was for the men at Walpole. A Norfolk officer who admitted he had been "scared shitless" on different occasions at his prison nevertheless understood how much easier the life of an officer was at Norfolk than at Walpole. "Sure, once in a while there is [tension here], but at least it eases off and things cool off. [The inmates] give you your own time to get your own head back together again. Where up [at Walpole] it never eases off."

Regardless of the prison in which they worked, many officers seemed haunted by their experiences inside the prison. They found they "could never get away from it. When I was out at night, I'd get thinking about the prison, flashbacks . . . I used to dream about it. I never felt I was away from it." Even officers who generally coped well were not immune. "I found myself . . . just lying in bed thinking of something and the next thing I know I'm going through a problem that I had and . . . there's sweat beads and everything else . . . You can be dreaming about anything in the world, but all of a sudden right in the middle of it you realize it's corrections oriented."

Some of the more extreme emotional effects of working in prison are discussed in the section on "Burnouts" in the chapter that follows.

## Physical Effects

Any job involving as much stress as that of a prison officer would be bound to produce physical disorders. In addition to injuries sustained at the hands of inmates, officers in this study reported having high blood pressure, heart problems, persistent and severe headaches, insomnia, indigestion, and blurred vision. They were apparently not atypical. A 1975 report on correctional employees in New York State found that the amount of time officers took off from their jobs for disability was 300 percent higher than the average for all state employees. Sixty percent of their disability leave was for heart, emotional, or drinking problems (Wynne, 1978, p. 62). An American Justice Institute study of sixteen states found that "the incidence of heart attacks among correctional officers is one of the highest among any group of state employees" (Wynne, 1978, p. 62).

Health problems relating to stress are an occupational hazard for all prison officers, but the medical risks for Massachusetts prison officers were greatly exacerbated in the 1970s by the excessive amount of overtime they were required to work. During the early years of crisis, officers

> were working twelve hours a day, seven and six days a week. One week alone, I personally worked seventy-two hours *overtime*—that's sixteen-hour shifts seven days a week . . . And you were like at the end of a string. You were bonzo by the time you got out . . . It drew you right out to the end of your rope . . . It was so unbelievable and so like in a dream world.

The situation improved during the latter part of the decade, but the prison system remained chronically understaffed, especially at Walpole and Concord. Throughout the decade, officers at Walpole were required to work a six- and often seven-day workweek. In addition, at all the prisons some officers were held over (usually without prior notification or consent) from almost every shift to cover vacant posts on the next shift. In 1979, the state secretary of human services noted that Massachusetts had

> the highest overtime in any corrections system in the United States . . . Although we were spending a lot of money on overtime, we were understaffed at the same time. People were unreasonably exposed. They were fatigued, worked too long, stressed and too much was demanded of them. They could not deal emotionally or physically with the circumstances around them. (Quoted in *Lowell Sun*, 25 September 1979)

That was not an understatement. Most officers were exhausted from the stress and overwork. "It's not like construction because I worked construction," recalled a former Walpole officer toward the end of the decade. "I was working [in construction] twelve hours a day . . . six days a week, and I never felt tired like I did when I was working the overtime up at Walpole." Even in normally quiet institutions the long hours took their toll. "I am mentally and physically tired," an officer at the Treatment Center wearily reported at the end of a sixteen-hour workday.

> You're sitting in here, the place is full of smoke, the place is filthy, your eyes are tired—my eyes are red right now. I've been here all day . . . The job just for some reason fatigues you. It wears you out. I'm more tired now than I would be if I worked sixteen hours hard. I would physically feel much better if I had.

Incredibly, some officers chose, *and were permitted*, to work double shifts seven days a week for months on end. One of the men I interviewed had done so for more than a year and he was not alone. The physical presence within the prisons of officers like him helped their superiors produce complete rosters of men, but as the months wore on, such officers were able to contribute little to the life of their respective institutions.*

The only way many men found they could "unwind and forget" the prison world was to "get together and go down to the local gin mill and juice it up." "I had to have a beer as soon as I got out, on the way home . . . just to calm myself." Rookies who were not drinkers soon found themselves staying out all night "drinking like fish." "I found myself looking for it just to unwind . . . You're so keyed up . . . It's the only way they can let down and get some enjoyment."

Officers typically hit the bars when they got off duty, but some could not wait until then. These officers were "always coming to work with bloodshot eyes, smelling of alcohol." Recalled one, "I

---

* As thanks for the long hours of overtime officers were in most cases being forced to perform, they then had to wait months, even years, to receive compensation. There were stories, perhaps apocryphal, of officers who purchased expensive cars with a single overtime check, of other officers who paid off their mortgages in two or three years. As the Governor's Advisory Committee on Corrections observed regarding the state's failure to pay either overtime or promised holiday pay on time, "We wonder how fast the state would haul a private company into court for such treatment" (Boston *Herald*, 14 June 1974). The inexcusable delays in paying overtime were the cause of considerable bitterness among officers. Worse yet, the department was notoriously late (and rumored to be miserly) in dispensing disability payments when officers were injured in the line of duty.

was drinking to get up enough nerve to go [in] and when I got out of work I'd get loaded just to forget . . . I'd go out at night and sometimes not come home, just stay out and get loaded all night long because I didn't want to think about going to work the next day. I'm ashamed of myself for doing it." Not surprisingly, men like him developed severe and lasting drinking problems. They saw what was happening to themselves but felt powerless to stop it as long as they remained in prison work. Another officer soberly reflected,

> I'm sure that everybody who's ever turned into an alcoholic or a drug addict has said, "Nothing like that will ever happen to me." But I do find myself going home at 11:30 at night, taking a shower, knowing I've got to be back here at six o'clock in the morning. And before I know it, it's one o'clock and I'm sitting here looking at the table with a quart of wine gone and three or four cans of beer . . . If I want to go out and socialize, I'm out to maybe two in the morning. Who says I'm not going to get drunker than a skunk? Because all of a sudden I find myself drinking and I say, "Wow, man, my troubles are going away. I'm not thinking about that place."

Alcohol was not the only drug abused. A Walpole officer reported, "A lot of guys used to smoke [dope] and stuff like that going to work." A former officer at a different institution who regularly smoked marijuana and hashish recalled of himself and some of his fellow officers, "We used to get high. Oh God, we used to get high before we used to go in. I didn't do it the first few months, but then my friend did and he told me, 'I come in jammed every day. That's the way I can handle this place. I just sit there jammed up for a couple of hours every day.' " Like the inmates in their charge, getting high was the only way some officers felt they could cope with the prison world. "Some people had to do it just to get {there}," recalled a Walpole officer. "Can't blame them. They had to take some kind of stimulant just to do their job. That's not saying much, is it?"

## Moral Effects

Officers in this study suffered in spirit as well as in mind and body. Abbott said of his captors, "guards *do not* have anything but 'cold' characters" (1982, p. 70, emphasis in original) and admonished anyone who might defend them, "There is no mistake made when

prison staffs are regarded as brutal sadists who spend all their working time creating and influencing prison intrigues of the most vile
sort" (p. 100). But like the one-dimensional view many officers hold
of inmates, Abbott's characterization badly misses the mark. Most
officers were horrified at the extent and sadism of violence within
the prisons and were troubled by the suffering they themselves
inflicted, directly or indirectly, on inmates. They characterized problems that they faced within prisons as *moral* dilemmas, ones involving discrepancies between their own ethical standards and
behavior expected of them as officers. Initially, many attempted to
avoid engaging in behavior injurious to inmates by refusing (openly
or surreptitiously) to carry out certain duties and by displacing their
aggressions onto others outside the prison or themselves. As their
involvement in the prison world grew, and their ability to abstain
from morally questionable actions within the prison declined, they
attempted to neutralize their own feelings of guilt by regarding
prisons as separate moral realms with their own distinct set of moral
standards or by viewing inmates as individuals outside the protection of moral laws. When such efforts failed, they shut their minds
to what others were doing and to what they were doing themselves.
Regardless of whether officers became active participants in the
worst abuses of the prisons or were merely passive observers of it,
the moral compromises involved exacted a substantial toll.

Few men in this study hated inmates from the outset or were
initially callous to their fate. Officers who came to prison work
never having witnessed violence before were at first shocked and
dismayed no matter who was the victim or who was the perpetrator.
An officer recalled the first stabbing he had witnessed.

> [An inmate] got stabbed in a fight. Blood was just pouring out of
> his head . . . I was the first one who saw him. He was hanging on
> the bars yelling and screaming, blood pouring out . . . [A] puddle
> filled up and then all of a sudden it started to coagulate . . . I was
> either going to pass out or puke, one of the two.

He was saved from doing either by a senior officer who arrived on
the scene and took charge. But his reaction was not uncommon.
Another officer recalled a brutal stabbing of an inmate a month after
he began working at Walpole.

> There was a guy, I don't remember his name, got stabbed up
> pretty bad. I was working the hospital that day and I helped the

medic patch him up. But after he was gone I felt like throwing up because he was really, really cut up bad . . . like maybe thirty or forty wounds in him . . . I saw the intent, the malice it was done with—different wounds, different cuts, different knives— and I just was kind of mad in a way . . . I thought it was really punkish of them to do something like that.

The lasting imprint of a murdered man's face, the shock at the sight of a mutilated body: these were images officers carried with them. Initially, at least, such events angered and sickened them. Some never ceased to feel awe and despair at such acts. One old-timer who never got used to the violence said, "When you stab a guy ninety times—I've seen them stabbed ninety-five, a hundred times—that sickens you. You've got to have real hate in your heart to do that."

Nothing, one officer observed, could prepare a man for the violence. But he was wrong. There were those who came to the prisons already inured to violence. They had seen it all before, not on the streets, but in war. "The veterans have seen it so much it doesn't bother them anymore." They had "seen human bodies where the biggest piece you could find was no bigger than [a fist], men with half their head gone, women and children lying dead by the road." A young veteran said of Walpole, "It does not affect me one bit, the brutality . . . I went to Vietnam and that's when I really first saw the many different forms and shapes the human body can take when it was introduced to different stimuli—bullets, fire, crashes, hand grenades, explosions . . . I know it turned me inside out, cold as far as that goes."

For officers who were not combat veterans, involvement in the prison world eventually had the same effect. The officer who was angered and sickened by the stabbing of an inmate thirty or forty times declared, "That stuck in my mind . . . But after that, nothing. When I saw them cut up it was just like nothing . . . It just didn't bother me. I got used to it, I guess. It's just a thing I had to get used to. And I knew it myself, if you're going to make it, you can't let it bother you." What was at first bizarre and frightening became normal, routine. "[People] just accept it as being part of their job . . . They know it's there, it exists. Hey, what can we do about it?" "It's something that's going to happen and you get used to that because it happens so often out there. You may be out there the night three or four guys may get stabbed; you may see them taken to the hospital. You ask them what happened, 'You just got stabbed ten times in this block?' Just like it's a normal conversation, nothing. So after a while you get used to it."

Yet officers who claimed antipathy to inmates and indifference to the violence inmates inflicted on one another (or that inmates inflicted on themselves) seemed at times to betray those sentiments in the interviews. One such officer described himself as harder and colder for having worked in prison. "Since I've been here I've seen so much. Now when I hear about some horrible crime I don't think anything of it, like someone cutting off someone's head. I'm indifferent." He spoke disparagingly of inmates. But toward the end of the interview he recalled the following incident. One night, an inmate in his block who had just a few years left on his sentence jammed his cell door closed and lit himself on fire. "It didn't kill him but he burned himself so bad that it makes your eyes water to see him." When the inmate was eventually transferred back to the prison hospital the officer stopped by to visit him. "I asked him why he did it and he said he just couldn't cope." After a long pause in the interview with me, the officer shook his head and added quietly, "I guess things don't bother me the way they used to."

He was not the only interviewee whose professed indifference to inmate-on-inmate violence conflicted with reactions to specific events. Shortly before I conducted one set of interviews at Walpole, an inmate scalded, gashed, and castrated himself. A dozen or more officers were required to subdue him. Almost every officer interviewed who had been on duty at the time spoke of the incident with shock and dismay. One officer involved had to be taken to the hospital with hyperventilation. Others felt nauseated. They disguised their feelings as best they could, even from one another. But, as a senior officer who was involved pointed out, such incidents took a tremendous psychological toll. "The officer who had to go into his cell and pick the testicles up off the floor and get blood all over him . . . He goes down to get a new shirt and clean the blood off him. And then maybe he goes to a bar and has one drink or maybe three or four because that's the only way he can forget. And maybe when he gets home he's roaring drunk."

While most officers soon became accustomed to the suffering inmates inflicted on other inmates, they came more slowly to accept their own role in that suffering. Their resistance eroded first to participation in the daily degradations of prison life. Skin-searching inmates, placing them in cold and barren cells, taking apart their rooms in search of contraband: these are ordinary tasks that officers must perform if they are to retain their jobs. But that does not mean they like performing them or are oblivious to the humiliation and hurt caused.

A Concord officer reported his reaction to doing shakedowns. "To me that was really dehumanizing. But I did it. I felt really shitty about it. But I did it. So, yes, it had an effect because I did it. I sure the hell couldn't have said no, first of all, okay, because I would have been out on my ear. But in that respect it had effect. I felt every inch of it." A Bridgewater officer objected to the treatment inmates received in seclusion cells with

> no bed, no clothes, just pajamas and it's cold in there. They have the windows open sometimes and it was freezing. Nothing on the floor except the . . . holes where you go to the bathroom. So that was really bad . . .
> *Did you find it bothered you at all . . . locking somebody up in that kind of room . . . knowing they're going to be cold?*
> Yes, it did.
> *How did you cope with that kind of feeling?*
> Defense mechanisms. Really, just say, "Hey, it's the way they do it here and there's nothing—I can't do anything about it." If you did, if you tried to throw a blanket in there, you'd get in trouble . . . If he hangs himself [with the blanket], you can be even worse off. I don't know. It's tough . . . A prison is tough both on an inmate and on an officer.

Avoiding the performance of objectionable tasks often brought officers into conflict with values such as honesty and duty. For example, many officers considered "skinning" (skin-searching) inmates "disgusting and degrading" for the inmates and themselves. One officer reported he regularly disobeyed orders to "skin" inmates if he felt it was "just to degrade the guy," but recognized that in the process he was being "dishonest" with his superiors. He was troubled by the constant "conflict in values" he faced on the job. "As an officer you're in many positions where you just can't control and you maybe don't want to act that way, but you have to . . . I constantly had to compromise." (I began making compromises with my own conscience the first day I worked as an officer. I was assigned to an old building, one in which each cell had to be individually locked and unlocked. The building was an obvious fire trap. Yet each night I carefully locked the women into their cells all the while knowing that in case of a major fire the two officers on the midnight shift could not possibly have unlocked all the cells in time to prevent loss of life. The only way for me to have avoided carrying out this duty would have been to resign. Numerous fatalities that have occurred in prisons and jails across the nation under the same circumstances suggest that thousands of officers must daily make this same compromise. Officers have virtually no influence over decisions such as whether or not to install expensive new locking mechanisms or replace old buildings. What they cannot change they come to accept, as I did.)

In order to cope with even their minimum daily duties officers found they "started developing calluses." Actions that at first were troubling eventually became routine and, in the process, lost much of their moral sting. A former officer recalled the appalling conditions in Walpole's punishment cells with urine and feces backed up onto the floor and maggots and roaches everywhere. Yet he got used to putting men in there.

> I know it was a real dump now, when I look at it. But at the time it was just where you go. It wasn't like I stood there every time I had to put somebody in there and I was totally emotional or something like that about it . . . The first time I saw it, it bothered me, and now it bothers me, but at the time it was just . . . an everyday thing.

As the Bridgewater officer who at first hated to put men into cold isolation cells reflected, "After a while you get immune to it. You have to. It's not that you're cold and all that—well, maybe some people are, but . . . you have to get immune to it."

Once having gotten used to their involvement in lesser acts of degradation, use of physical violence also lost some of its repugnance. The Bridgewater officer just quoted continued, "It's [like] a war. You have to get used to getting shot at and before you know it, you're shooting back. You've got to shoot or be shot."

The desire to "shoot back" often seemed overwhelming. *Yet many officers went to great lengths to restrain themselves from using violence within the prison.* They sought to control their aggressions through such legitimate outlets as boxing, judo, and weight lifting. One officer "got a couple of tires set up and . . . beat on the tires once in a while. It does me a world of good because when you got so much anxiety inside of you, it is good to lose a lot of it."

When inanimate objects provided insufficient release, some officers still avoided using violence *within* the prison, but found themselves using it outside instead. Men who had never fought before became regular participants in barroom brawls. "It was not out of dislike for the poor guy who owned the barroom . . . [but because of the] pent-up anger that builds up from being an officer here. Many times it's hard to keep your temper." Some turned their aggressions onto themselves. "I took it out on myself, on walls, punch walls. That's what I did. Because that [way] I took the anxiety out on me." Others took it out on those they cared for most—their families and their friends. One officer who had come to hate inmates and felt considerable aggression toward them nevertheless abstained for more than a year from the violence at his institution. As an accomplished hockey player, however, he found himself taking his hostilities out on the ice. For the first time in his life he played "dirty and aggressive," deliberately injuring opponents. "I lost a lot of friends . . . people I've known all my life. I got into . . . fights; I got thrown out of games. I did everything. I was crazy. I could've hurt some people really bad and I didn't care. No way did I care. I didn't care what I did to them. I *couldn't*."

Officers who resisted the use of violence within the prison did so not merely out of a sense that such violence was illegal or unjustifiable under the circumstances. Their feelings persisted even in the one situation in which they might have lawfully maimed or killed an inmate. Twenty-four hours a day, officers are stationed in gun towers with orders to shoot if necessary to prevent inmates from escaping. A majority of officers felt they had an obligation to follow those orders, however reluctantly, to ensure the safety of individuals outside. "I'd hate to have someone go over the walls and then go down the street and kill somebody and that would be my responsibility if I couldn't pull the trigger. I mean, right now I'm saying I'd do it—I hope I'm never put in that position." A few (mainly those who had been in combat) saw no moral conflict. "I would shoot him . . . I was taught that when I was in the military. Those are the rules and regulations. I wouldn't think twice. You don't let your moral feelings come between you and the rules in that situation."

To an extent that might have surprised their superiors, however, many officers reported that their "moral feelings" placed them in serious conflict with "the rules" when they were on gun tower duty. An experienced officer who had worked the gun towers from time to time over a period of years and was well respected within his prison responded to my query,

*Would you have shot anyone?*

I don't really know . . . I'd probably be so scared that I'd lose my job [that I would say], "Okay, I know it's you, Jones. I see you going over!" and pray he'd go back without shooting, and then give the warning shots. I don't think I could, though. I would say I shot at him, or I would try and hit his toe or something. I'd be so scared of permanently hurting a guy unless, maybe if it was a certain individual who I knew was really vicious or someone that I was deathly afraid of that if he got into society someone would really be hurt.

This officer was "scared of permanently hurting" an inmate not only because of what that would mean for the inmate, but also because he believed that in the process he would destroy what he valued about *himself*. Like other officers, he had no doubts as to the nature of the moral dilemma he faced.

I think it's like a lot of things that they say, "This is your job and it's right." I can't see it as being right. I can't accept it. I can't. I couldn't live with it . . . Inside of me there's two parts. One that says I read the post orders and I [am] standing here with my loaded gun and I know what to do. But then there's always that other guy that's inside and it says, "If you do it, what happens to *you* afterwards." I mean, you can take my uniform and hang it up in the hall of fame for correction officers and say I hit the guy three times in the head. But it's an empty uniform. The person that was in there is gone, is destroyed and is no longer. Some guys can live with it and say, "Yup, that's my uniform." But I couldn't. I just couldn't accept that.

As officers found themselves becoming more and more a part of the prison world, many expressed genuine dismay at changes they saw in themselves, especially their decreasing resistance to the use of violence and a corresponding willingness to violate their own consciences. An officer who regularly worked the gun towers reflected,

When you get someone missing and they notify all the towers, I found myself grabbing for that shotgun. And I would catch myself standing out of my window. "——, what the fuck are you doing?" I really would question myself. "Suppose he did come your way?". . . I don't think I ever would have lived with myself. That would have really tore me up if I had blown somebody away. But was I ready to? Yeah. If it ever went down. I *still* don't know . . . Things like that really started really getting to me. Like what happens if you are put in a situation, how would you react to it? Too often the answer was coming up "guard." Again, that individualism was slowly being eaten out of my soul.

A mild-mannered colleague, a pacifist at heart, experienced much the same effect:

It was weird, I found myself up there just playing with guns. And I don't even like guns and I don't even think I could shoot anybody. Here I am seeing how fast I can empty all the shells out of the shuck . . . If I had spent any more time in the tower I felt I would have become immune to it. I would have waited for it, waited for them to try an escape so I could fire at will. That's the kind of emotional state I was getting to. It wasn't a question of whether I would shoot them or whether I wouldn't shoot them but when are they coming? . . . How soon will I wait before I start blasting? . . . It didn't matter whether the inmate lived or whether the inmate died, it was just, put a notch in the gun for me. And I don't think it was just me who'd go through that kind of mental thing. I'm sure everybody who . . . is stuck out in the tower would go through that.

*Neutralizing guilt.* Regardless of their own moral inhibitions regarding violence, substantial numbers of officers eventually came to use it against inmates. They sought to neutralize their guilt over violating moral laws *to which they subscribed* by postulating that the prison world constituted a separate moral realm or that inmates were beings beyond the embrace of moral laws.

An officer asserted, "This is a prison and it's not society. When you step in here, you step into a different world." He used this logic to defend a moral code for prisons based on an eye for an eye (or, more accurately, two eyes for an eye) while simultaneously rejecting that moral code for the world he lived in outside.

It's brutality anyway you look at it, even {in terms of} getting a beating for giving a beating is brutality. But you got no other choice. If there was any other way open to us, we'd take it . . . So it is cruel and I guess if I was on the outside I would disagree with it. But I can't, not from my standpoint at the moment.

A colleague agreed, "As far as I'm concerned, this is a different world in here. It operates under different principles that you can't carry on outside over here."

But attempting to construct and inhabit simultaneously two separate moral realms has serious drawbacks, not least of which is that actions appropriate to only one realm are susceptible to judgments emanating from the other.* For example, an officer who engaged in the practice of cosigning disciplinary reports regarding events he had not actually witnessed labeled his own actions as "morally wrong" and indefensible outside the prison context. An officer at a different institution who was heavily involved in the violence of his prison also characterized his behavior as "wrong" and said of colleagues who engaged in similar behavior, "if they acted like that out on the streets, I wouldn't even want to be associated with them."

An alternative (and apparently more successful) technique of neutralizing guilt was to postulate that inmates constitute a class of individuals beyond the claims of morality, that they are not, in fact, persons to whom one owes moral obligations at all. Men behind bars were seen to have relinquished their claims to moral consideration by virtue of their status and behavior as inmates. An officer characterized his colleagues' reasoning about all inmates, " 'This guy is bad. The court put him here. He cannot be good. There's no reason other than that he is evil that he is here.' " Inmates were "moral morons," incapable of moral thought or moral action inside prisons or out. Nowhere was inmate depravity demonstrated more convincingly than in the mutilated corpses of their fellow inmates. "I can't believe how unhumanly the inmates act," mused one officer. "The cons kill the cons—that's their own—over nothing!" Are not those who dismember their own on a whim, who live in excrement, and who respond to violence but not reason more animal than human? "They're just programmed. These guys have nothing in their brains or nothing in their lives other than violence and danger . . . Those aren't really like people. Most of them are animals." From such a

---

* I am referring here to *internal* judgments, ones officers make of themselves. But they are also, of course, subject to *external* judgments, ones made by people outside the prison. Part of the anger and bitterness officers felt in the 1970s regarding judicial intrusion into the internal affairs of prisons derived from the fact that such intrusions violated the moral separation between society and its prisons. The consequences for a society of creating and maintaining institutions with moral standards distinct from and substantially lower than those of the society as a whole are considered in the concluding chapter.

perspective officers concluded, "There's only one way to handle an animal, right? And that's what they are, I guess. They live in an animal atmosphere so they must be classified animals. And you've got to, you've got to, you've got to treat them what they are. And you've got to railroad them."

The perception that a class of individuals constitute a breed apart, " 'that those people are the scum of the earth and there is not even a slight resemblance to me,' " plays an important part in lowering barriers to violence in prison, as it does on the battlefield. Soldiers "go to war and they say, 'Well, I killed this gook and I shot this commie.' " Officers went to prison and they spoke of maggots killing each other, of *inmates* bleeding and dying, not men. "What happens here to the inmates does not bother me now in the least. I have no compassion for the inmates as a group . . . I used to pass out at the sight of blood. Now it doesn't bother me. It's *inmate* blood."

A former officer understood the power of such metaphors in permitting officers to victimize inmates.

> If you can put yourself in a frame of mind that they're animals—I'm a human being; I'm a good human being and they're bad human beings; or make that separation—whatever feels comfortable in your own head, it's easy to perpetrate that feeling of animosity, that hatred, that fear. Because there's a lot of fear in guards, believe me—that fear that turns into hate. You're scared five days a week. How do you deal with that fear? By three or four dudes beating up on somebody? Yeah, that's one way because that makes you strong and makes you feel good. But also by making him *less* than you because if you're better then you don't need to fear him as much. And that's a mentality, guards are better than the inmates.

This officer rejected the " 'us' against 'them' philosophy" yet believed that "that's the kind of mentality you have to go in with in order to succeed or survive . . . You have to give up that feeling that that's a human being you're dealing with and not just a piece of meat."

The tendency to view inmates as nonhuman was particularly marked at the Bridgewater State Hospital, where many inmates looked and behaved unlike anyone officers had ever encountered outside. There were inmates who in their anguish had destroyed their own faces and no longer had eyes, noses, foreheads; there were others who themselves believed they were not humans but devils, werewolves, or a variety of earthly and unearthly creatures instead. A Bridgewater officer recalled an inmate who

> started yelling and screaming like a wild animal. We had to put a towel around his neck and arms and take him down to seclusion ... There was a full moon out, too, big, big moon right above seclusion ... I had that [towel] tight as I could hold it ... He was a wild man. He wasn't human. There was no way. He wasn't a human being. We weren't dealing with a person. He didn't even *feel* like a person. It was weird. I'll never forget that.

Such inmates seemed devoid of characteristics that were essentially human; not surprisingly, some officers came to treat them as if they were not humans at all.

An inescapable flaw in efforts to evict inmates from the moral realm exposed officers once again to self-judgment and guilt. Regardless of what inmates had done in the past, how they behaved in the present, even how they looked, they were still fellow human beings, a fact that all officers readily acknowledged when pressed. Unable to justify fully what they were doing either by restructuring the moral world or determining its membership, officers attempted to shut off feeling and conscience by becoming "disassociated, nonemotional, noncaring, unconcerned." Doing so became a matter of physical and psychological *survival.* "I guess I put it in my conscience not to feel anything because I knew in the long run it would only be damaging to me ... I had to get used to it or I wasn't going to make it. It was a point of survival. Either me or them, and I decided it was going to be me."

*Long-term moral effects.* "You can't think of a person as an individual or even as a real human in a situation like that without ultimately being damaged somehow," an officer reluctantly concluded. But in the long run such a strategy proved most damaging of all to officers, for it eventually impaired their capacity to care for anyone. An officer spoke of the effect Vietnam and Walpole had had.

> After you see so much, you can't tolerate it. So you blot it out ... There's a shutter there that says, "All right, you've killed and you've killed and you've killed, and you've seen your buddies' heads blown off and everything like that. Now I'm just cutting that off. That don't bother you." And you, you're not the same person ... Some guys readjust to a degree. I don't think that lid or whatever it is that closes don't ever open all the way

again. Something's different about you. There's a character change . . . The mind just says, "I've seen all I can take." Click!

Most officers in this study recognized the damage. One observed of his colleagues, his friends, "They have become hard as rocks. Their personalities have just turned cold." They felt they had to become hard. An officer of ten years said of his wife, "She calls me a sadist. She says I don't care about people. In here I *can't* care about people." Concurred an officer near retirement who despaired at what Walpole had done to his life, "You can't be a positive person in a place like this. A prison is a place of hate." Exposure to such an environment had lasting effects on some men. Two years after the officer who saw his colleagues "become hard as rocks" had resigned, he spoke of what the prison had done to his own capacity to care for anyone. Shortly before I interviewed him for the last time he had happened upon an automobile accident. Though instrumental in extricating the badly mangled victims, he found himself utterly indifferent to their fate. "I used to have a lot of compassion I felt for people and now I don't have as much . . . It just doesn't bother me the way it used to and it bothers me that it doesn't bother me! . . . I just can't get the feelings back for certain things."

Another former officer who had become heavily involved in the violence at his institution recalled, "When you get in there and you're new you say, 'No, no, it's not going to happen to me.' But when you go in there day in and day out and get ten years in and you're watching it, seeing it all the time, you become just like them. And the next thing you know, you're a heavy hitter and the whole bit." After this officer finally left the institution, he groped for insight into what had happened to him. "I lost something. I don't know what it is. I'm still trying to find out. It's something definitely missing there."

Even officers who did not actively participate in the violence found their passive acquiescence in it destructive for themselves. They spoke of feeling ashamed and degraded by what happened around them. I asked an officer who had worked throughout the worst crises of the 1970s what was the worst an inmate had ever been hurt at the hands of officers that he had witnessed. He described a particularly brutal beating of an inmate by a group of officers. And then he said,

Maybe I feel, what I'm saying on his hurt, is my hurt. Because I felt so lacking, so missing something that I didn't do something. I was really totally ashamed, totally embarrassed that I had to say that I seen, and I'm really, really sorry. And I'm not sorry for him, I'm sorry for me that I didn't have the guts or the balls or whatever you want to say, to do something at that time. And it, it eats away afterwards. So maybe when I say hurt I don't mean him, but I mean me.

These were not Abbott's "cold characters" and "brutal sadists." They were men who feared their very souls were being destroyed by the violence and their own complicity in it.

## Social Effects

When I asked officers what effect prison work had had on them, many replied, "You should ask my wife!" Officers who had learned to cope, if only marginally, inside prison often found themselves unable to cope outside. Nearly all carried home with them characteristics that made prison life more tolerable but made home life less tolerable for everyone—qualities of being hard, cold, callous, gruff, suspicious, indifferent. As discussed in earlier sections, officers often displaced aggressions onto those they loved "because you're holding everything in here, you've got to let it out somewhere. {Where} you going to let it out? Your home, your wife." They did not like what they had become as husbands and fathers.

I hated being there, and you know how you are when you're mad and somebody comes up to you and you don't want to hear it and you just bite their head off? I did that a lot, not because I wanted to, I was just very unhappy. I was really miserable . . . I was bringing it home. I was so mad and so upset that I had to go to work every day that I'd be mad at my wife. I really put her through a lot of hell.

It was a common tale, officers coming home in a "piss-poor mood and taking it out on the wife and kids."

Officers who successfully adjusted to the demands of prison work by adopting an aggressive, commanding stance regarding inmates often found themselves unable to leave those traits behind. One officer humorously characterized such men, "I think these are the kind of guys that go home, call count time to their kids, 'Count time!' If they don't go in [their rooms] they get a ticket. Put the wife in isolation for ten days." There was an element of truth in his jesting.

An officer highly rated by his superiors for his strong-arm tactics at work reported his home life in shambles. He found he had to "concentrate" at home in order not to behave there as he did in the prison. He cautioned himself, "You don't give an order at home; you don't give the same kind of responses. You can't be blunt. You need to give more descriptive answers." Other officers, emotionally exhausted from working in the prison, became apathetic and withdrawn at home. "I didn't care about the mortgage payments; I didn't care about any bills; I didn't care about anything." It is little wonder that "so many guys got divorces." "Take one hundred officers in here," remarked a Walpole officer, "and ninety-five have home problems."

Most painful for some officers was the deterioration in relations with their children. Some were too emotionally strung out by what they were experiencing at work to participate in their children's upbringing. "My daughter was at a real good age back then," sadly recalled one former officer, "and I didn't have anything to do with her." Others found themselves becoming authoritarian with their children, partly carrying over behavior appropriate only in a prison, but also partly acting out of fear for where a wayward youth could lead.

The isolation suffered by many officers was exacerbated by their inability to make others understand what was happening to them inside the prison. A gnawing sense that "no one can understand what goes on in [a prison] . . . unless they've worked there" led officers to turn more and more to fellow officers for companionship and solace and less and less to their families and those who had been their closest friends. "Who am I going to talk to about this place? Nobody would understand what it's like to work in here. They couldn't possibly."

Some officers initially tried to talk with their wives about their prison work but found that the topic led to arguments, misunderstandings, and an eventual resolve not to discuss work at home. Others found that when they spoke of what was happening in the prisons, "People don't believe it. [My wife] won't believe any of that stuff if you come home and tell her." Most officers were not sure they wanted their families to know what was happening. When I suggested that wives should perhaps be given a tour of Walpole, the officer whose wife "didn't believe" him replied,

You wouldn't want them to come. I think it's better off them not knowing what it's like than having to go in and experience it. Because I don't think the average human being should have to go into an environment like that because it leaves a scar on everybody that's involved in it . . . If it's being sheltered, you should be sheltered. I'd rather be sheltered than be exposed.

Many officers chose to tell their wives as little as possible. But their silence was rarely successful in protecting their families from worry, or their marriages from stress.

That was my biggest problem. During that time when I went through it I didn't want my wife to go through it and I seen no sense in me telling everything. And she'd say, "I heard over the radio, I'm worried sick, what happened?" "Nothing. There was just an incident." "Were you there?" I'd say, "Well, yes, but I didn't have to do anything. We just went in and took the guy out." She'd press me. I felt nervous about telling her. I figured she's got enough to worry about. And then she'd get mad because the guys would come over to pick me up and they'd say, "Hey, that was really something yesterday where so-and-so swung and just missed you with this or got you that." And then she'd say, "How come you don't tell me. Please share it with me." And I'd say, "I feel very uncomfortable about having you go through that. I know how I feel going through it and I feel uncomfortable about you going through it."

And that was the only real problem, in that she figured I wasn't telling her everything. And I wasn't. I didn't think no need to [say] . . . "I really feel shitty. The tension is unbelievable." I just couldn't see me doing that. It would be like me hurting her and I didn't want to do it. But she really didn't like understand . . . Some marriages were already shaky and that was the straw that broke the camel's back.

If officers felt they could not share with their families what was happening to them, they might still have found emotional outlet among friends and individuals unconnected to the prison world, but the opportunity for such social contacts was severely limited. Prisons by their nature are insular places. Officers have virtually no contact on the job with persons unrelated to the prison. Social relations *outside* the prison were also greatly constrained for the officers in this study by the hours they were forced to work. As already noted, officers, especially those at Walpole, were required to work long hours of overtime every week throughout the 1970s. To make matters worse, shift and days off were determined exclusively by seniority bid. Thus, an officer typically had to work for years before he acquired weekends off or could bid onto the day shift. (House officers at Norfolk worked swing shifts and had variable days off, thus allowing them more normal contacts with the world outside the prison.)

Working the 3–11 shift with weekdays off wreaked havoc with an officer's family and social life.

> A new guy . . . comes in and he's put on a shift where he doesn't see a weekend in I don't know how long . . . They're expecting you for the younger years of your life, for the first four or five years, to take Tuesday and Wednesday or a Thursday and a Friday off . . . What can a guy look forward to on a Tuesday and Wednesday? On weekends when his family are going out, people are socializing, he's in working. And when he comes during the middle of the week, nobody wants to do anything.

They felt they had no alternative but to seek companionship with fellow officers. Their social life centered on Wednesday fishing trips, midday ball games, and drinking at the pub with the car pool after work. Men working the 3–11 with no weekends off scarcely saw their friends or school-aged children. Those who stopped to drink and forget on the way home hardly saw their wives either. "You get out of work at eleven and you could be home at twelve, quarter past twelve. You stay out and drink half the night away and you get home at two or two-thirty and on top of that you come home {half in the bag}, it doesn't help your marriage any."

Even when officers had the opportunity to socialize with people outside of the prison world, they often found themselves unable or unwilling to do so. Negative stereotypes about prison officers abound. Many officers came to avoid strangers for fear they would be treated with derision or hostility. When they did deal with others outside the prison they often found themselves being suspicious and aggressive. A Norfolk officer recalled the effect prison work had on him:

> It makes you very wary. In fact, I think it hurts you making tight personal relationships . . . Outside I think you have less of a compassion for your fellow man because . . . you're constantly associating with people who are ready to get you on the slightest slip of your words. And you become very positive [in] what

you say. You say only what you want people to hear . . . I wasn't inclined towards letting somebody put something over on me without bringing it to their attention.

Nor was it just relations with strangers that were impaired. Friends were often avoided, too. Many officers found they had lost the ability to communicate about anything other than the prison. "I'd meet someone I hadn't seen on the street and I had nothing to say," recalled one officer. Those who made an effort to say something found they couldn't communicate without using language and metaphor appropriate only to the prison. "I was with people I hadn't seen in a long time and they weren't correctional oriented . . . [I kept] cracking jokes about, 'Well, you should be locked in Block 10 or something.' And they didn't understand what I'd say." Many eventually gave up trying to communicate. "I'd see friends," explained another officer. "But what do you talk about? What do you say to people? 'Well, we locked this guy up?' You don't want to talk to them about what goes on up there." When this officer finally quit he found, "I had lost a lot of friends, and it was tough."*

Especially when the system was in turmoil, the prison world consumed their whole lives and left little for those outside. A Walpole officer recalled some of the worst days of the 1970s.

When you are working at Walpole, especially during the trouble times, you ate, sleep and drank Walpole . . . You went down to the [local bar] and you went to the package store, picked up a six-pack, and all the guys from Walpole that you rode with that's all you'd talk about. You went home, you'd catch a few hours sleep that was necessary, and then you'd go back and you'd be in that car pool. Your friends were Walpole, especially if you were on the 3-to-11 . . . and you had Tuesday-Wednesdays off . . . So your whole total "you" was Walpole . . . You just got

---

* I, too, came to avoid former friends and acquaintances while I was working as a prison officer. The prison in which I was employed was about an hour's drive from the college from which I had recently graduated. Although some of my college friends and acquaintances were supportive and interested in what I was doing, others proved unsympathetic and hostile. I recall one encounter in particular. I was walking on the campus green with my house keys pinned to my clothes, a practical arrangement since there were holes in all the pockets of my faded jeans. A law student I knew announced loudly that I had always struck her as the type who "liked keys" and demanded to know if I got a thrill out of locking people up. During those days, visits back to my old college haunts often filled me with greater trepidation than did the prison on a tense day.

so involved it was the whole *everything*. Everything was Walpole . . . And it was just so totally the picture that it was really scary . . . Jesus that was a time that was . . . I don't know how I went through it and I don't know how anybody else went through it.

Isolation of officers from the world outside did not just have implications for themselves and their families. It also strengthened the claims of the officer subculture and made more plausible the idea that the prison was a physical, moral, and social world unto itself.

## Escape

"Walpole is a dismal place for officers as well as inmates," sadly commented a senior officer who had spent a major part of his life working there. A Bridgewater supervisor with more than twenty years on the job was more succinct. "The job sucks. I wouldn't recommend it to anyone . . . Who in his right mind would be a correction officer?" The Norfolk officer who made perhaps the happiest adjustment to prison work of anyone in this study nonetheless considered his institution "a very grey place" in which to work. "You still got the walls to look at. You're still in prison as much as the inmates are."

The parallels between keeper and kept were obvious to men for whom working in prison was like "doing time." "Guards get paid for being cons. You're a con in there, you're not a guard in there." Officers plotted their escape from prison as desperately as did the men they guarded. "Everyone is looking for an out . . . I'd quit tomorrow [if I had another job]. I wouldn't even give them notice. I'd just walk out." Older officers counseled their younger colleagues to get out while they still had a chance. " 'If you're smart, you get out of here right now.' . . . What they're saying is, 'I made a mistake and I don't want you to do it.' " In an effort to heed that advice, each year scores of officers took exams for jobs in the post office and fire and police departments and applied for anything else that offered an alternative. "You watch these guys, they get the 'help wanted' ads. I don't think there's hardly an officer in here that doesn't study them." What would it take for one interviewee to quit? "A job offer! . . . Offer me a job, watch me take it. When you come up with something, let me know!"

Under the circumstances, it should come as no surprise that turnover rates among officers were high. Nearly half of the officers in my longitudinal sample left the department within two years. Nor did they seem atypical. According to a Department of Correction study, 10 percent of all officers hired between 1975 and 1980 left the department within six months, and 20 percent left by the end of their first year (Massachusetts Department of Correction, 1981a, p. 27). More than half of all officers employed by the department in any capacity had less than five years service (Massachusetts Department of Correction, 1981b, p. 28). Predictably, of the four major facilities for men, retention rates were lowest at Walpole (Massachusetts Department of Correction, 1981a, p. 35).

Those who stayed "had nowhere else to go." A young Norfolk officer who found nothing rewarding about his job other than his paycheck asked plaintively, "If I could find something better I'd consider it, no doubt about it. I did not have goals in my life to become a correction officer. But what can you get on the street? . . . I have no college education. I have no trade . . . Where do I go? What do I turn to?" An older officer at Walpole echoed his plea. He had originally come to Walpole two decades earlier when the mills had closed. Over the years he had become consumed with hate. A priest to whom he went for advice urged him to leave the prison. "But where can I go? I've worked here twenty years. What else can I do?" And so he stayed, despairing that life and happiness had irretrievably passed him by. Officers like him were melancholy when they spoke of what they might have been—teachers, football coaches, firemen. Young and old, they felt trapped. A Bridgewater officer lamented, "I can see myself never getting out of here, *never*." A young Walpole officer who did not feel he had the "guts" to quit observed of his colleagues in words that applied to himself, "There are some good guys working here, some really super people. I don't know why they work in a place like this and ruin their lives. You can tell they aren't happy." Why did he stay? "The security is it. That's all there is. My inner feelings are being destroyed. I just want to be happy. I don't think that's too much to ask." For such men, the financial security offered by their job was a trap. As he put it, "They are paying me good money to ruin my life."

When unable to find another job, some officers sought alternative means of escape, such as medical or psychiatric retirement. A few officers even considered early retirement, courtesy of the inmates. "I had a couple of cons that were going to put me out. Talked about it, said, 'We'll put you out, no problem.' And I was close to saying,

'Yeah.' . . . There's a lot of guys in there really hoping they were going to get hit." Men like him were so desperate for a way out of their situation that they entertained inviting assault on themselves. Some men, even those "with a lot of years and time in, just left. They quit their jobs without any future job prospects, not another job in hand." But most officers, even young ones, felt bound to stay unless they could find an honorable way out.

I think the saddest thing about the interviews I conducted was the pain with which some officers suffered the censure of their families for their failure to cope with the prison environment and for their desire to quit regardless of future prospects. Their families were usually too isolated from other officers' families and too removed from what was happening in the prisons to appreciate how destructive the prisons were for nearly everyone who worked inside them. In their ignorance they pressured their men to stay, blaming them for the problems they were having at the prison and for what they were becoming as husbands, fathers, and sons.

An officer who as a rookie was enthusiastic about his job but two years later was "totally unenthusiastic" about it recalled the pressure he had been under not to quit. "Everybody was saying, all my family, my wife and everybody, 'You have a good job.' And I just didn't want to blow it and have everybody think, 'There he goes, he's blowing a good job.' I had that on my mind a lot." He stayed for several years because "there was no place else to go." And then one day he abruptly quit.

> I just wanted to get out of there so bad. I didn't even have a job to go to. I hated it so much that I quit right on the spot . . . My parents and [my wife's] parents were completely disgusted with me when I quit. But they didn't know what was going on. All they cared about was that it was a civil service job, state job. It was a pretty good job as far as they were concerned because of the money and I guess the title and everything . . . Her mother and father like disowned me when I quit, not even knowing anything about it. It was just like a major cop-out . . . "He wasn't happy so he just left. He didn't care about the children or the wife or anything. He just said to hell with everything." I didn't say to *hell* with everything. It was just the job was making me sick, turning me into somebody that I really am not.

Members of his family were not the only ones who did not understand.

A lot of people . . . they just can't understand why I quit. "Boy, you're crazy—good money, good benefits." I get really, really mad. I really do. I jump off the gun and I shouldn't. I just say, "Hey, look, *you* go up there and *you* see what it's like. Don't tell *me* what it's like if you haven't been there." As far as the conditions themselves, nobody knows. But they're always right there to say you're stupid for quitting.

Officers suffered their families' censure deeply and often shared their families' judgment of themselves as failures whether they resigned from the prison or not.

## Life after Prison

"There was nothing that felt better than when I called in and told them I was leaving . . . It was like a rush." But all too often quitting provided but a momentary high. By the time they finally left prison, many officers were spent, finished. "I was done." "I was a complete mental and physical wreck." Their marriages often had already broken up. Those who had quit without another job in hand found they could not easily get one.

I quit my job. I had nothing. Couldn't get a job after that . . . I figured, ah, heck, I could find a job somewhere, I've been a screw for two years. But they don't want me. They don't want a screw, nowhere, nobody. Except police—that's the only place, maybe security guards. But if you go to another job and you say you've been a guard, they don't want you . . . It's a combination of the reputation you have as being a guard, as being a jerk and a drunk and dope and everything else I guess. That's the impression from most people. I couldn't even get a job for minimum wage at [the factories] . . . I couldn't believe it!

And they still had with them the memories. They were still plagued by nightmares and flashbacks. "I dream about it a lot. I find myself driving the car and I'll be in [the cell] block—and I'll wake up and I'm on the highway driving. I'll find myself walking down the tier in [the] block while I'm driving—my wife's here, the kids, and I've blocked everything out. I'm *right in* the block!" The sights and sounds of the prison were still with them. "That sound [of a slamming door], I still can hear it now. Because you knew—Bingo! you were going [in] . . . Just the word 'slam,' phew! it opens up really what was going on."

Some continued to feel the effects for years. "I'm still depressed," reported a Bridgewater officer more than a year after he had left. "I can't slow down anymore. I'm always like nervous all the time." Their whole outlook on life had been distorted. A former Norfolk officer described the impact of his two years at the prison, "It's like a rude awakening. I don't have a trust, the optimistic views of humanity anymore." For some, the damage seemed permanent. "I probably will never forget about Walpole, I don't think. I really don't. Maybe I'm wrong. I'm trying to, but it's kind of a real shock. It's like unexplainable. I mean I *know* why they're in there, but I can't explain in my own head why everything's happened like that." For men like him—former prison officer, former infantryman—leaving Walpole "was like coming home from Vietnam."

No one had cared what happened to them inside the prison other than their fellow officers. When they left, they found no one cared at all, least of all that society they once thought they were serving. As one officer bitterly concluded, society still owed him something for the years he had worked at Walpole, but never would deliver.

> I should get a disability from that place . . . I don't see why not. Put you through hell for a couple of years. It'll ruin your life. It'll ruin everything around you. Everything you touch is ruined. They don't care. They'll just get some other jerk to work there. They don't care.

# = 10 =

# A Typology of Officers

The passage through which one enters the Massachusetts state prison is called "the trap." It is appropriately named. Few avoid for long the changes prisons wreak on those who pass inside their walls. Prison work affected most of the officers who were part of this study in ways discussed in the preceding chapter. Despite similarities in what prisons do to men who work within them, ways in which officers respond to and seek to cope with the prison environment vary. These variations are the subject of this chapter.

The many and colorful "argot roles" assumed by inmates have provided interesting material for those who study prisons. "Real men," "ball busters," "rats," "center men," "gorillas," "merchants," "wolves," "fags," "punks," "toughs," and "hipsters" populate scholarly accounts of the prison world. Those who guard this entertaining assortment of prisoners, meanwhile, "remain a faceless, undifferentiated group, their grey homogeneity unrelieved by any colorful argot role-playing" (Hawkins, 1976, p. 81). But the officers' "grey homogeneity" is a facade. Beneath it are attitudes and responses to the prison world as distinct among officers as are differences that exist among inmates.

## The Officer Facade

The facade most officers adopt at prisons like Walpole is that of the "Hard Ass," coldly indifferent to inmates and to the violence and sadism around them. "We all change a little bit when we come in the front door for roll call. You put on your cap and assume a different disguise for eight hours a day . . . You got to kind of knuckle down and be the tough guy." They seek to maintain that "disguise" regardless of the circumstances they are in or the company they are keeping. "The whole thing is going around . . . [acting like] you're not affected by it all. So what these officers are doing the whole time is putting on a big front. They're constantly working on that and making sure they don't let this down whether it's subconscious or not." (Officers, of course, are not the only ones inside prisons who disguise their feelings. Inmates, especially those at Walpole, put on a facade as coolly indifferent as that of the officers.)

Officers put on "a big front" for a number of reasons. First and foremost, they seek to disguise their true feelings because they fear for their own physical safety. A common perception, especially at Walpole, was that any officer who indicated he was intimidated or distressed placed himself in great danger from inmates. "You can't be nervous in there because they sense it and they eat you alive."

> So that used to be the biggest thing, was if you heard something behind you, don't turn around fast because that's a cue, "This guy is nervous. I'm going to start getting on his case." . . . Even though you were scared as hell, which sometimes you were . . . you just for some reason within you, you kept on saying, "You can't show it, you can't show it, you can't show it."

Officers who were shocked and revolted by the violence of the prison strove to appear casual, preferably callous, in order to protect themselves. An inmate was stabbed one night in a block and was bleeding profusely. Officers

> dragged him out and while we were taking care of him one of the other inmates takes the blood and writes "kill" on the wall. I had that block the next night and to try not to let the inmates know that it actually did affect me I says, "Hey, you stupid bastards, I see you forgot to dot the 'i.'" So one of them came over and dotted the "i."

Cool in public, this officer privately resolved, "That's it. I'm through. I am going to hit the want ads tomorrow."

Second, officers seek to "cover up" their feelings because they fear that otherwise they will not be able to cope emotionally with situations in which they find themselves. An officer recalled his own hostility as a rookie to fellow officers who seemed cold and indifferent to inmates and explained why, as a seasoned officer, he came to adopt that same facade himself.

[At] first [when] I was here I found a lot of conflicts with different officers because of their attitudes towards the inmates. That
was then. Now there are very few people that I have a conflict
with because I'm able to look at them objectively, to see where
they're at . . . The way that I perceived their attitude before I
think was wrong. The way that I perceive it now is a little bit
different in that they're copping a little attitude in certain re-
spects to cover up for something else. It's not them. Before I
thought it was them. I said, "Oh, I don't like him." But I can see
through that now because a lot of times I come out with that
kind of facade myself.

This officer recalled the incident (described in Chapter 9) when an
inmate scalded, gashed, and castrated himself. All of the officers I
interviewed who had been on duty that night had been distressed by
the incident, but that surely was not the impression they gave
publicly.

I came in the next day to punch in. There is a thing over the
bulletin board saying, "Any officer in need of a pair of balls
please contact the office." . . . The guy was a big brawny guy. He
was a Hell's Angel. And then some [officer] will say . . . [in a
high-pitched voice], "Hi, I used to be a bikie," and making jokes
like that, just joking about the situation basically . . . They
thought it was quite comical and humorous. I didn't. I didn't at
the time. But now that I look back on it I can see that they have
to draw some kind of humor out of it in order to cope with the
job. Because most people here are married and have kids and
they need the job so they have to handle it in some humorous
type of way.

So when they talked about such incidents among themselves, "some
take it seriously, but then, at the end of the serious note, a little
chuckle or joke would come out to sort of cover it over."

Whatever they felt inside, officers believed they had to adopt a
cold, indifferent exterior, jesting about blood on the walls or testicles on the floor, sitting by a mutilated corpse nonchalantly drinking coffee, laughing about an inmate suicide. "Inside it may bother
them but outside they don't show anything."

Third, officers adopt the stereotyped facade of the prison guard
because they fear rejection by fellow officers. An experienced officer
known for his sympathetic attitudes toward inmates observed that

many officers "kind of thought like you but were a little too afraid of not being accepted by the rest of the group to admit it"—much less act on it. Younger officers were particularly prone to voice attitudes that they thought other officers wanted to hear. An officer who saved the life of an inmate who had overdosed on drugs got a mixed public reception from his colleagues for his efforts.

> You hear a lot of [older officers] say, "Well, it deserves him right if he's going to mess with the drugs, and good for him and maybe next time he'll kill himself." A lot of the younger guys *say* it, but if you talk to them they don't really mean it. I think most of the younger guys, they feel bad for them ... Here it seems to be everybody's out to make a name for themselves, be put in the class with the older guys who have had to deal with major problems over the years, because those are the guys that we look to for assistance and help and knowledge. And so they want to be put in the same class and naturally they talk what they think these guys would say and would want to hear. But when you talk to them one-on-one [when] there's not a lot of people around, they're completely different. They're them- selves, they're not putting on the show.

The interviewees just quoted were particularly keen observers of their colleagues. But officers "put so many disguises on" that they often succeeded in fooling one another as well as the inmates. As officers attempted to conceal their own feelings and attitudes and to conform in word and action to what they thought most officers expected of them, they contributed to misunderstandings among themselves about what members of the officer corps actually be- lieved. Such erroneous beliefs about the beliefs of fellow officers are instances of "pluralistic ignorance," the phenomenon in which members of a group systematically misperceive the attitudes and beliefs of their fellow group members.

Norms of the officer subculture reflect, of course, what officers believe most other officers believe. In Chapter 5 I discussed conse- quences that officers thought would befall any officer who violated the norm "don't rat" by testifying against fellow officers in the event of an inmate death. It may be worth recalling here what one Walpole officer had to say of the role of "pluralistic ignorance" in that context.

> A lot of guys put on a good front ... They'd probably feel something for you. But I don't think—they *couldn't* show it ...

I think it'd be a lot that would feel something for you. To what degree I haven't the slightest. But I would like to think that it would be a lot. *It could be the whole group.* But no one's willing to make the first move. No one's willing to make the first step because of that unwritten code that says that I violated them or I violated their code and I'm a correctional officer. (Emphasis added.)

Stanton Wheeler (1958, 1961) and others have found substantial pluralistic ignorance among inmates, and I have found it in studies of officers in Connecticut and Massachusetts (Kauffman, 1978, 1981). In one of these earlier studies (1981, pp. 291–292) I concluded that it was not surprising that considerable pluralistic ignorance should exist among both prison officers and inmates.

Indeed, pluralistic ignorance may be most characteristic of groups in which group members feel solidarity is essential to their survival. In such situations, mere expression of dissent may appear so threatening to the group's well-being that it is not tolerated even by those who may be silently sympathetic to the particular opinions being aired. Individuals voicing dissent will have to contend with those who legitimately oppose their position as well as with those who feel a need to appear as if they oppose it. In addition, dissenters may also have to contend with those who agree with their particular position, but who frown on dissent itself. Under such circumstances, even majority views may go unspoken and thus unheard.

"Pluralistic ignorance" appeared to be greater among officers at Walpole than at any of the other prisons I have studied in Connecticut and Massachusetts.

## Five Types of Officers

Beneath their facade, officers vary significantly in their attitudes toward inmates and officers, and they respond to the prison environment in characteristically different ways. In earlier chapters, I have used *white hat* and *hard ass*—terms common in prison argot— to denote officers either sympathetic to inmates and hostile to officers or those with the opposite orientations. But such a dichotomy oversimplifies. There were a few officers in this study who were sympathetic to both officers and inmates; many more were sympathetic to neither group. Perhaps a majority (at least of long-termers) were largely indifferent to both groups. Figure 2 classifies

Attitude toward Officers

|  |  | Positive | Ambivalent | Negative |
|---|---|---|---|---|
| Attitude toward Inmates | Positive | Pollyannas |  | White Hats |
|  | Ambivalent |  | Functionaries |  |
|  | Negative | Hard Asses |  | Burnouts |

Figure 2. A typology of officers according to attitudes toward officers and inmates.

officers according to their attitudes toward the two most important groups within the prison world: inmates and officers. Their attitudes toward these two groups are useful in understanding how they responded to prison life and how they sought to survive.

As discussed in Chapter 7, most recruits who were part of this study held predominantly positive attitudes toward both officers and inmates before they commenced their prison work. These men entered their respective institutions prepared to be what I have labeled "Pollyannas." In addition, some recruits held positive attitudes toward inmates and negative ones toward officers (White Hats) and perhaps an equal number held negative attitudes toward inmates and positive attitudes toward officers (Hard Asses). Because virtually all officers began their careers as Pollyannas, White Hats, or Hard Asses, these may be considered "primary" types. Officers became Burnouts (those negative toward both salient groups within the prison) and Functionaries (those indifferent to both) largely as a consequence of prison work. Hence, Burnouts and Functionaries may be considered "secondary" types. (Transitions from one type to another are discussed at the end of this chapter.)

*Pollyannas.* Positive attitudes toward both officers and inmates by members of either group were virtually impossible to sustain in Walpole's polarized atmosphere. Only one of the thirty Walpole officers interviewed for this study clearly fit into the Pollyanna model. This officer liked and cared deeply about his colleagues although he was critical of the way they often behaved toward inmates. His affection for his co-workers helped sustain him. He coped with an environment he did not like principally through the enormous satisfaction he derived from helping those down and out.

> I felt really sorry for those guys [the inmates in his block] . . . They had nothing, nothing whatsoever. And if they asked me to do a legitimate thing . . . I'd do it, or I'd try to do it, make an effort and then come back . . . I felt I was their only link of communications. If they needed or wanted something I had to meet that need. I'm the only guy walking the blocks or walking the tiers. They can't tell it to their hopper in the corner and get any response. They are going to tell it to the correction officer . . . and if I didn't relieve that I didn't think I was doing my job.

Rather than finding the job a thankless one, as so many of his colleagues did, he found in it the "ultimate reward."

> You got people that for the littlest things show so much—if you can read into that, if you can see what they are saying. Because they're not the type of guy that'll say "thank you" in words. It comes in other things. And that is so much of a joy inside to say I'm doing a job that I really, really like and I'm getting back from it, not money, but something that means so much more to me. And it's just what makes you the happiest . . . That's what makes your chest stick out. It's just something that's awful hard to explain. You don't like that environment and the situation that you are in, but you get what you need out of that, so much more than you could anything else that I can think of . . .
> *It's really interesting that you say that because if I think if there is one term that's been used more often by [officers] describing their job, it's a "thankless job."*
> They're in the wrong job.
> *You don't find it that way at all?*
> Nope, not in the least, not in the least.

This officer survived at Walpole because of an extraordinary personal resilience and equally extraordinary insight into all of those around him, officer and inmate alike. He was, in fact, one of the most unusual and compelling individuals I have ever encountered inside prisons or out.

The Pollyanna role was somewhat more viable at the other prisons studied. The three non-Walpole officers I classed as Pollyannas were low-key, congenial individuals able to get along well with inmates and officers. Although critical of the way their respective institutions were run, they did not set out to revolutionize the system. ("I don't really like the idea of prisons. If there's a better way, I'd like to see it done. But like most things, you sort of have to take it as she rolls. Life's not perfect.") Their capacity to have positive attitudes toward inmates stemmed in part from their ability to focus on the individual, not the group.

> If you stood back and looked at them, you could say they're bad. What could you say good about them just as a general class of people? They murder, rape, shoot. You name it, they do it. And how can you stand back and say they're nice people? But I really didn't stand back. I just looked at a guy here, looked at a guy there. I tried to avoid standing back and looking at them.

Though they found they liked most inmates as individuals, they were not particularly lenient as officers. While it "paid to be sensitive," it did not pay to be weak. Theirs was an approach to prisons and prisoners that they saw not only as "humane, but also good sense." Two of these officers survived happily at their institutions; the third concluded that an "understanding, compassionate" person was not suited for the job. All eventually left prison work. None felt he could have survived for long at Walpole.

*White Hats.* Officers who held positive attitudes toward inmates but negative ones toward officers were derisively labeled "White Hats" (or "goody two shoes") in the officer subculture. For reasons detailed in Chapter 8, theirs was an even less likely prescription for survival than that of the Pollyanna.

The sole Walpole officer whom I classified as a "White Hat" was near retirement when I interviewed him. He, too, derived great satisfaction from the help he could give to inmates, many of whom he considered friends. "I like it here. I like the [inmates] I work with. I like meeting different people. I enjoy talking to the [inmates], meeting them, getting to know them. I like helping guys. It makes me feel good." More than anything else, he had enjoyed in the past working with new inmates, trying to "make them feel at ease. It's the worst day of their lives for some of them [when they first come in]. You have to be understanding . . . to have compassion." Compassion was something he felt most other officers lacked. Unlike Pollyannas who were sympathetic to both officers and inmates, this officer had little positive to say about those who were presently his colleagues—men different in kind, he felt, from those with whom he had begun work decades before. This officer survived in part out of a quiet compassion, but he also had had sufficient seniority *before* the turmoil of the early 1970s to distance himself from the ensuing crises and demands for solidarity by his embattled colleagues.

Five officers who were part of the longitudinal sample assigned to Norfolk, Concord, and Bridgewater expressed predominantly positive attitudes toward inmates and negative attitudes toward their fellow officers when they were interviewed two years after joining the Department of Correction. Four of the five were college educated. They couched their attitudes toward prisons and their own experiences as officers largely in political terms. Each had hoped to help change the penal system from within. In less than a year, three had been forced out by their fellow officers and a fourth had resigned of his own accord.

The fifth officer was different. He and his friends had spent their youth headed not for college but for the penitentiary. "Before I took this job, and growing up, I did a lot of things that they could have put me in jail for . . . So I'm no different from them, no different at all." He was mystified neither by the causes of criminality nor by the behavior of inmates inside prison. "You're behind bars all the time and you're told, 'You do this and you do that and that's it. And if you do anything else, you're in trouble.' And you're living in that environment, of course you're going to act up, you're going to rebel. *Anybody* would."

He was one of the few officers who enjoyed his job. "I look forward to coming to work . . . I enjoy working with people and working here I can work with all kinds of people, not just select groups." It was not inmates, but rather officers and administrators, who got on his nerves. The former seemed too often to revel in their authority while the latter seemed mired in incompetence and indifference. "The only negative thing about the job is that I've got another thirty-some-odd years I have to deal with people like that. They're the worst kind. I'd rather deal with somebody that's trying to con me than somebody that knows something should be that way but just don't give a damn." He kept these views largely to himself as he went about quietly doing his tasks while enjoying his interaction with most inmates. He planned to spend his entire career at a prison where he saw his approach as a viable one. But, once again, this officer believed he could not have survived as he was if he had been at Walpole.

*Hard Asses.* At the opposite extreme from the White Hat is the Hard Ass, hostile to inmates, identifying strongly with fellow officers. Typically young and inexperienced, Hard Asses viewed Walpole as an adventure, and its violence as exciting. "Some of the new officers—just like me—it was a new adventure for them. 'Man! Did you see! Man, do you see how he was stabbed!' And take this, the excited type atmosphere about it." Theirs was an uncomplicated view of prisons, one in which officers were pitted against inmates in a contest of good against evil. At least at first, they thrilled to the battle, fired by a belief that they had both right *and* might on their side. They saw themselves as part of a "special breed" of officers and derived great satisfaction from their ability to exercise control by whatever means. "You have to show these inmates that you can give them business when it comes, and you can be right when the time comes, too; that you can show some force when it's needed, and that you can keep your cool at it, too." These were men who "like having action" and found strength and comfort in their membership in the brotherhood of officers.

As was discussed in previous chapters, Hard Ass officers played a pivotal role in Walpole's violence and in the transmission of cultural values at that institution. But even at Walpole, Hard Asses were relatively few in number. The truth of the matter is, in an institution where "payback is a motherfucker," the Hard Ass role is a poor way to survive. Acting "like a drill instructor down at Parris Island" might be effective in cowing submission in the short run, but in the long run it is an open invitation for a shiv in the back. As one officer sardonically observed, "It's effective except when he gets killed and his wife and kid are home without any father. What the hell sense is that?" As the thrill wore off and the fear and aggravation seeped in, almost all Hard Asses at Walpole became Burnouts and either retreated to a safe post within the prison or, more commonly, resigned.

The Hard Ass role was in some senses a more viable one at other institutions. At Norfolk and Concord, violence was muted on both sides; officers with antipathy to inmates were less likely to engage in excessive behavior and thus to suffer consequences at the hands of inmates. Furthermore, officers who were unusually belligerent or punitive risked censure by fellow officers who did not want trouble. Especially at Norfolk, where job assignment was not determined by seniority bid, officers who consistently caused trouble were likely to be pulled from the yard by their superiors and placed for months in the towers. It was a move other officers with Hard Ass orientations frequently supported. A Norfolk officer who disliked inmates and identified strongly with fellow officers nevertheless said of colleagues who too readily aggravated inmates, "We've got guys like that and they are sitting in towers right now, tonight, sitting there because they're trouble makers. The deputy will find out who that is and get rid of him. Myself, I don't want to work with a guy like that, because he's the one who's going to cause me trouble."

Officers at Norfolk and Concord who wanted more excitement aspired to be members of their institution's "tactical team," a hand-picked group of officers trained to handle emergency situations within their own institution. Membership conferred status, held out the possibility of adventure, and offered esprit de corps at institutions where officers frequently complained it was lacking. (Officers who were not members were inclined to dismiss the tactical team as "a clique" whose members "try to put themselves a little bit above you.") Said one who was a member of his institution's team, "I love it. I really do. It's good physical training and you build a closer relationship with the officers on the team than you do even with the officers you work with . . . Everything is 'we'—'we' do this and 'we' do that . . . I just enjoy it, I really do. And I feel more confident with myself." Since the tactical teams were rarely called into action at these institutions, members were able to enjoy a heightened sense of adventure and conflict without taking many risks. As the officer who "loved" being a member of his team commented, "I'm glad I'm here at Norfolk instead of up at Walpole because I'm {beaming here} yet still do everything that's expected of me."

Unlike officers at the other prisons, Hard Asses at Bridgewater State Hospital did not risk reasoned retaliation from inmates. Furthermore, at least in parts of the institution on certain shifts, they did not risk censure by administrators or fellow officers for acting aggressively toward inmates. It is ironic that the Hard Ass role may have been most viable as a long-term strategy at the institution that was intended to be as much "hospital" as "prison."

*Burnouts.* Inside prisons and out, the term *burnout* is used colloquially to suggest severe emotional fatigue. In the context of the typology of officers proposed here, I use it to imply that and more. The defining characteristics of a Burnout in this typology are negative attitudes toward both officers and inmates. Coinciding with that orientation, as both cause and effect, is the psychological distress associated with one who has "burned out." Unable to find solace in relations with either officers or inmates, Burnouts experienced the full horrors of the prison world unsupported and alone. For them, psychological survival within the prison was a tenuous matter indeed; most barely coped at all.

Some men come to prison work too anxious and emotionally isolated from the start. They are few in number. Those who become Burnouts as a consequence of working in prisons like Walpole are many, probably a majority of those who originally enter the institution. A Walpole officer recalled his own gradual decline. "It got to me in ways that I didn't know it was getting to me. People were telling me I was getting a little weird." The officers with whom he worked "were going through the same thing I was going through. So we kind of went to the wayside altogether." But it was a fate they shared in silence. "We never really talked about that, about burning out or anything . . . We knew we were burnouts but we didn't really care."

Such men did not just burn out as officers, they burned out as *people*. The prison came to dominate their behavior everywhere—in restaurants, supermarkets, classrooms, parks. A slamming door in Walpole was the recognized signal of trouble. Outside the prison, officers found "a door would slam and I'd jump, ready to go. And everybody would look at me, 'What's the matter?!' " Inside Walpole, the cautious man—officer or inmate—kept his back to the wall warily watching all who passed before him. Once outside the institution many officers did the same:

> I didn't realize what I was doing, but when I went to class on my days off I always . . . had to sit in the back of the class, with my back to the wall . . . There were seats up front, loads of them, and I would squirm my way against the wall. There was one time I couldn't get to the back of the class. I took a chair and turned it sideways against the side wall and still everyone was in front of me. And I think that was like in Walpole because always you'd have your back against the wall or against something that you knew was there and have everything in front of you so you can observe that. And I found myself doing that *all* the time.

They found themselves unable to cope with crowds on city streets, in stores, even in their own apartment buildings. Recalled one, "For a long time I couldn't even go into a supermarket. I was *that* paranoid." This officer described Walpole as "more like a zoo than a prison." One day while still employed at the prison he took his small son to a real zoo and "absolutely freaked out" seeing all the animals behind bars. For such men, anything that recalled Walpole became intolerable.

Officers already burnt out were bitter about what they had become. Those who had not yet joined their ranks feared they one day would. I asked a five-year man who once enjoyed the challenge and excitement of Walpole but now had "a little more fear in me" how Walpole would affect him if he were to stay for twenty years. "I'd be burnt out. I'd be a vegetable . . . You need your youth. It's a young man's job . . . You can't keep coping with it. Your nervous system wouldn't allow you to . . . There's no way I could put in twenty years . . . The place would become where it would suck the life out of me." An officer already far gone put things more bluntly. "If I'm here for twenty years, I won't be worth shit." I had no doubt he was right.

As might be expected, the number of Burnouts was not as great nor the consequences usually as severe at the other institutions as they were at Walpole. Officers at Bridgewater, Concord, and especially Norfolk who were disillusioned with inmates and fellow officers often settled directly into the Functionary role. But some Burnouts at other prisons were worthy of Walpole. One officer who had been working long hours of overtime in high-inmate-contact positions liked the money,

> but in the meantime, what do I do to my head? What do I do to my body? What do I do to my thinking? I run myself {ragged} a year, two years. By then maybe I'm so bent up that I can't even recuperate anyway. So I'm done. What is the deputy [superintendent] going to do? Come over here and say, "Jeez, boy, he was a nice guy for two years—all that overtime. It's really too bad you're burnt out like this."

This officer thoroughly disliked inmates (and administrators); his relations with fellow officers were strained. He found prison work "makes me paranoid, makes me wonder what's going on about me all the time . . . I don't sleep right . . . thinking about being here." He felt trapped, and had considered suicide. Prison work was not what he had hoped or anticipated it would be. "I don't come to work here to be fighting with somebody every day. Came to work here to survive, like anybody else. To live, like anybody else. To see what it's like; to try it out. It's a hole; it's a rat hole." He fantasized about quitting.

> To be honest with you, I don't know what I'm going to do. There will come a day when I'm tired of being shit on . . . and I might just pick up the telephone and tell them to "stick the job up your ass" because I'm tired of being shit on . . . My mind is deteriorating. I'm not going to ruin myself for two hundred dollars a week . . . ruin my mind, thinking, physical, everything.

Yet, for two hundred dollars a week he was doing just that. Year after year he stayed, a Burnout in every sense of the word.

*Functionaries.* White Hats and Pollyannas rarely took root in Walpole's hostile environment. Hard Asses seemed at first to flourish and dominate but they, too, soon withered away. Walpole's landscape was littered with the charred remains of men who were Burnouts. Only those who successfully shut themselves off to events around them took root and survived over the years, although theirs was a stunted growth.

Those I have labeled "Functionaries" were at best ambivalent, at worst indifferent, to officers and inmates. They coped by closing their minds to the prison world around them and everyone in it. Functionaries were free of illusions that they were serving a useful role in society, whether it be to help inmates or protect the public. "You don't accomplish a bloody thing in this place." "It's a dead end . . . You are basically doing a nonproductive type of job. You are not doing anybody any good. You are just maintaining that human warehouse . . . I don't feel like I am doing anything for society at all." They held their job because they needed a job, not because there was anything they liked about it or found rewarding in it.

> Especially now, the way the economy is, you have to have a job. That's what was keeping me there, was the money. I'm not doing it because I like it. And a lot of people aren't doing it because, that's not what they grew up to want to be, is to be a prison guard. They're doing it because they have to do it. Hey, you've got a job where you can make two hundred fifty dollars a week and work overtime as much as you want. Guys are making twenty grand there . . . because of the overtime. Insurance, all your benefits, retirement . . . Fifty thousand if you get killed . . . It's just like I had a job to do and I had to get a

paycheck and I had to go in and I had to put up with {the stuff}
... Somebody has to do it and I was in the circumstances where
I had to do it, to survive. And I just did it. And it was really
nothing more than that. My dream when I was growing up
wasn't to be a correctional officer.

They insulated themselves as best they could from events around
them not because they were callous at heart but because they recognized that was the only way they could survive. Few pretended to
be happy. "I can tell just by the way they're talking that they feel
like they're missing something in life. A down attitude. Hey, they'll
laugh and joke, but it's a down attitude still. It's not speaking from
the heart."

One man's story exemplifies the perspective and role of the Functionary. When interviewed as a trainee, this man had been determined to be "different" from other officers, to "maintain some kind
of humanity within myself." His first months in Walpole's "extremely depressing atmosphere" were a shock. Originally a White
Hat, he quickly became a Burnout, alienated from everything and
everybody within the prison. One day an inmate in his block was
brutally assaulted.

> I said right then and there, I'm getting another job ... There's
> got to be an easier way. I figured, why should I subject myself to
> this kind of environment because I know that it does have some
> kind of profound effect that I really can't describe and it prob-
> ably won't even show itself for a while, manifest itself. But I
> knew that something was there that shouldn't be there ... It is
> like watching violence on television or in a movie. I mean, it
> can't have a *positive* effect on you ... And I am seeing all this
> stuff here and saying that can't have a good effect on me. I will
> get something that isn't as bad.

But getting something that wasn't as bad proved a fruitless quest.
After months of effort, and with his wife pregnant, he finally resolved he would have to stay at Walpole, at least in the short run,
and adjust to the realities of working there. "Rather than getting
wrapped up in all the problems, in the depressing types of things
that bothered me [at] first [when] I was here, I just sort of stayed on
the other side of that invisible wall, like mental anesthesia."

In coping, he anesthetized himself to the inmates' situation and to
his own role in the prison.

Before I almost felt sorry for [the inmates]. But now I realize, why should I feel sorry for them? They did it themselves. We all determine our own course of existence and this is the course that they determined . . .

*What made you change on that—you said when you first came in you felt sorry for them.*

Necessity. I didn't want to become so depressed and beat my head against the wall every time I came walking in the door. So I think I just sort of developed this type of an attitude which I think is a very realistic attitude.

*So the one that you had before was unrealistic?*

It was realistic. It *was* realistic. But it was somewhat detrimental to my well-being. So I had to adjust it a little bit.

He adjusted it by adopting the perspective and role of the Functionary. What would happen now if another inmate were brutally attacked in his block?

Knowing that I am married and my wife is pregnant and I need the job, I would muster all the mental anesthesia I could possibly get because I couldn't just walk out. I've got responsibilities . . . Before, when I was single, hey, fine, you can do what you want. But wife and kids to me right now is the epitome of human responsibility.

Like most officers, he stifled his regrets as best he could. "I think about it, but then I try not to think about it too long because I don't want to get depressed because I need the money." He counted on being able to anesthetize his mind just long enough to find another job, "something that isn't as bad," but feared the consequences if he could not. "If I don't [get out] then I am going to be very disappointed and I will probably end up just like these twenty- or twenty-five-year guys, filled with resentment. And I don't want to do that because I can see that it could possibly happen."

His was the story of most men who went to Walpole and stayed. As he explained, "The typical officer right now, I would describe him as being one who is not satisfied with his job, always looking for different alternatives to make a living, and gets frustrated practically every day . . . The typical officer is basically myself."

The "typical officer" who remained employed at the other prisons was not much different. He stayed in prison work for the same reason he had come to it, "it's a job." Gone were any vestiges of "social work" or "law enforcement" motivations. An officer who had had some of both as a rookie responded to my query, "Why do I stay? That's a damn good question. I'll tell you, well, there's nothing out there on the streets that I'm going to make the money the way I'm doing right now . . . I've got a family to worry about." As far as the rest of the job, "I don't give a damn." Men like him had ceased to care about anything other than their paychecks and their own physical well-being. Another officer explained,

> When I first started, I wanted to do really well up there and as it went along, I could care less . . . I used to come home absolutely ripping about working there. And finally I said to myself, "Jesus, what am I doing? I only want to put in eight hours up there." Then I got to the point where I didn't care what happened. As long as I wasn't involved in it, I didn't care. If there was a lockup or something . . . fine, don't put my name on the report, I don't even want to go near it. Just let me put my forty hours in.

## Transitions

As suggested earlier, an officer's "type" usually evolved over time. A few men in this study came into prison work as a Pollyanna, or a White Hat, or a Hard Ass (or, less frequently, as a Functionary or Burnout), and retained their initial orientation for the duration of their prison career. More commonly, officers in this study started out as Pollyannas, White Hats, or Hard Asses (in approximately that order of frequency), became Burnouts (some Pollyannas and White Hats became Hard Asses along the way to becoming Burnouts), following which they either settled into the role of the Functionary or resigned. Generally speaking, movement was from positive attitudes toward inmates and/or officers, to negative attitudes (first toward inmates, then toward officers), to physical or emotional withdrawal from the prison and everyone in it.

There were, of course, variations in these patterns. For example, officers at prisons other than Walpole often "mellowed out" instead of "burning out," that is, they became Functionaries without first becoming Burnouts. (Thus, an officer who had started out as a Hard Ass in a prison other than Walpole concluded after a year of confrontation with inmates, "You just have to decide for yourself, 'Do I want to be a hard ass or do I want to make life easy for myself?' I decided I wanted to make life easy for myself. For what they're paying me, it's not worth it to come in here every day and then go home and take it out on my family." He reported making the transition from Hard Ass to Functionary smoothly and apparently displayed none of the symptoms of a Burnout along the way.) Despite variations in paths that officers followed, one pattern did *not* emerge. No one in this study started out holding negative attitudes toward inmates and later developed positive attitudes toward them. In other words, Hard Asses and Burnouts did not become White Hats or Pollyannas. The transformation from Pollyanna or White Hat to Burnout or Hard Ass, on the other hand, was common.

Like the Walpole officer discussed above who went from being a White Hat to a Burnout to a "mentally anesthetized" Functionary, men in this study readily understood and were able to articulate the transformations that had occurred in them. "I've changed some attitudes," recalled a non-Walpole officer who as a rookie had looked forward to helping inmates but had worried about relations with fellow officers. "I'm not so liberal as I thought I was, especially in my attitudes. I think I've gone through two or three different stages since I've been here." The first stage lasted only three months and involved genuine efforts to help inmates,

> Just by listening and talking. I'd talk out a few things. I'd talk out the family problems and I'd try to put myself in their place.
> *What happened?*
> It didn't work.
> *They wouldn't talk?*
> Oh yeah, talked all kinds of talk. Too much. After a while, day after day, it was the same thing. I'd hear the same stories over and over again. It's like a big scam.

"Too many con jobs" led to a second, "cynical" phase that lasted almost a year. "I wouldn't do anything for anybody. It was always 'no, no, no.' " During that phase, he identified strongly with fellow officers and became involved at least at the periphery in hostile actions against inmates.

> *Why did you get out of the cynical stage?*
> Because it was too much of a hassle for myself, causing too many problems ... I was putting myself through too much aggravation.

So, he adjusted his thinking again.

> I think at this point I'm right in the middle. Some people I'll give some things to, other people I won't do anything for, pick-

ing the people as I go. It's probably not a good attitude because [it] really isn't that fair. It's just "people treat me good, I treat them good." It's as simple as that.

*People who treat you bad—*

Get the same . . . I've just learned to flow with the tide.

By "flowing with the tide" within the prison (and undertaking a vigorous physical exercise program and other activities outside the prison) he slowly accommodated himself to a lifetime of prison work with few rewards other than a paycheck and a roof over his head while on the job.

What do I like best about the job? Whew! I don't know. It's got to be—every night I think about this—I compare it to my last job [in construction] and working in the extremes of cold weather and hot weather . . . I can't say I'm cool [here] in the summer, but I'm not out in the hot sun. That's the only thing I can come up with right away. But as far as the job itself, I can't think of anything that I really, really like. I just {put up with} a lot of things.

*Why do you stay?*

Responsibility to the family . . . It's a living, I guess. It's a living.

This officer began prison work as a White Hat. He was quickly disillusioned by inmates and found to his surprise that he liked most of his fellow officers. In an abrupt reversal, he became a Hard Ass. Eventually the long-term liabilities of being a Hard Ass manifested themselves and he was in danger of becoming a Burnout. For his family's sake, he was determined to remain at the prison. Therefore, he made a conscious decision to distance himself from fellow officers (especially Hard Asses), to moderate his hostility toward inmates, and to withdraw emotionally from the prison. In short, like most officers who stayed, he became a Functionary.

Transitions from one type of officer to another reflect the socialization process discussed in Chapter 8. New officers at Walpole typically spent their first months on the 7–3 shift working a cell block alone or with other, equally inexperienced rookies. This devastating introduction to the prison world served to extinguish positive attitudes toward inmates, and very nearly extinguished them toward fellow officers as well. By the time rookies were transferred to the 3–11 shift, scarcely a Pollyanna or White Hat was left among them. Those who were not already Burnouts could be temporarily spared that fate by the possibility of membership in the dominant Hard Ass subculture on the 3–11 shift. Even so, their tenure as Hard Asses was usually brief. By the end of their first two years, most Walpole officers were Burnouts or had resigned. Of those who, by necessity or choice, remained at the prison more than three or four years, virtually all became Functionaries. By that stage they had sufficient seniority to bid for and get positions removed from contact with inmates, and often from fellow officers as well.

Transitions from one type of officer to another also mirrored the moral transformations in officers discussed in Chapter 9. Moral, as well as personal, regard for inmates was characteristic of Pollyannas and White Hats. Most rookies were shocked at conditions of confinement within the prisons and initially opposed victimization of inmates by any party. As officers abandoned the Pollyanna and White Hat perspectives, they searched for justifications for their own hostile or violent behavior against inmates. Efforts to deny moral obligation to inmates (either by postulating that moral laws applicable to society as a whole did not apply to prisons or that inmates were not persons to whom one owed moral obligation) were characteristic of Hard Asses. The inadequacies of efforts to "exclude" inmates from their sphere of moral responsibility were in part what eventually alienated officers from the Hard Ass role and led to their moral (in addition to their emotional, physical, and social) breakdown as Burnouts.

The solution of the Functionary to problems of self-judgment was "mental anesthesia"—the refusal to consider moral consequences of one's own (and others') actions. Officers "mentally anesthetized" themselves because they had no alternative strategies for coping with the prison environment. "It's a tough job. It's a tough job to try and rationalize—like 'I'm going to help someone,' or 'I'm going to do something good,' or 'This is good.' It's a job that's hard to believe anything [in]. You can't really think about your job." Functionaries were not men who were hard by nature or morally indifferent from the start. For the most part, they were products of the prisons in which they worked. "Most officers, even though it seems to be cold the way we treat people . . . it's the tools you're given and the training you're given and the attitudes that you have and the attitudes you've been given that makes you that way. And you don't feel good about yourself."

# 11

# Prisoners All

Officers and inmates are the chief antagonists in prison conflict. As such, they are typically blamed for problems that plague prisons. Just as prisons are regarded as deviant environments, those who live and work in them are dismissed as possessing deviant characters and interests. But are inmates and officers really culpable for the failures of their own institutions?

Inmates who tyrannize other inmates may benefit from violent and chaotic conditions within prisons, but the vast majority of inmates suffer terribly from such conditions. Their goal is not to instigate trouble, but rather to survive it. When the situation within a prison becomes intolerable for inmates, as it clearly was at Walpole and Concord throughout much of the 1970s, they have no constructive means of effecting change. As the Massachusetts Governor's Advisory Committee on Corrections pointed out (1974, p. 3), inmates are in a "no-win" situation.

> The inmate population has been patient beyond human endurance. The only real "demand" is for help in the broadest sense. They are in a trap. When the institutions are quiet, nothing changes. When violence erupts the typical response is: "if inmates act that way they don't deserve help." . . . The cycle continues. The status quo is maintained.

Officers, too, are in a trap vis-à-vis the world outside. As far as the public is concerned, "The guards are either easy and lugging [drugs], or they're tough and they're beating up somebody. You don't hear about the other guys that have to put up with the crap every day and do . . . a good job."

This study does not support the conventional wisdom that men who go to work in prisons are predisposed to violence, or revel in authority, or have unusually punitive attitudes toward lawbreakers. Most men in this study became officers because they needed a job; those who stayed did so because they felt they had no alternative. As recruits they voiced their commitment to a humane system of corrections and their own hopes of playing a constructive role within that system. As officers they voiced bewilderment over conditions within the prisons and despair over what had happened to themselves and all of those around them. They had found themselves in a prison world that was not of their own making. As one former officer lamented, "I never thought something like that would ever exist up there. I never dreamt of that in my wildest dreams."

Recruitment of "better" prison officers would not serve as an antidote to the poisonous environment of prisons like Walpole. It is not only that men in this study who engaged in violence and other abuses were "terribly and terrifyingly normal," as Hannah Arendt described Adolf Eichmann (1977, p. 276). More important, these men possessed attributes that made them poignantly human: their capacity for suffering and self-judgment, for loyalty and humor, for insight and growth. In their foibles and aspirations they differed little from men who have never walked a prison tier. Critics of prisons should not comfort themselves with the idea that, forced into the same circumstances, they would behave more nobly—or more effectively—than did the officers of the Massachusetts prison system.

The intractable problems posed by prisons are not rooted in the identities and characters of officers or inmates. The problems are much more fundamental. They are rooted in the nature of the goals prisons are erected to serve. In appreciating this point, it is worth considering in what ways and to what extent the Massachusetts prison system fulfilled four widely prescribed goals of incarceration: punishment, isolation, deterrence, and rehabilitation.

Incarceration in prisons like Walpole, Concord, and Bridgewater during the 1970s unquestionably constituted substantial *punishment*. But the degree of pain inflicted on individual inmates within these prisons was highly unpredictable and often wildly disproportionate to the crimes for which each inmate had been sent to prison. While court officials and prison administrators helped determine the length of each inmate's stay in prison, neither they nor officers inside had much influence on what happened to a man once incarcerated. An inmate's safety could not be guaranteed even if he chose to serve his time in solitary confinement. No doubt in violation of societal intentions and expectations, those inmates who suffered most within the prisons at the hands of fellow inmates were often the meekest and least violent among them, and those who had committed the least serious offenses outside the prison. Punishment so capricious and inequitable does a disservice to any system of justice.

Despite the tumult within the Massachusetts prison system during the 1970s, escapes from within the major prisons were rare. Thus, the prison system was reasonably successful in *isolating* offenders from the outside world during the duration of their sentences. But by no means were the most violent among them incapacitated from committing new crimes while in prison. They were merely restricted to less visible and less popular victims—in this case, fellow inmates and officers.

Capriciousness of punishment and victimization of those already inside prisons are not matters that concern everyone. The editors of the Lowell *Sun* (26 November 1978) suggested that

> the people of this state couldn't care less if the violence takes place within Walpole ... as long as the murders are not committed outside of its walls. Let the bastards stew in their own juice. That's the feeling of most people in this state today about Walpole and the conditions that its inmates face.

Prisons, according to editors of the *Sun*, "need be hardly more than concentration camps closely guarded by all the paraphernalia available to modern security systems." They found "a lesson in Walpole ... The lesson is this: stay out of it ... Walpole is supposed to be tough and so is imprisonment of all kinds in order that this may serve both as a deterrent to and a punishment for crime."

But does a prison like Walpole serve as a *deterrent* to crimes committed outside its walls? The average man contemplating life in Walpole during the 1970s would surely have thought more than twice about doing anything that he believed might have resulted in incarceration in that prison. (Whether the average murderer, rapist, extortionist, or drug abuser actually makes such calculations is another matter, one to which criminologists pay considerable attention.) Even if Walpole served as a deterrent to crime for those who had never done time behind its walls, it almost surely served as a stimulus to the commission of other crimes, especially violent ones, by men who had been there and gone.

Prisons are often charged with being "schools for crime," producing alumni skilled in burglary and up-to-date in the latest rackets. Whether or not that old maxim applied to Walpole (and somehow it is difficult to imagine men concerned with sheer survival expending much energy on the acquisition of such skills), those who lived and worked inside that prison considered it a "school for violence." As a former Walpole inmate observed, "Walpole can do nothing for those men inside but teach them that violence is the quickest and their only way to resolve serious everyday problems" (*Boston Globe*, 9 December 1978). His was a judgement with which most officers agreed. Everyone within Walpole was forced to accustom himself to the violence and sadism around him. To survive, each inmate had to have ready access to a lethal weapon *and* demonstrate a willingness to use it at any time. It is not logical to assume that men forced into those circumstances for years on end, without relief or alternative, easily shed such attitudes and behaviors once they walk out of the gates, more bitter and alienated than when they walked in. A Walpole officer observed of the typical inmate, "not too bad when he went in," but "hard-core" when he came out, "Boy if he had a grudge against the world before he went in there, {see him} [just] before he gets out!"

Speaking of his experiences in prisons of the "caliber" of Walpole, Jack Abbott (1982, pp. 143–146) wrote,

> For almost twenty years I have seen prisoners come and go. There is not *one* of them who comes to prison for the first time who is *capable* of the vast repertoire of crimes he is capable of when he finally gets out of prison. I'm not talking about the fine technicalities of, say, safe-cracking or the mechanics of murder . . . No one learns those things in prison, contrary to the government's claims . . . What is forced down their throats in spite of themselves is *the will* to commit crimes. It is the *capability* I am speaking of . . . Why do you commit crimes you never dreamed of being able to commit before you entered prison? You have changed so that you are not even aware there was a time you were incapable of such things.

The overwhelming majority of those sent to prison eventually return to society; most do so within a few years. Citizens and policymakers should carefully consider the logic and the wisdom of subjecting thousands of their fellow men to environments such as that in Walpole and then of expecting these men to return and "sin no more." Victims of Walpole's violence no doubt include many people who have never seen the inside of those blood- and excrement-stained walls.

Most important in regard to the goal of deterrence, the prison system served as the stimulus for crimes committed by state employees within the prisons. Throughout the 1970s, some officers and their superiors at Walpole, Bridgewater, and perhaps Concord engaged in unlawful behavior in their efforts to control their respective inmate populations. The systematic brutality documented in this book is unjustifiable regardless of the behavior that provoked it. These crimes were arguably the most serious of all because in the minds of both victims and perpetrators they were committed in the name of society itself.

Efforts to *rehabilitate* inmates ranked high on the agendas of prison reformers and administrators during the 1960s and 1970s. Most of these efforts were sooner or later judged failures—in Massachusetts and elsewhere—and by the 1980s rehabilitation had fallen into disrepute as a goal of prisons in the United States. (The relative emphasis on the various goals assigned to prisons has proved to be cyclical over the years. Rehabilitation will no doubt regain its former status within a decade or two.)

Far more important than the failure of prisons in rehabilitating inmates, however, is their marked success in *debilitating* virtually everyone inside them. The emotional, moral, social, and physical debilitation of officers in the Massachusetts prison system described in this book applied at least as much to the inmates in their charge, and probably applied with varying force to administrators, social workers, and others whose lives were connected with the prison system.

Nor do I think the effect stops there. Most American prisons operate according to moral and legal principles that are markedly inferior to those that apply to the larger community. The presence of enclaves of brutality and deprivation, created and sustained by governments on behalf of citizens, literally demoralizes—that is, corrupts the morals of—the society as a whole. Contradictions inherent in maintaining such morally "inferior" institutions are no less apparent for the society that creates them than they are for the individuals who work within them. Inevitably, the moral standards of the greater community are undermined.

I do not believe, to paraphrase the Attica Commission, that "Walpole is every prison and every prison is Walpole." The extremely high levels of violence and open conflict experienced in Massachusetts during the 1970s do not characterize most prisons most of the time. (Indeed, they have not, for the most part, characterized Massachusetts prisons during the 1980s.) Prison officials often can succeed in the short run in staunching the brutality and degradation that proved so devastating for officers and inmates in this study. But they can rarely, if ever, alleviate such suffering on a long-term basis. Regardless of the level of open conflict evident at any particular time, I believe we rely on systems of mass incarceration at our peril. Those outside the walls cannot escape responsibility for what happens inside them any more than they can, in the long run, avoid the moral and social problems such systems inevitably create for the greater community.

At the very least, those men and women hired as prison officers should not be blamed for the often tragic outcomes of our prison policies. As a former Massachusetts prison officer admonished,

> If you're going to point the finger, you have to point it at yourself as much as anyone else. Because we built the walls, and we said to the officer, "Go in there and just take care of it. We don't want to hear anything about it." So if *you're* disgusted with it, then . . . be disgusted with yourself, because you're the one who allows this to happen and it's not the guards.

# Procedural and Ethical Problems of Prison Research

As Gresham Sykes has pointed out, "the social system of the prison is a difficult thing to uncover ... A prison is founded in part on secrecy and the observer from the free community is inevitably defined as an intruder, at least initially" (1958, pp. xix, xx). Efforts of researchers to overcome problems presented by their forays into the prison world are part of the folklore of penology. During the course of my research on Massachusetts prison officers, I encountered a number of procedural and ethical problems.

The initial problem for the prison researcher is to secure access to and cooperation from the individuals to be studied, an effort complicated by the presence of three mutually antagonistic groups within prisons. Those wishing to study inmates must first secure cooperation from administrators and, to a lesser extent, officers. They then must immediately and publicly distance themselves from both those groups, especially the officers, without at the same time jeopardizing access to the prison. For example, James Jacobs noted that while doing research at Stateville prison, he was "anxious to keep staff contacts (especially with guards) to a minimum. However, it was necessary to maintain cordial relations with staff and administration in the face of considerable skepticism about the 'advisability' of this research" (1977, p. 216). Unfortunately, not all researchers studying inmates have attempted to maintain "cordial" relations with officers. One of the ways they have sought to demonstrate independence from the official regime, and thus ingratiate themselves with inmates, is by open displays of hostility to officers. For example, Richard McCleery, in his otherwise commendable studies of prisons in Hawaii and North Carolina in the 1950s, sought "to dissociate himself from the official power structure as far as possible" in the eyes of the inmates. In accomplishing this task, he "deferred to the guard's requirements with apparent ill-will" (1961a, p. 273). I recall similar displays of ill will, whether real or feigned, on the part of researchers when I was working as an officer in Connecticut. Although open discourtesy to officers may be an effective strategy for researchers studying inmates, at the very least it complicates the task of those who later seek to study officers.

Researchers who desire to study *officers* need not, of course, concern themselves with cooperation from inmates; indeed, they must give no hint of personal or organizational affiliation with inmates. Yet cooperation must be secured from administrators and supervisors while a careful and obvious distance from them is maintained.

During the years I was interviewing officers in Massachusetts I minimized contact with administrators for two reasons. First, I did not want officers whom I was interviewing to associate me with their superiors or think that I had close ties with them. I had learned what the consequences of suggestions to the contrary could be. I was once in the middle of interviewing an officer at a prison unconnected to the research reported here when the head of the institution entered unannounced, greeted me warmly, and made reference to mutual friends. When he left a few minutes later, the interview, which until then had been progressing well, continued in monosyllables and ended a scant fifteen minutes later.

Second, I was wary of jeopardizing access to the prison system either by letting administrators know what officers were telling me about events within the prison that would reflect badly on their administration or by expressing views on prison management that administrators might perceive as antagonistic to their own. I had learned that lesson in a different state prison system. A superintendent I knew, liked, and admired, who ran a relatively scandal-free prison and was secure in his job, had denied me access to his prison over what I considered to be a fairly innocuous newspaper article that I had written about prison officers. I easily imagined how much more quickly I might wear out my welcome in Massachusetts if I appeared overly interested in such sensitive matters as violence by officers against inmates and administrators' complicity in it.

Once having gained access to the prison population to be studied, the researcher faces the difficult task of deciding who is telling the truth about what. Deceit is practically a way of life in prison. In Massachusetts during the 1970s it was regularly practiced by inmates, officers, and administrators—and with good reason. Members of all three groups had a lot to hide. In the case of the officers, even the suggestion of abuse of inmates seemed likely to lead to more adverse publicity or, worse, to further investigations, lawsuits, even indictments.

Despite obvious incentives to conceal what was happening, I believe most of the officers I interviewed presented honest (if not necessarily accurate) accounts of their prison world and their lives within it. (See Chapter 6 regarding some officers who were either not telling the truth or were unusually ignorant of events within their own institution.) Some were remarkably candid and critical about events that they had witnessed or in which they had participated. Most of their accounts proved to be consistent not only within and between interviews, but were also generally consistent with news accounts and, perhaps most surprising of all, with inmates' accounts of what was happening within the prisons. (Officers, inmates, and news reporters often differed, of course, in their interpretations as to *why* such events were taking place.) In fact, the only versions of events within the prisons that the officers' accounts consistently contradicted were those given by department officials. (Unlike officers, administrators rarely seemed willing to stray from official renditions of events when I interviewed them. Prison administrators regularly lost their jobs in Massachusetts during the 1970s. Accounts that reflected badly on their administration jeopardized their jobs regardless of whether the specific sources of reports were known.)

Inevitably, I had to rely on my own judgment regarding what interview material should be used and what should be discounted. Some officers whom I interviewed stood out in the degree to which their versions of events and analyses of conditions were substantiated by other sources. These interviews became baselines by which interviews with officers from the same institution could be judged. With respect to serious charges of abuse and mismanagement, I required confirmation of information. (Thus, for example, I have not reported allegations of one type of official abuse discussed by an otherwise reliable interviewee because he was the last officer I interviewed from his institution and no other officer had raised that particular topic.) Doubtless, some material that should have been discounted has been reported here; probably more often, information that was accurate has been excluded.

Given the incentives officers had to conceal what was happening within the prisons and their own role in it, how can I account for their apparent openness and honesty during the interviews, especially while being tape recorded? I cannot definitively answer that question for the interviewees, but I think there are at least three plausible reasons.

First, as countless interviewers have learned before me, people are often remarkably forthcoming when asked in private, in a nonjudgmental way, about their lives and their perspectives on critical events involving them. This tendency toward openness is likely to be enhanced when in-depth interviews are conducted between the same interviewee and interviewer over a number of years, creating an ongoing, personal relationship.

Second, my own background as a prison officer probably served to defuse initial hostilities to me as an outsider and a researcher. I used my prison background as a way of introducing myself to officers, and at times during interviews referred to parallel or contrasting experiences that I had had as an officer. I hoped that the officers would, thereby, view me as someone with empathy for their own attitudes and situations. However, I tried to make it clear to them that my pledge of confidentiality was based not on our shared background as prison officers but rather on my role as a researcher.

Third, and perhaps most important, many of the officers I interviewed were anxious to talk with someone in private about what was happening to them, but had few, if any, opportunities to do so. For reasons discussed in the text, officers felt isolated from their friends and often from their families as well, and felt unable to share with them the trials and traumas of their work. Doubts and fears were best left unspoken among officers, and, with rare exceptions, their superiors seemed indifferent. As one officer complained,

> Why couldn't it just be somebody from [the central office in] Boston who had the guts to come down here and sit down and talk to one of us guys . . . I can say that I feel better because I'll be able to sit here tonight and explain myself to somebody who wasn't even my superior how I feel about things, when somebody who is my superior can't even sit down and talk to me about how the job here is running.

The simplest explanation for why the officers spoke openly and passionately about their work and their lives is that someone actually asked them.

Officers apparently were not the only ones anxious to talk with someone about what had happened to them and their families as a consequence of prison employment. During the course of contacting officers and making appointments with them, I occasionally spoke with their wives. They knew of my research and were invariably courteous and curious. Several expressed a desire to speak with me about what had happened to their husbands and their marriages as a consequence of their husbands' prison work. I felt that by speaking with them at any length I risked compromising the pledges of confidentiality I had made to their husbands and thus I declined to see them. In the brief exchanges that we did have, I tried to reassure them that they were not alone, that theirs were not the only marriages that had suffered, that the changes they had seen in their husbands were changes that countless wives had seen in their men who had gone to work in prisons. What I have written regarding the effects of working in prisons on officers is what I would have liked to (and perhaps should) have shared with their wives then.

The candor and intensity of the interviews created problems of their own. First, participation in the study clearly had effects on at least some officers ranging from making them more reflective about their jobs to influencing career decisions. After I had interviewed the longitudinal sample at the training academy, for example, several recruits recommended to the director that the interview become a regular part of the "training" program. When I reinterviewed the longitudinal sample two years later, I was surprised at the number of officers who clearly recalled questions I had asked the first time and said they had thought about issues raised in the first interview during the interim. When I contacted men who had left the department after the second round of interviews, several reported that the first follow-up interview had provided a stimulus for them to quit their jobs.

Possible effects of the interviews themselves were of concern regarding validity of the research and, more important, the well-being of officers involved. Regarding validity, Campbell and Stanley noted, "It has long been a truism in the social sciences that the process of measuring may change that which is being measured . . . The reactive effect can be expected whenever the testing process is in itself a stimulus to change rather than a passive record of behavior" (1966, p. 9). Interviews with the longitudinal subjects in this study clearly were complicated by "reactive effects."

A more serious problem concerned emotional risks to the officers from their involvement. One of the hazards of conducting interviews such as those reported here is that they entail brief and intense intrusions into individuals' lives without promise or prospect of more sustained involvement. Some officers seemed to benefit from the opportunity to talk about what was happening to them, but for others I felt it deepened their despair. I did not regard the interviews as counseling sessions, but in those cases in which officers asked for my opinion or, more rarely, my advice, I gave it to them honestly. In a few cases, I suggested that an officer seek professional assistance.

Finally, the candor with which interviewees discussed one aspect of their prison world—officer violence—raised a troubling question: To what extent is a researcher justified in guaranteeing anonymity to individuals engaged in violence against others?

My experiences as an officer and researcher in the comparatively nonviolent Connecticut prison system had not prepared me for what I would find in Massachusetts. Although violence became a major topic of this book, it was not a subject with which I was initially concerned. The first few interviews I conducted at Walpole forced me to assess not only the focus of the research but also my responsibilities as a researcher. Without a guarantee of confidentiality, officers would understandably not discuss officers' use of violence or other serious abuses, thus foreclosing any real attempt to understand the Massachusetts prison system or the lives of officers working in it. (In an effort to protect the interviewees and myself, midway through the first series of interviews I modified my promise of confidentiality to exclude specific, first-hand information about actual, attempted, or intended homicides.)

I believe that as a society we must come to grips with the brutality of our institutions—not only to recognize it, but also to try to understand it. But we cannot understand that portion of prison violence that involves officers unless we can, to some extent, see that violence through the officers' eyes and experiences. Failure to do so has blinded us to what I believe is the inevitability of violence in prisons as they are presently constituted and has prevented us from seeing the extent to which the officer is also captive and victim of the system. I believe that research has to be done that engages prison officers in thoughtful discussion of the violence of their own subculture while simultaneously shielding them from legal repercussions.

*     *     *

A final note: An interview is a product of the personality and background of both the interviewee *and* the interviewer. My experience as a prison officer influenced the questions that I asked and the answers that I received, as did my being young, white, and female. Some would see these attributes as an impediment to research of the sort I carried out. Indeed, a grant proposal I submitted to the Law Enforcement Assistance Administration in 1978 was rejected by an anonymous reviewer who expressed concern about bias "introduced" by a female researcher studying male guards. I have no doubt that my being a woman had an effect on the interviews, for better *and* for worse. Prisons are a world of pretense. My guess is that, all else being equal, most of the men I interviewed were more inclined to drop that pretense in talking to a woman than they would have been talking to a man when discussing such things as their own fears, anxieties, guilt, and despair. On the other hand, I sensed that they were less forthcoming about details of violent events, especially those in which sex was a factor (for example, rapes and castrations), and that they made some effort to moderate their language in my presence.

While these likely effects should be noted, I do not think they are cause for much concern. In research of the type reported here, interviewers gain nothing more than snapshots of the lives they investigate. A different camera, a different lens, a different setting, a different day all influence what they see and what they report. More is learned from a collage than from a single photograph, an argument not only for more research, but also for diversity among researchers.

# Bibliography

Newspaper articles cited are listed separately, beginning on page 282.

Abbott, Jack Henry. 1982. *In the Belly of the Beast: Letters from Prison.* New York: Vintage Books.

Arendt, Hannah. [1963] 1977. *Eichmann in Jerusalem: A Report on the Banality of Evil.* New York: Penguin Books.

*Attica: The Official Report of the New York State Special Commission on Attica.* 1972. New York: Bantam Books.

Bachrach, Peter, and Morton S. Baratz. 1970. *Power and Poverty: Theory and Practice.* New York and London: Oxford University Press.

Bettelheim, Bruno. 1960. *The Informed Heart: Autonomy in a Mass Age.* Glencoe, Ill.: The Free Press.

Boone, John O. 1973. Memo from Commissioner Boone to Kenneth Bishop, Acting Superintendent, MCI Walpole, regarding "Phased Supervised Return of MCI Walpole Personnel." Boston: Massachusetts Department of Correction, 19 March.

Brim, Orville. 1968. "Adult Socialization." In *International Encyclopedia of the Social Sciences,* ed. David L. Sills, vol. 14, 555–562. New York: Macmillan Co. and The Free Press.

Campbell, Donald T., and Julian C. Stanley. 1966. *Experimental and Quasi-Experimental Designs for Research.* Chicago: Rand McNally and Co.

Campbell, W. Donald. 1976. *Department of Correction,* 3 pts. Case study prepared under the direction of Professor John R. Russell. Boston: Boston University School of Management.

Clemmer, Donald. 1940. *The Prison Community.* New York: Rinehart and Co.

Cloward, Richard A. 1960. "Social Control in the Prison." In *Theoretical Studies in Social Organization of the Prison,* Richard A. Cloward et al., 20–48. New York: Social Science Research Council.

Crouch, Ben M. 1980. "The Book vs. the Boot: Two Styles of Guarding in a Southern Prison." In *The Keepers: Prison Guards and Contemporary Corrections*, ed. Ben M. Crouch, 207–224. Springfield, Ill.: Charles C. Thomas.

Delahunt, William. 1978. "Statement of William Delahunt, Norfolk County District Attorney, before the Joint Legislative Committee on Human Services and Elderly Affairs." In *Testimony Delivered at a Hearing on Violence in Prisons*, 37–45. Boston: Joint Committee on Human Services and Elderly Affairs, 20 November.

Easton, David. 1958. "The Perception of Authority and Political Change." In *Authority*, ed. Carl J. Friedrich, 170–196. Cambridge, Mass.: Harvard University Press.

Friedrich, Carl J. 1958. "Authority, Reason, and Discretion." In *Authority*, ed. Carl J. Friedrich, 28–48. Cambridge, Mass.: Harvard University Press.

Governor's Advisory Committee on Corrections (Robert M. Palmer, Chairman). 1974. *1974 Report of the Governor's Advisory Committee on Corrections*. Boston: State House, 18 December.

———— 1978. *1978 Report of the Governor's Advisory Committee on Corrections*. Boston: State House, 28 December.

Hawkins, Gordon. 1976. *The Prison: Policy and Practice*. Chicago: University of Chicago Press.

Jacobs, James B. 1977. *Stateville: The Penitentiary in Mass Society*. Chicago: University of Chicago Press.

Jacobs, James B., and Mary P. Grear. 1980. "Dropouts and Rejects: An Analysis of the Prison Guard's Revolving Door." In *The Keepers: Prison Guards and Contemporary Corrections*, ed. Ben M. Crouch, 273–290. Springfield, Ill.: Charles C. Thomas.

Jenkins, Ernest F. 1978. "Statement by Ernest F. Jenkins, Jr., Senior Correction Officer, Massachusetts Correctional Institution, Concord—28 November, 1978." In *Testimony Delivered at a Hearing on Violence in Prisons*, 82–87. Boston: Joint Committee on Human Services and Elderly Affairs, 28 November.

Kauffman, Kelsey. 1978. "Prison Officer Attitudes and Perceptions of Attitudes." Doctoral qualifying paper. Cambridge, Mass.: Graduate School of Education, Harvard University.

———— 1981. "Prison Officers' Attitudes and Perceptions of Attitudes: A Case of Pluralistic Ignorance." *Journal of Research in Crime and Delinquency*, 18 (July): 272–294.

———— 1985. "Prison Officers and Their World." Ed.D. diss. Cambridge, Mass.: Graduate School of Education, Harvard University.

Kogon, Eugen. [1950] 1960. *The Theory and Practice of Hell: The German Concentration Camps and the System Behind Them*. Trans. Heinz Norden. New York: Berkley Publishing Co.

Konefsky, Alan, Richard Peers, and Donald Simon. 1977. *Massachusetts*

*Department of Correction*, 3 pts. Case study #C94–77–165 to 167; prepared under the supervision of Professor Philip B. Heymann. Cambridge, Mass.: John F. Kennedy School of Government, Harvard University.

Lewis, Orlando F. [1922] 1967. *The Development of American Prisons and Prison Customs, 1776–1845*. Montclair, N.J.: Patterson Smith.

*Libby v. Commissioner of Correction*. 1982. 385 Mass. 421.

Lindblom, Charles E. 1977. *Politics and Markets: The World's Political-Economic Systems*. New York: Basic Books.

Martin, Robert E. 1978. "Violence in Massachusetts Prisons." In *Testimony Delivered at a Hearing on Violence in Prisons*, 66–76. Boston: Joint Committee on Human Services and Elderly Affairs, 28 November.

Massachusetts Department of Correction. 1977. "Evaluation of Levels of Violence at MCI-Walpole." Prepared by Joseph Landolfi, Research Analyst. Boston: Massachusetts Department of Correction, October.

——— 1981a. "Patterns of Career Mobility and Retention Among Correction Officers of the Massachusetts Department of Correction." Prepared by Linda K. Holt, Senior Researcher. Boston: Massachusetts Department of Correction, March.

——— 1981b. "Some Background Characteristics of the Staff of the Massachusetts Department of Correction." Prepared by Linda K. Holt, Staff Researcher. Boston: Massachusetts Department of Correction, February.

McCleery, Richard. 1961a. "Authoritarianism and the Belief System of Incorrigibles." In *The Prison: Studies in Institutional Organization and Change*, ed. Donald R. Cressey, 260–306. New York: Holt, Rinehart and Winston.

——— 1961b. "The Governmental Process and Informal Social Control." In *The Prison: Studies in Institutional Organization and Change*, ed. Donald R. Cressey, 149–188. New York: Holt, Rinehart and Winston.

Mills, Theodore M. 1967. *The Sociology of Small Groups*. Englewood Cliffs, N.J.: Prentice-Hall.

Mitford, Jessica. 1973. *Kind and Usual Punishment: The Prison Business*. New York: Alfred A. Knopf.

Moore, Wilbert E. 1969. "Occupational Socialization." In *Handbook of Socialization Theory and Research*, ed. David A. Goslin. Chicago: Rand McNally and Co.

Morris, Terence, and Pauline Morris. 1963. *Pentonville: A Sociological Study of an English Prison*. London: Routledge and Kegan Paul.

National Institute of Corrections. 1979. *Technical Assistance Report of Massachusetts Department of Corrections*. Boston: Office of Human Services, October.

Orwell, George. [1949] 1974. *Nineteen Eighty-Four*. London: Secker and Warburg.

Powers, Edwin. 1973. *The Basic Structure of the Administration of Criminal Justice in Massachusetts*. Boston: The Crime and Justice Foundation.

Rothman, David J. 1980. *Conscience and Convenience: The Asylum and Its Alternatives in Progressive America.* Boston: Little, Brown.

Speer, Albert. [1975] 1977. *Spandau: The Secret Diaries.* Trans. Richard Winston and Clara Winston. New York: Pocket Books.

Sykes, Gresham M. 1958. *The Society of Captives: A Study of a Maximum Security Prison.* Princeton, N.J.: Princeton University Press.

Wensley, Howard S. 1978. Letter to the Superintendent of Walpole Prison reporting the results of an inspection of Walpole. Boston: Department of Public Health, 6 November.

Wheeler, Stanton. 1961. "Role Conflict in Correctional Communities." In *The Prison: Studies in Institutional Organization and Change,* ed. Donald R. Cressey, 229–259. New York: Holt, Rinehart and Winston.

——— 1958. "Social Organization in a Correctional Community." Ph.D. diss. Seattle: Department of Sociology, University of Washington.

Wynne, John M. 1978. *Prison Employee Unionism: The Impact on Correctional Administration and Programs.* Washington, D.C.: National Institute of Law Enforcement and Criminal Justice.

## Newspaper Articles Cited

| | |
|---|---|
| 23 March 1972 | *Boston Globe.* "$1.3m Asked to Repair Prison Unrest." |
| 5 May 1972 | *Boston Globe.* F. B. Taylor Jr. "Boone Soft on Inmates, Say Officers." |
| 1 Aug. 1972 | *New York Times.* Bill Kovach. "2 Slain by Convict in Break Attempt." |
| 3 Aug. 1972 | *Boston Globe.* Rachelle Patterson. "Sargent Backs Boone on Prison Incident." |
| 3 March 1973 | *Boston Herald American* (late ed.). Tom Sullivan and Ed O'Connor. "Porelle Quits at Walpole." |
| 10 March 1973 | *Boston Globe.* Jerry Taylor. "Boone Blames 'Guard Culture' for Walpole Troubles." |
| 17 March 1973 | *Boston Globe.* "Walpole Guards Given Chance to Return." |
| 18 March 1973 | *Boston Globe.* Jerry Taylor. "The View from Both Sides of the Cell Door at Walpole Prison." |
| 21 March 1973 | *Boston Globe.* Jonathan Fuerbringer. "Strike Led Walpole Guards into Sargent Hammerlock." |
| 25 April 1973 | *Boston Globe.* "Habit-forming Drugs Doled Out at Walpole Prison." |
| 20 May 1973 | *Boston Globe.* Stephen Wermiel. "State Police Quell Riot at Walpole." |
| 14 June 1974 | *Boston Herald American.* Bob Hassett. "Mass. Prisons Scored in Report." |
| 26 Jan. 1975 | *Boston Globe.* "The Prison System: Good for Guards Only." |

| | |
|---|---|
| 24 Nov. 1977 | *Boston Globe*. John F. Cullen. "3 Convicted, Given Life in Murder of Fellow Walpole Inmate." |
| 10 June 1978 | *Boston Herald American*. "3 guards Fired for Ku Klux Prank." |
| 12 Aug. 1978 | *Boston Globe*. Editorial. "Avoiding a Prison Crisis." |
| 19 Aug. 1978 | *Boston Globe*. Marvin Pave. "Walpole Union Asked to List Safety Proposals." |
| 20 Sept. 1978 | *Boston Globe*. Lonnie Isabel. "Walpole Prison Abuses Alleged." |
| 14 Oct. 1978 | *Real Paper* (Cambridge, Mass.). Letter from John F. Hurney, MCI Walpole. "Prisoners' Plight." |
| 12 Nov. 1978 | *Lowell Sun*. Joanne D'Alcomo. "State Report Says Half of Cells at Walpole 'Unfit for Habitation.' " |
| 20 Nov. 1978 | *Boston Globe*. Editorial. "No Security at Walpole." |
| 26 Nov. 1978 | *Lowell Sun*. Editorial. "The Fight Against Crime." |
| 9 Dec. 1978 | *Boston Globe*. Letter from James E. Jackson. "Walpole Reinforces Lawlessness in Prisoners." |
| 20 Dec. 1978 | *Boston Globe*. "Guards at Walpole Cleared of Brutality." |
| 3 Jan. 1979 | *Boston Herald American*. Eleanor Roberts. "Duke's Last Day—or Is It the First?" |
| 23 Jan. 1979 | *Boston Globe*. Editorial. "Hall's Prison Stewardship." |
| 27 March 1979 | *Boston Herald American*. Bill Dooley. "Walpole Guards, State Negotiate." |
| 30 March 1979 | *Boston Globe*. Letter from Michael A. McLaughlin. "Security at Walpole." |
| 6 May 1979 | *Boston Globe*. Lonnie Isabel and Timothy Dwyer. "How Insiders Look at the Walpole Mess." |
| 7 May 1979 | *Boston Globe*. Editorial. "Ten-Block: Intolerable Conditions." |
| 31 July 1979 | *New Bedford Standard-Times*. Jim Walsh. "For Walpole Guard, Siege was 'Traumatic' 10 hours." |
| 16 Aug. 1979 | *Worcester Telegram*. "State May Discipline Walpole Guards." |
| 28 Aug. 1979 | *Boston Herald American*. R. A. Zaldivar. "The Question at Walpole: 'Who's in Charge?' " |
| 25 Sept. 1979 | *Lowell Sun*. "A Conversation with Charles F. Mahoney." |
| 11 Dec. 1979 | *Boston Globe*. Timothy Dwyer. "Isolation Cell Case Rested." |
| 7 March 1980 | *Boston Globe*. Lonnie Isabel. "A Prisoner Gets Married." |
| 16 April 1980 | *Boston Globe*. Mike Barnicle. "She Won't Let Them Forget about Him." |

# Index